Empowering Society

An Analysis of Business, Government and Social Development Approaches to Empowerment

Usha Jumani

FOUNDATION®
BOOKS

Delhi • Bangalore • Mumbai • Kolkata • Chennai • Hyderabad

Published by
Foundation Books Pvt. Ltd.
Cambridge House, 4381/4 Ansari Road, Daryaganj, **New Delhi** – 110002

FOUNDATION BOOKS PVT. LTD.
C-22, C-Block, Brigade M.M., K.R. Road, Jayanagar, **Bangalore** 560 070
Plot No. 80, Service Industries, Shirvane, Sector-1, Nerul, **Navi Mumbai** 400 706
60, Dr. Sundari Mohan Avenue, 1st Floor, **Kolkata** 700 014
21/1 (New No. 49), 1st Floor, Model School Road,
Thousand Lights, **Chennai** 600 006
House No. 3-5-874/6/4, (Near Apollo Hospital),
Hyderguda, **Hyderabad** 500 029

First Edition 2006

ISBN 81-7596-317-4

Published by Manas Saikia for Foundation Books Pvt. Ltd. and printed & bound at Raj Press, R-3 Inderpuri, New Delhi - 110 012.

Contents

Preface

People and their behaviour always fascinate me. This has led me to interact with a range of people and deal with situations from all sections of the society. Capacity building of individuals and organisations has been my primary professional interest, and in this task my training in management and organisation development has been of great help. Through my work with organisations of different kinds, spanning over more than two decades, I have often wondered why some sections of people and business organisations generate wealth from the same economy which also has millions of people struggling to eke out a living. This I think has much to do with the capacity or the lack of it, and creating opportunities for all to generate wealth. For, the different worlds of the rich and poor in India are more than just structural differences.

This has been the inspiration behind this book. I have had close interaction in some way or the other with three different types of organisations – business, social development, and government. All the three systems work for capacity building of their stakeholders and through that of the larger society. The term 'empowerment' has become a key word to depict any positive change in the lives of people. I felt that by comparing the functioning of the three systems – all concerned with the future of the country – we would have a better appreciation of various nuances and shades of meaning associated with empowerment. At a time when organisational boundaries are getting increasingly blurred, such an exercise, I felt, would be all the more rewarding and meaningful.

The result is this book.

Usha Jumani

Acknowledgments

I wish to express my sincere thanks to the Business and Community Foundation, New Delhi for providing me an opportunity to undertake this study through the Fellowship for Corporate Partnerships Award, 2001–02.

I also sincerely thank the managements of Excel Industries Ltd., Gujarat Ambuja Cements Ltd., Tata Chemicals Ltd., Gujarat Cooperative Milk Marketing Federation Ltd. and Indian Farmers Fertiliser Cooperative Ltd., Kalol Unit, for agreeing to participate in this study. I am grateful to all the individuals in these organisations who have very generously shared their experiences and insights with me during my visits to these organisations. They have all contributed to making this book a reality.

The many individuals and staff of organisations whom I have interviewed for their understanding empowerment have also been very helpful. My sincere thanks to them.

Professor Dwijendra Tripathi has provided valuable comments and inputs in shaping this book and has been a constant source of guidance and support. His contribution in making this book a reality has been very important. Jyoti Jumani has provided continuous support and help throughout the period of conducting this study. Meenakshi and Anil Nayar and several friends have been very generous with their contacts and resources for meeting various people. Sandeep Shah and his team have been very helpful with the computer applications. Prakash Balge and Shiv Mandapa have contributed in preparing the graphics and computer images for the text. I sincerely thank all of them. Finally I wish to thank my family members for their support.

Usha Jumani
Ahmedabad

Part I

The Setting

This part has three chapters The Context of Empowerment, The Indian Realities, and Empowerment and Corporate Social Responsibility, which together provide the setting for developing a conceptual framework for empowerment.

1

The Context of Empowerment

The evolution of a mature democracy can be directly related to the level of empowerment experienced by its citizens and institutions. To understand this correlation, it is necessary to develop clarity about the process of empowerment in any given society. However, the term 'empowerment' is used widely in a variety of contexts with an equally wide range of meanings. The growing emphasis on participative systems of governance and management at all levels of organisational functioning in society is an important factor that has contributed to the wide use of the term 'empowerment' today. The world of business, the field of social development, the sphere of government and legislation are some of the more prominent contexts where this term has gained currency. Independently, these contexts address different segments of society in their thrust of empowerment and strive to achieve different objectives in their respective fields of action. The following randomly selected sample of available definitions, pertaining to different contexts, provide a fair idea of the varied connotations of the term.

Business Organisations

In the business context, empowerment is generally visualised as the process which generates and continually sustains a working environment that provides for individual creativity to express itself to the maximum possible extent. In the words of D. C. Kinlaw (1995), it is 'the process of achieving continuous improvement in an organisation's performance by developing and extending the competent influence of individuals and teams over the areas and functions which affect their performance and that of the total organisation'. According to him, 'empowerment is clearly coupled with the idea of continuous improvement in an organisation's total performance, is concentrated on making the most of all the mental resources represented in all the people, and creates conditions and initiatives that go far beyond anything that was ever contemplated within the context of earlier ideas like participative management and employee involvement'.

Applegarth and Posner (1998) identify three sets of people in any team or organisational framework: (i) the empowered, where they have the freedom to act within known boundaries to achieve agreed results (ii) the disempowered, where the freedom they once enjoyed has been taken away and (iii) the unempowered, where the freedom has never been granted in the first place.

How to empower the unempowered? Conrad Lashley (2001) identifies four different managerial strategies for empowering the unempowered which he calls empowerment through participation, involvement, commitment, and delayering.

What route or a combination of routes an organisation takes to empower its people would much depend on the quality of its leadership as emphasised by J. A. Conger (1989). Defining empowerment as the 'process of enabling and motivating subordinates by increasing their personal efficacy', he adds that it is 'the leaders's responsibility to help each subordinate reach his or her full potential'. He further emphasises that, 'effective organisations hold leaders accountable for the development of all subordinates'.

Business organisations view empowerment as a concern for all their people across various levels, incomes and also gender, and not limited to any specific segment.

Social Context

In the social context however, the term 'empowerment' assumes a much broader connotation. For Mahatma Gandhi, for instance, it signifies the upliftment of the poorest of the poor. The Mahatma's 'search for power was accompanied, and in fact superceded, by his keenness for the empowerment of everybody around him, and in particular, for the empowerment of the weak and helpless' (Gandhi, 2001). Following is Gandhi's oft-quoted maxim in this context:

> I will give you a talisman. Whenever you are in doubt, or when the self becomes too much with you, apply the following test. Recall the face of the poorest or weakest man whom you may have seen, and ask yourself if the step you contemplate is going to be of any use to him. Will he gain anything by it? Will it restore him to a control over his own life and destiny? In other words, will it lead to *swaraj* for the hungry and spiritually starving millions? Then you will find your doubts and yourself melting away.

Elaborating the above talisman, Rajmohan Gandhi observes:

> Note that he is not asking for coins or leftover food to be thrown before the starving. He wants the starving to have control over their lives and their destiny. Gandhi employs here the language not of charity or of condescension but of empowerment. He is calling for the empowerment of the weak and the humble. And note too, parenthetically, that he not only wants doubts to leave us, he wants the self too to melt away. He wants empowerment, control, power – yet he wants the self to go. (Gandhi, 2001)

Although Gandhi himself did not go into specifics about what should or could be done to empower the downtrodden, the question is well worth asking. Debal Singha Roy (2001) answers this in the following words: 'Empowerment ... is not simply a mechanical process of sharing, distribution or redistribution of power. Rather, it involves far wider changes in social and economic institutional arrangements, political ideologies, traditional practices and even in the mindsets of the marginalised people through conscientisation'. Virginius Xaxa (2001) implies the same when he says that 'empowerment means endowing individuals, groups or communities with power'.

Many others have argued on similar lines with regard to women. Kumud Sharma (1991–92) for instance, defines empowerment as 'a range of activities from individual self-assertion to collective resistance, protest and mobilisation that challenge basic power relations'. She asserts that for 'individuals and groups where class, caste, ethnicity and gender determine their access to resources and power, their empowerment begins when they not only recognise the systemic forces that oppress them, but act to change existing power relationships'. Empowerment for her therefore, 'is a process aimed at changing the nature and direction of systemic forces which marginalise women and other disadvantaged sections in a given context'.

Srilata Batliwala (1994) likewise defines women's empowerment 'as the process of challenging existing power relations, and of gaining a greater control over the sources of power', while for Sandra Morgan and Ann Bookman (1988) 'a spectrum of political activity ranging from acts of individual resistance to mass political mobilisation that challenge the basic power relations in our society' constitutes empowerment.

Some others, however, have a less radical view. For Marilyn Carr et al (1997) women's empowerment is simply 'economic change/material gain plus increased bargaining power and/or structural change which enables women to secure economic gains on an on-going and sustained basis'.

These definitions emphasise that empowerment processes should address the reality of the poor and the disadvantaged sections of society to improve their material conditions and status in society. The focus of these definitions is that the process of deprivation is endemic to the social system and empowerment has to provide a systemic response to alleviate the material deprivation of people. Simultaneously, it has to address the psycho-social consequences which such deprivation inflicts on the affected people. Notwithstanding this emphasis, there is an implicit assumption in several of these definitions that empowerment primarily addresses women's reality in society and the term is equated to women's empowerment.

Governmental Systems

The approach to empowerment in the social context is also linked to the role of the government. Though little has been written about empowerment in the context of the government system, there is ample indication to suggest that empowering the hitherto underprivileged sections of the population is now considered to be the legitimate function of the government. Significantly enough, the Ministry of Social Welfare of the Government of India has been recently renamed as the Ministry for Social Justice and Empowerment. Likewise, the 73rd and 74th Amendments (1992) in the Indian Constitution, devolving powers to the Panchayati Raj Institutions in rural and urban areas, have been hailed as vehicles of political empowerment. These amendments focus on providing the population as a whole a larger role in governance at the grassroots level in rural and urban areas. They also have provisions for reservations for women, scheduled castes, and scheduled tribes, to enable them to play a greater role in these forums of local self-governance.

The government has also launched special efforts for empowering specific segments of the population. For instance, the Department of Women and Child Development, Ministry of Human Resources Development, Government of India announced a 'National Policy for the Empowerment of Women' in 2001, with the following objectives:

i. Creating an environment through positive economic and social policies for full development of women, to enable them to realise their full potential.

ii. The *de jure* and *de facto* enjoyment of all human rights and fundamental freedom by women on equal basis with men in all spheres – political, economic, social, cultural and civil.

iii. Equal access to participation and decision making of women in social, political and economic life of the nation.

iv. Equal access of women to health care, quality education at all levels, career and vocational guidance, employment, equal remuneration, occupational health and safety, social security and public office, etc.

v. Strengthening legal systems aimed at elimination of all forms of discrimination against women.

vi. Changing societal attitudes and community practices by active participation and involvement of both men and women.

vii. Mainstreaming a gender perspective in the development process.

viii. Elimination of discrimination and all forms of violence against women and the girl child.

ix. Building and strengthening partnerships with civil society, particularly women's organisations.

As can be seen, the Policy attempts to operationalise the goal of 'changing the nature and direction of systemic forces' that some writers on women's empowerment have suggested. This also reinforces the assumption that empowerment primarily concerns women's reality. Focusing on specific groups, like women, does not detract from the government's concern to empower the population as a whole. It only means that such groups need special attention.

International Scenario

Documents produced by international conferences and institutions have added their own inputs to the meaning and scope of the term. The World Summit on Social Development, Copenhagen, 1995, for instance, emphasised that 'empowering people, particularly women, to strengthen their capacities is the main objective of development and its principal resource. Empowerment requires the full participation of people in the formulation, implementation and evaluation of decisions determining the functioning and the well-being of our societies'. The tone of the International Conference on Population and Development held in 1994 was somewhat different. It gave the following definition specfically with reference to women:

> Women's Empowerment refers to the process by which women gain inner power to express and defend their rights and gain greater self-confidence, self-identity, self-esteem and control over their own lives and personal and social relationships. Although the extent and circumstances vary

> across societies and over time within a particular society, girls and women typically have less power than boys and men in both private and public spheres. Women's empowerment is the process by which these unequal power relations are transformed in women's favour.

A few years later The World Bank (Narayan, 2002) defined empowerment in the context of poverty reduction initiatives as 'the expansion of assets and capabilities of poor people to participate, negotiate, influence, control, and hold accountable institutions that affect their lives'.

The international organisations tend to view empowerment as a thrust area for poor and underprivileged people in general and women in particular.

Need for Conceptual Clarity

What these randomly selected examples highlight is that empowermnent is viewed differently in different contexts. In fact, one can see differing perceptions even within a particular context. With a view to sharpening the understanding of the meaning and scope of the term and the process of bringing it about, the author interviewed a cross section of persons associated with business organisations, academic and professional institutions, government, and social development interventions. Their responses, included as Appendix I to this volume, are as varied as the available written literature. The reproductions of perceptions of empowerment, representing a variety of contexts and appearing as Appendix II to this volume, illustrate the same thing. The wide ranging and sometimes even flippant use of this term thus highlights the need to analyse the variegated use and meanings of this term with a view to providing conceptual clarity and focus in its application to different societal contexts.

Given the fluidity in the use of the term empowerment, some very basic questions arise: What after all does empowerment mean? What are the differences in the application of this term to different contexts? What are the changes which can be seen as a result of empowerment?

What is the scope and coverage of empowerment efforts? What is the sustainability of these efforts? And above all, how does society as a whole change in the process of these different segments of society being constantly empowered? This book seeks to answer some of these questions which can be meaningfully addressed only in given organisational and societal contexts. For this purpose, three major organisational spheres of business, government, and social development in Indian society have been selected for a comparative study. Collectively, they represent the whole society in the form of economic, political, and social entities. The selection of these spheres is further justified by the fact that practically all the major initiatives leading, directly or indirectly, towards empowerment in some form are being attempted within the rubric of business, government, or social development organisations.

Businesses in India have been pursuing their core interests, but they are also active in the realm of social development. Trusts and foundations set up by them undertake a wide range of activities directed to serve society in ways other than merely producing goods and services for the marketplace. Through these endeavours they fulfill a part of what is generally referred to as their Corporate Social Responsibility (CSR), which is gaining legitimacy in the world of business everywhere. It is important to focus on the concept of CSR to understand the changing nature of business organisations in the present times and its relevance to empowerment through business organisations.

The social and work realities of the people in a given society circumscribe the development challenges facing it and government organisations, particularly under a democratic set-up, are mandated to address them. Their functions are related to the empowerment process, for, improving the capabilities of their people is considered to be one of the main functions of a government. In between the business organisations and government are the social development organisations. They are engaged in a variety of activities directed at improving the quality of life of the segments of population they are working with. Business and social development organisations (running independently of business) also engage with each other and with the government in a variety of partnerships to deal with various development issues.

The differential understanding of empowerment in various organisational contexts plays an important role in analysing and addressing the development challenges in a given society and lead to empowering society as a whole. The study attempts to capture this differential understanding of empowerment in the Indian reality. A comparison of the empowerment approaches adopted by business organisations in their business operations as well as in their community development initiatives, juxtaposed on the nature of empowerment achieved by the other two organisational systems should sharpen our understanding of the empowerment process. Such a comparison would also help to calibrate the term 'empowerment' in the Indian ethos and context to facilitate its application to the larger population of the country. This is what is sought to be achieved through a study of organisations active in these different types of societal contexts, as listed below:

- Business organisations
- Social development organisations
  - i. Trusts and Foundations set up by business
  - ii. Organisations running independent of business
- Government organisations

Case studies are the principal source of insights for this study. An adequate number of cases, covering a variety of situations focusing on empowerment, are available in published sources relating to the government and social development organisations. Such materials with regard to business organisations, focusing specifically on empowerment, are practically unavailable. It therefore became necessary to develop empirical case studies relating to the empowerment efforts through business organisations. These are included as Appendix III in this volume. The state of Gujarat in India is the geographical focus for developing our case studies of business organisations. They pertain to a purposive sample of businesses which are doing well, have set up separate organisations for community development work, and which have some *prima facie* element of empowerment in their approach to business as well as to community development work.

The analysis of empowerment emerging from the case studies (developed by us as well as those from published sources) has been integrated with the author's own insights of intensive work experience for more than twenty-five years with the social development and government organisation systems. Hence, a combination of empirical and secondary data as well as the author's first hand experience form the basis for analysing and understanding the empowerment approaches of the three organisational systems included in this study.

Organisation of the Book

The book is organised in the following three parts:

Part I has three chapters which provide the setting for empowerment. The introduction to the subject and the objectives and methodology adopted for the study are presented first. This is followed by a description of the Indian realities and the overall social development indicators, in Chapter two, to highlight the major development concerns of the country. This chapter also explains the nature of organisational functioning in the Indian economy and the work reality of the majority of its population, and of women, as social development efforts primarily focus on this section of the population. An overview of the literature on corporate social responsibility, in Chapter three, explains the current focus of this concept and its relevance to empowerment.

Part II presents the nature of empowerment through the three organisational systems of business, government, and social development. The meaning of empowerment through business organisations emerging from the case studies is described in chapter four. The conceptual frameworks currently being used for understanding governance and government along with cases from published sources are discussed in Chapter five to highlight the nature of empowerment through government action. The main features of non-governmental organisations (NGOs) and civil society in the country are broadly described in Chapter six and illustrated with cases from published sources to develop an understanding of empowerment through social development organisations.

Part III presents our analysis of empowerment, based on these empirical and conceptual insights. Five principal strands of empowerment – Process Orientation, Bases of Power, Organising and Organisation,

Mainstreaming, and Representative Organisations – have been discussed in Chapters seven to eleven with a separate chapter for each strand. These five strands are woven together to present an integrated view of Empowering Society in Chapter twelve, which is the concluding chapter.

References

Applegarth, Mike and Posner, Keith, *The Empowerment Handbook,* New Delhi: Research Press, 1998, p. 8.

Batliwala, Srilata, 'The Meaning of Women's Empowerment: New Concepts from Action' in Sen, G, Germain, A. and Chen, L. (eds) *Population Policies Reconsidered: Health, Empowerment and Rights,* Boston, MA: Harvard School of Public Health, 1994, p. 130.

Carr, M., Chen, M. and Jhabvala, R. (eds), *Speaking Out – Women's Economic Empowerment in South Asia,* New Delhi: Vistaar, 1997, p. 11.

Conger, J. A., *The Charismatic Leader,* San Francisco: Jossey-Bass, 1989, pp. 171–172.

Gandhi, Rajmohan, 'Management of Power –The Approach of Mahatma Gandhi' in Chakraborty, S. K. and Bhattacharya, Pradip (eds) *Leadership and Power,* New Delhi: Oxford University Press, 2001, p. 152.

Government of India, *National Policy for the Empowerment of Women, 2001,* New Delhi: Department of Women and Child Development, Ministry of Human Resource Development, 2001, p. 7.

International Conference on Population and Development, 1994, *Programme of Action,* para 4.1.

Kinlaw, D.C., *The Practice of Empowerment,* Aldershot-Hampshire: Gower, 1995, pp. 6 and 21.

Lashley, Conrad, *Empowerment – HR strategies for service excellence,* Oxford University Press: Butterworth-Heinemann, 2001, p. 56.

Morgan, Sandra and Bookman, Ann (eds), *Women and the Politics of Empowerment,* Philadelphia: Temple University Press, 1988 as cited in Carr, M., Chen, M. and Jhabvala, R (eds) *Speaking Out – Women's Economic Empowerment in South Asia,* New Delhi: Vistaar, 1997, p. 226.

Narayan, Deepa (ed.), *Empowerment and Poverty Reduction – A Source book,* Washington D.C.: The International Bank for Reconstruction and Development, 2002, p. 14.

Sharma, Kumud, 'Grassroots Organisations and Women's Empowerment: Some Issues in the Contemporary Debate' in *Samya Shakti,* Centre for Women's Development Studies, New Delhi, Volume VI, 1991–92, p. 29.

SinghaRoy, Debal (ed), *Social Development and the Empowerment of Marginalised Groups: Perspectives and Strategies,* New Delhi: Sage Publications, 2001, p. 14.

World Summit for Social Development, 1995: *Declaration of the World Summit for Social Development,* Geneva: UN, point 26.0.

Xaxa, Virginius, 'Empowerment of Tribes' in SinghaRoy, Debal (ed) *Social Development and the Empowerment of Marginalised Groups: Perspectives and Strategies*, New Delhi: Sage Publications, 2001, p. 203.

2

The Indian Realities

Empowerment cannot be divorced from, but is specific to, social realities. The nature and process of empowerment would be different in different societies. What are the realities that impinge on the empowerment dynamics in a country like India? For one thing, India is a multi-cultural, multi-ethnic, multi-linguistic, multi-religious, pluralistic society with a deeply entrenched caste-based, hierarchical stratification. Some important social indicators of well-being of the population as a whole in India are presented below to focus on the challenges faced by the country and consequently the implications of empowering society.

Social Indicators

Population and Sex Ratio

India's population as per the 2001 Census stood at:

Persons	1,027,015,247
Males	531,277,078
Females	495,738,169

The rural-urban break-up of the population is:

	Numbers	Percentage
Total	1,027,015,247	100.00
Rural	741,660,293	72.22
Urban	285,354,954	27.78

The number of females to thousand males fluctuated between 924–934 between 1971–2001. This is much lower than the sex ratio of 980 in the early part of the twentieth century.

Literacy, Schooling, and Health

The literacy rate has been defined by the Census of India as the proportion of literates to the total population in the age group of 7 years and above. On the basis of this criterion, literacy in India has grown from 43.6% in 1981 to 65.38% in 2001. The male literacy rate was 75.85% while the female literacy rate stood at 54.16%.

The adult literacy rate, defined as the proportion of literate population in age group 15 years and above, has grown from 41% in 1981 to about 49% in 1991. As per the National Sample Survey Organisation (NSSO) 54th Round, Jan–June 1998, the adult literacy rate was 57%.

The gross enrollment rate in schools for class I–V was 94.9% in 1999–2000 as per the Annual Report of the Ministry of Human Resource Development. For children in class VI–VIII it declined to 58.8%. The net enrollment ratio for children in the 6 to below 14 years group was 57.5% as per the Educational Survey, 1993. This means, that out of all the children in the country in age group of 6 to below 14 years, 57.5% were enrolled in classes I–VIII. The ratio was 64% for boys and 50.4% for girls. Intensity of formal education was 4.03 years for students enrolled in 1978. It increased to 4.64 years in 1993. For both the years it was less for girls in comparison with boys. For boys, it increased from 4.19 years in 1978 to 4.7 years in 1993. For girls, it increased from 3.76 years to 4.46 years. During this period thus, the gender gap vis-a-vis school education declined from 0.43 years to 0.31 years.

Life expectancy at birth increased from around 30 years at the time of Independence to over 60 years in 1992–96. Life expectancy at age one has improved from 60.9 years to 64.9 years over the period 1981–85 and 1992–96. Infant mortality rate (IMR) is the probability of the death of a child dying before reaching the age of one year. The IMR was 115 per thousand live births (122 for males and 108 for females) according to the 1981 Census. In 1999 the IMR was 70 infants per 1000 live births. The under-five mortality rate was 152 children per 1000 live births in 1981. It fell to 94 children per thousand live births in 1991. The maternal mortality rate defined as the number of maternal deaths per hundred thousand births was 408 in 1997 as per the Registrar General of India.

Over half the children under age of five years are moderately or severely undernourished. 30% of new-born babies and nearly 60% of women are anaemic. This is despite the country being self-sufficient in food production for over a decade, with mounting public food stocks at its command.

Basic Infrastructure Facilities

All households had access to safe drinking water as per the 2001 Census as compared to 62% of the households as reported by the 1991 Census. 36.1% of the households (22.8% in rural and 70.4% in urban areas) had bathroom facilities and 36.4% households (21.9% in rural and 73.7% in urban areas) had toilet facilities within the premises of their residence as per the 2001 Census. Less than one-fourth of the households in the country had toilet facilities within the premises of their residence, according to the 1991 Census.

The 2001 Census reported 55.8% of the households had access to electricity against 42.4% in the 1991 Census. 50% of villages with population under 1000 are yet to be connected to roads.

GNP

The Gross National Product of the country was Rs. 2,230,272 crores in 2002–03 at current prices and Rs. 1,306,811 crores at 1993–94 prices. The per capita Net National Product was Rs. 18912.1 at current prices in 2002–03 and Rs. 10964.1 at 1993–94 prices (Quick estimates).

National Gender Equality Index (GEI), and UNDP Development Indices

There has been a marginal improvement in the index of gender equality measuring the attainments on human development indicators for females as a proportion of that of males. At the national level GEI increased from 62% in the early eighties to 67.6% in the early nineties. This implies that on an average the attainments of women on human development indicators were only two-thirds of those for men in the country.

India ranks 115 out of 162 countries in terms of the Human Development Index (HDI) developed by the United Nations Development Programme (UNDP) and is classified in the Medium Human Development group of countries with an HDI of 0.571 in 2001. The HDI has improved from 0.439 in 1992.

The Gender Development Index for India has improved from 0.401 in 1992 to 0.533 in 2001. This is still low in comparison with the country's HDI.

The Gender Empowerment Index has also improved from 0.226 in 1992 to 0.240 in 1999. Considerable improvement is still needed on this count.

(The sources for the figures quoted in this section are the *National Human Development Report 2001,* Planning Commission, Government of India, *The Economic Survey* 2001–02, 2002–03, 2003–04 of the Government of India and *Annual Report 2001–02 of Ministry of Health and Family Welfare*, Government of India).

These overall social indicators for India highlight the scale of efforts still required to be invested to provide basic facilities of education, health, and infrastructure to the entire population. A major concern of development interventions is how and when these facilities will become accesible to those deprived of them. Besides other parameters, the meaning of empowerment for those sections of the population deprived of even the basic facilities is linked to being able to avail them. Their work and income reality is also intricately interwoven with the deprivation of basic facilities.

Work Reality

After the discussion of some of the important social indicators for India, the complex work reality of the people has to be discussed to lay out the economic canvas of the country and its relationship with empowerment.

The terms 'self-employment' and 'other-employment' are used to designate respectively those who work for themselves and those who work for somebody else in an established employer-employee relationship, recognised and supported by law (Jumani, 1992).

Fig. 1 is a graphic representation of the total working population in India, divided into high income, middle income, and low income groups. The approximate share of each income group in the working population is designated by the three horizontal lines in the circle. The proportion of people engaged in other-employment, constituting barely 7% of the total, is represented by the small section cut off by chord ab in the circle.

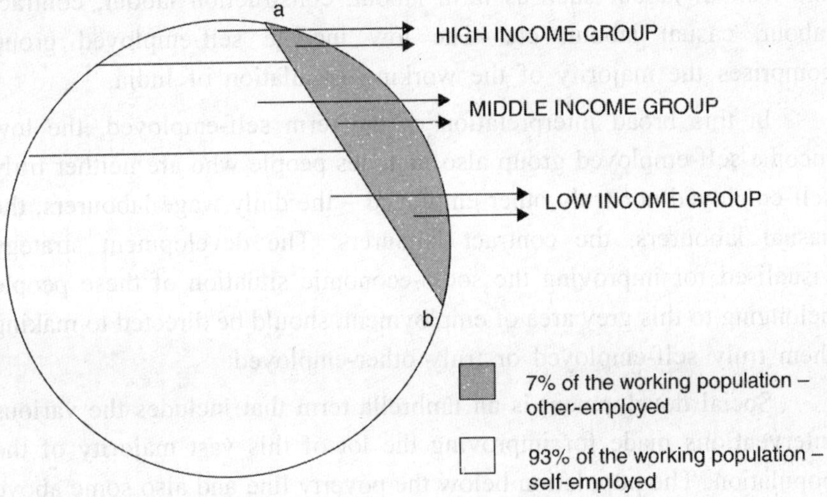

Fig. 1. Graphic representation of the total working population in India.

People in other-employment fall across all the three income groups. The remaining population, which is self-employed, earns its livelihood by finding its own self-created niche in the economy and fending for itself. The self-employed people also fall across all the three income groups.

People in other-employment from the high and middle income groups include managers, officers, administrators, professionals such as doctors, lawyers, teachers, architects, engineers, accountants, information technologists, etc. The low income other-employed group includes factory workers, peons, clerks, etc.

Self-employed people from the high and middle income groups include manufacturers and industrialists, entrepreneurs, consultants, professionals, traders, dealers, various contractors, big farmers, etc.

Self-employed people in the low income group include small producers engaged in land based, livestock based, and manufacturing based activities; vendors engaged in vending and trade of various commodities such as food, cloth, garments, shoes, household utility items; providers of services such as cleaning, transportation, washing, cooking, and manual labour such as farm labour, construction labour, contract labour, casual labour, etc. The low income self-employed group comprises the majority of the working population of India.

In this broad interpretation of the term self-employed, the low income self-employed group also includes people who are neither truly self-employed nor truly other-employed – the daily wage labourers, the casual labourers, the contract labourers. The development strategy visualised for improving the socio-economic situation of these people belonging to this grey area of employment, should be directed to making them truly self-employed or truly other-employed.

Social development is an umbrella term that includes the various interventions made for improving the lot of this vast majority of the population. The population below the poverty line and also some above the poverty line are included in this category. The Planning Commission estimates the proportion of the population below the poverty line in India at 26.1% in 1999–2000 (260 million people). According to the UNDP Human Development Report 2002, on the other hand, 44.62% of the population was living on less than U.S. $1 per day in 2000.

Reality of the Low Income Self-Employed People

Five types of work/production relationships mark the economic activities of the low income self-employed people. These are discussed below:

Wage work is where a person is paid daily wages for doing a particular work. There is no assurance of work for any length of time; the arrangement being fixed for the day only. Some types of agricultural labour work like weeding, land levelling; casual labour work in mines, construction sites, factories, offices is done in this way.

Piece rate work is an arrangement where the payment is fixed for a certain quantum of work irrespective of the time taken to complete it. Farm work like transplantation, harvesting, post harvest processing, nursery raising; forest produce collection; producing handicrafts, leather goods, bricks, food products, garments; contract work like cleaning, loading-unloading, building construction is done in this way.

There is no investment of capital by the worker in wage work and piece rate work, but sometimes the worker uses his/her own tools and equipment and some materials for doing the work.

Unpaid family work is where several family members assist in a work while only one person is considered a worker and gets paid for the final output – be it wage work or piece rate work or own account work. Women and children are more commonly engaged as unpaid family labour in the work which the male members of the family take up.

Own account work is where a person invests his/her own labour and capital to produce goods and/or services for a return. The person does not employ any other worker to do the work – it is done by him/her alone or with the help of unpaid family labour. Carpentry, weaving, handicrafts, agriculture, trade, transportation services, cooking and food processing, catering, teaching, can be included in this category.

Small entrepreneur is where the worker engages his/her own labour and capital to produce goods and/or services for a return and also engages one or more other paid workers to assist. Farming, manufacturing, trade, services are some of the examples of this type of work.

A particular industry can have all the above five production relationships in different aspects of the work.

Increasingly the small entrepreneur activities belong to the middle income and high income population in India. The remaining four work relationships where low income group people are concentrated and the kind of occupations they are engaged in have to be understood if the issue of poverty has to be addressed and if the economic activities of poor people have to be strengthened through development as a planned effort.

The life of the low income self-employed people (men, women, and children) in India is very difficult. They have to fend for themselves to somehow generate income in cash and/or kind to sustain themselves and their families. Their occupations are a combination of subsistence and commercial work. The production relations they are engaged in are a combination of own account work, piece rate work, wage work, and unpaid family work at different times of the year. For example, a poor person may be engaged in agricultural labour on daily wages for a part of the year, she may have a few poultry which lay eggs for a part of the year, and may also be involved in weaving cloth on piece rate basis for another part of the year. The consumption and production needs of the poor for generating income/returns are intermingled because day-to-day survival is the most crucial aspect of their lives. They have very low staying power and accept unfavourable trade terms in their work transactions. Their incomes bear little relationship to the hours they spend on work, to the market prices of goods and services, to the value of output and profits they help produce.

The economic activities of the poor include small farm agriculture, tree growing, nursery raising; dairy farming, fishing, raising poultry, goats, pigs, silk worm cocoons; collecting forest produce like leaves, grasses, seeds, gum, medicinal herbs; handloom weaving, silk reeling, cotton and wool spinning, stitching garments, making handicrafts, pottery, carpentry, working in smithy, masonry; vending food, cloth, garments, toys, shoes, kites, household utility items; providing services like sweeping, cooking, laundry, childcare; domestic labour, casual work in mines, factories, fields, construction sites.

People engaged in these economic activities are dispersed over so many households and workplaces. They work individually. The economic activities they are engaged in are small in size, require traditional labour intensive skills, and generate small incomes/returns. These activities are highly decentralised, depend on verbal transactions with a few people based on mutual trust. Many of them are illiterate. They, thus, feel handicapped in dealing with formal institutional avenues of the economy and have very little policy support for their work.

The multiple roles, multiple occupations, multiple production relationships, cash/kind income base all contribute to the complex reality of the livelihoods of the poor.

The economy of a place does not respond because one is poor or underprivileged or because one is woman – it responds to the forces of demand and supply. Poor and underprivileged men and women have not been able to understand and take advantage of the changing forces of demand and supply in an economy like that of India. The challenge for poor countries is to enable this vast majority of people to improve their socio-economic situation. The reality of women in this scenario also needs to be understood in greater detail.

Women's Reality

Almost all societies, including India, have traditionally ascribed a lower status to women, and therefore ascribed more power to men to control the lives of women in their society (except in the matriarchal societies). Consequently women have been underprivileged as well as undervalued. The subordination of women is manifested in the social, cultural, economic, educational, and political fields. In the biological realm, nature has endowed only females with the capacity of childbearing. Ironically, this biological reality is the root cause of the various subordinations faced by women.

Social inequality gives a lower status to women as being less important, less capable, less central, and less valuable than men in a society. This is just by virtue of being born a woman – a reality over which she has no choice.

Economic inequality gives a lower status to poor people (men and women) as being less important, less capable, less central, and less valuable vis-a-vis the rich in a society.

A majority of women in India suffer from social and economic inequality, which adds up to political inequity also. To enable poor people to overcome the handicap of poverty implies economic change. To enable women to overcome the handicap of subordination implies social change. To enable underprivileged people (men and women) to overcome the handicap of being underprivileged implies social and economic change.

The forces of social and economic change are increasingly coming to grips with gender equality as a central issue. The experience of development initiatives over the decades has highlighted the reality that women suffer the most from the existing inequalities of being poor, of being women, and of being underprivileged. The nature of gender inequality is experienced differently by women from the various socio-economic strata of the society. Rich women (if at all) mainly suffer the social subordination of being women. Their reality therefore is different from that of poor women. The discriminations suffered by women are manifested in the following major issues grouped in social, economic, and political categories:

Control over own body	
Food and nutrition	Social
Health care	
Education	
Skills and vocational training	
Work	
Income	Economic
Formal and institutional transactions	
Ownership of wealth	
Investment for self-development	
Investment for capacity building	Political
Leadership and decision making	
Political representation	

The outcome of such discriminations is a society where half the population – women – are excluded in various ways from the mainstream of society. The gaps in the statistical picture between the lives of men and women is also an outcome of the above discriminations between them. Such discriminations lead to different

- – Social role determination for men and women
- – Life choices for men and women
- – Control over resources for men and women
- – Level of power in the hands of men and women.

All these forces together create multiple role responsibilities for poor women. The roles of wife, mother, homemaker, citizen are in addition to the worker roles for poor women in most cultures. Hence all the household chores, plus childcare, plus looking after the husband and menfolk and other family members, have to go hand-in-hand with the income earning and work that sustains livelihood.

Most of the activities that poor women do are not normally included in 'work', and they are invisible as workers in official statistics. Women are responsible for a greater share of non SNA (System of National Accounts) work in the care economy which is difficult to measure. This work is neither recognised nor considered adequately in socio-economic policy making. They put in more hours of work and they get paid less than men for similar work. They rarely own assets in their name.

A recent study commissioned jointly by the Department of Women and Child Development and UNIFEM to analyse the Union budget of the Government of India from the gender perspective for the year 2001–02 reflects some of these aspects (*Report on Gender Diagnosis and Budgeting in India*, National Institute of Public Finance and Policy, December 2001). The study identified three categories of public expenditure on women:

i. expenditure specifically targeted to women

ii. public expenditure which has earmarked pro-women expenditure

iii. mainstream public expenditure that has gender impact.

The analysis shows that out of the total budget of Rs. 75,223 crores, the amounts in the first category were limited to Rs. 3,260 crores and those in the second category to Rs. 10,596 crores. Due to paucity of gender disaggregated data of most mainstream programmes and services, the study made only an illustrative analysis of the third category of expenditure on elementary education. It found that girls received 40 per cent of the public expenditure on elementary education.

Many efforts have been made over the past three decades to address this reality of women. The situation is improving very slowly as reflected in the various development indicators and indices mentioned in the section on 'Social Indicators'. However a lot more effort is still needed to achieve equality between men and women.

The social and work reality of the majority of the population in India, described in this chapter, can be explained through the concept of Informal Systems of Work.

Informal Systems of Work

Basically the poor in India are part of the informal system of work. Informal systems of work are essentially based on verbal transactions as opposed to formal systems of work where written transactions predominate. The more the aspects of an individual's work and life are dependent on written transactions for validity, the more that individual is likely to belong to a formal system of work. The more the aspects of an individual's work and life are dependent on verbal transactions for validity, the more that individual is likely to belong to an informal system of work. There is a continuum between informal systems of work at one end and formal systems of work at the other end. Semiformal systems of work fall somewhere in between this continuum and reflect the reality of individuals with a mix of written and verbal transactions. The economies of countries like India have been functioning substantially as informal systems of work for centuries. This is the way the majority of the working population is familiar with and this is the basis on which the work of the majority is structured.

Informal systems of work prevalent in India have been traditionally structured around generating self-employment for the majority of the population. A positive social and cultural value has been attached to ownership of one's resources in order to earn a livelihood. Selling only one's physical and manual labour and working for somebody else as an employee has been seen culturally as the least preferred way of earning a livelihood. The economy has been structured in such a way that the majority of the population is in a buyer-seller relationship. A sense of involvement in work; maintaining high motivation; developing accountability and responsibility to do one's work well; linking productivity and work performance to income; developing a sense of identity and belonging through the primary social system of family and kinship; are all sought to be achieved by reinforcing self-employment for the majority through buyer-seller relationships. Informal systems of work and self-employment for the majority have therefore gone hand-in-hand.

Development interventions for the poor and penetration of the market economy in their work is shifting this reality towards semiformal systems of work. The middle income and high income groups of the self-employed people also are engaged in semiformal systems of work, but they are increasingly becoming a part of the formal systems of work.

Addressing the Reality of the Poor

In social development efforts the major actors have been governments and inter-governmental organisations, the communities of people for whom development interventions are made, funding agencies, experts and non-governmental organisations. There has been a shift in orientation from welfare to development to empowerment in social development work over the past fifty years. Empowerment of people has become very current in the perspective on development per se and also in the efforts for poverty alleviation. Gender and development interventions have been particularly advocating empowerment approaches to address the lower status of women in society.

Special attention is being directed by the Government of India to improve the situation of workers who do not have a recognised employer-employee relationship. The specific anti-poverty programmes are also intended to improve the lot of these workers.

Development interventions for socio-economic changes in India have been designed around issues of consciousness raising, training and education, health care, child care, domestic violence, water and sanitation, credit, work and income, legal rights, gender relations, consumer action, housing, communications, social security, natural resources, environment.

All the three types of organisations included in this study are active in addressing the reality of the poor. They are also equally vocal about empowering the people they work with. Even though all the actors have taken up the development challenges faced by the country, their efforts are piecemeal and scattered with little commonality in the situational analysis done by them. Consequently, there are low synergies of efforts to take on the challenges jointly. The reality of this vast majority of the Indian population has to be systematically addressed for improving their lot and for facilitating their sustained empowerment.

The process of empowerment has to take into account the diverse realities of the people in the country as well as the differential levels of strength and capability to create a more egalitarian and prosperous society. Each segment of the population requires a different mix of interventions for empowerment and a different set of sensitivities to empower themselves and facilitate the empowerment of others. Together, the three organisational systems of business, government, and social development do cover all the segments of society and contribute to improving their reality. A comparative understanding of their approaches leads to a qualitative shift in all the interventions for empowerment in society.

References

Government of India, *National Human Development Report 2001,* New Delhi: Planning Commission.

______, *The Economic Survey 2001–02, 2002–03,* and *2003–04,* New Delhi.

______, *Annual Report 2001–02, Ministry of Health and Family Welfare,* New Delhi.

Jumani, Usha, *Dealing With Poverty – Self-employment for Poor Rural Women,* New Delhi: Sage, 1992, pp. 13–34.

3

Empowerment and Corporate Social Responsibility

The *raison d'etre* of business is its economic contract with society – to create wealth through the production of goods and services which are consumed by the people. Conventionally, the success of business has been viewed in terms of profits it generates i.e. a purely financial, single bottomline measure. This has, however, changed over the years to view the success of business from several other measures besides profit. Profits are necessary and inevitable for the success of business but the way the profits are generated is equally important. The social, environmental, ethical, informational means and methods employed to generate profits have a bearing on the responsible and accountable behaviour of business. Thus, a concept of multiple bottomlines has evolved from these concerns to measure the success of business as multipurpose organisations set to achieve multiple objectives.

The Stakeholders Focus

Accompanying this change is the shift from viewing business as shareholder focused organisations to stakeholder focused organisations. The various stakeholders that a business is held accountable to include owners, customers, employees, environment, regulatory authorities, community, and society, at large. Business has to maintain a careful balance between the demands and pressures of these various stakeholders, which can sometimes be conflicting in nature.

Peter Pruzan (2001) succintly identifies the distinctive features of these two views of organisation which he calls 'shareholder value perspective' and 'stakeholder value perspective':

> From a shareholder-value perspective, the goal is to maximise shareholder value, primarily via a maximisation of profits. To achieve this end, the most efficient use must be made of the 'instruments' available. These include not just technology and capital resources, but also employees, customers, suppliers, the media, the community, the physical environment, etc. From a stakeholder-value perspective this relationship between ends and means can be said to be shifted to 180 degrees. The goals of the company will often include having satisfied employees who take pride in the organisation; customers who feel confident that they get their money's worth; products which not only are safe to use, functional, and of good quality, but are also produced in a manner which recognises human rights and does not unduly harm the environment; suppliers, and local communities that experience positive symbiotic relationships with the company; shareholders who receive a satisfactory return on their investments and are proud to own a share of the company; and so on. In order to contribute to the achievement of these goals, a high level of profits is required. Here the roles have been reversed. Income is no longer the primary *goal,* but a vital *means.*

Another scholar, Bruce Lloyd (2001) too argues the value of a responsibility-driven approach. He sees the exercise of corporate power as a critical element in the long term competitive advantage of successful organisations. When responsibility is internalised in the exercise of power, its focus shifts from 'What is really important?' to 'What should be really important?', leading to responsible corporate citizenship. Decision making in the organisation is thus motivated by the positive influence of an underlying sense of values or ethics and moves away from the legalistic approach to compliance. To quote him: 'In the responsibility-driven approach there is a genuine concern with reconciling the interests of all the stakeholders within the decision making process. Recent research has confirmed that organisations that are able to undertake this reconciliation effectively are those that produce the best long-term benefits for any stakeholder group, including the shareholders'.

The concept of Corporate Social Responsibility (CSR) is rooted in the stakeholder value perspective of business organisations. That the stakeholder value perspective has made some impact on the actual working of businesses is clear from the following views of a few principal practitioners.

According to Thomas G. Burns (1998) of Chevron, 'although the primary function of a corporation is wealth creation, an effective corporation must endeavour to focus on multiple bottomlines, and wealth creation is only one of them'. He, therefore, argues that involvement in social development projects is an investment opportunity and not a charity. D. K. Dey (1998) of Tata Steel highlights the same thing when he says that, 'Social Responsibility is not a question of cost. The cost of not doing is far greater because the benefits accrue over a period of time and cannot be immediately measured'. Ian Scott (1998) of Boston Consulting Group, emphasises a similar view by saying that corporate social responsibility must increasingly be seen as integral to the role and expectations of the corporation and not as a tangential or narrowly defined concept. Phil Watts (1997) argues that 'Business and industry are not just economic actors nor can be social activists. Their roles lie somewhere in between'. Likewise, Howard Shields (1998) of Shell International Petroleum Company, states that the objective should be to achieve clarity both inside and outside the organisation about what the organisation must do, what it may do and what it simply cannot do. Anjali Hazarika (1998) sums up the argument quite forcefully:

> The global companies of tomorrow will have to actively work today to integrate social accountability issues into their key business processes in order to meet – and in some cases exceed – customer expectations. 'The neighbour of choice strategy' must become an integral part of a company's

culture. Companies will know that they have succeeded in organising corporate social responsibility activities when they automatically include corporate social responsibility considerations in their decisions.

In fact the international nature of the business environment means that these responsibilities exist in those areas where business operates or seeks to operate. This is a global responsibility which lies at the heart of the business contract. The economic function of business and its wider responsibilities are integral features of this contract. By crossing the boundary between business and the community, the community will become a key stakeholder in business and business will be encouraged to give up the traditional mode of resource utilisation and adopt a sustainable mode for resource enrichment of the planet.

Enlightened self-interest is an important factor in operationalising corporate social responsibility and has shaped corporate investment decisions in sectors such as education, arts and culture, health, and community projects. This kind of concern is not confined to the private sector alone. A government document relating to public enterprises in India – *XXIV Report of the Committee on Public Undertakings (1993–94)* – identifies the following areas deserving support from public sector companies in the country:

- Education and culture
- Health and family welfare
- Housing and schemes of rural upliftment
- Development and infrastructure facilities
- Recreation and communication programmes
- Pollution and environment aspects
- Rehabilitation of project affected persons.

The nuances implied in the CSR concept are articulated through several other terms in management literature such as corporate responsibility, responsible business, socially responsible business, responsible corporate citizenship, corporate social performance, business and social development.

All these terms basically underline the principle that business organisations have to be concerned about several motives in addition to the profit motive.

Frameworks for CSR Activities

Some of the frameworks for CSR activities are described here to sharpen our understanding of the concept.

The Prince of Wales Business Leaders Forum Approach

This approach, developed in collaboration with The World Bank and The United Nations Development Programme, (Nelson, 1996), indicates that a company can serve its stakeholders through:

- Its core business activities, which looks at its policies, operations and production activities (in terms of safety, quality, environment implications, etc.), both within the business as well as its backward and forward linkages such as suppliers, distributors and customer relations.
- Social investments and philanthropy i.e. moving from ad hoc giving to strategic approaches to building community partnerships, looking for 'win-win' solutions, applying core competencies to such investments and linking community investments to mainstream business strategy.
- Public policy dialogue wherein business advocates with the state for changes in public policy that may benefit the business but its core motivation is public interest.

Built up on this framework is the concept of SVA^2 (Nelson, 1998) described through the following equation:

Shareholder value addition × *Societal value addition* = SVA^2

Jane Nelson elaborates this concept as:

> Our vision for SVA^2 is about value creation: but value defined in its broadest sense of economic, human, natural and social capital. SVA^2 rests on the fundamental premise that profit is absolutely essential and that the primary role of business in Society is to create or add value through sourcing,

development, production and delivery of products and services that meet customer needs. The approach therefore does not challenge the role of business, but it does challenge the way we think about, measure and manage that role and the different types of value which it creates. The goal of SVA^2 is to offer a strategic framework and a set of tools for analysing and managing this value creation process in a way that creates value for the owners of the business i.e. the shareholders, but within the parameters of ensuring that societal value especially for host countries and communities (measured economically, socially and environmentally) is also created as an integral result of this process.

The SVA^2 approach visualises five interdependent SVA^2 Pillars of Performance as critical value drivers in a company's creation of shareholder value-added and societal value-added, and each one of them influences and is influenced by the others. These pillars are identified as follows:

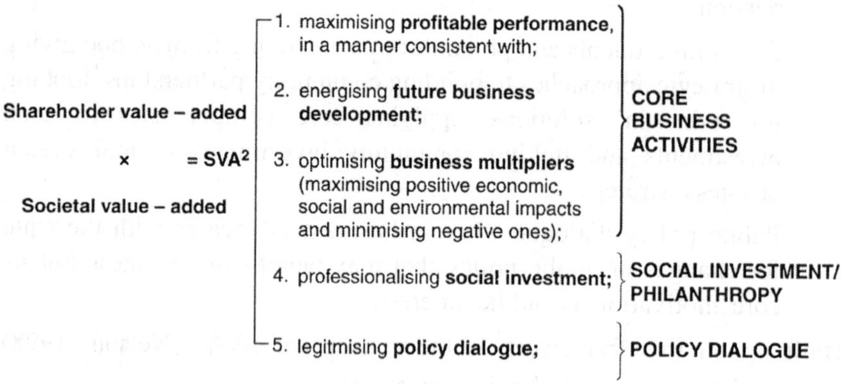

Source: Jane Nelson, *Building Competitiveness and Communities*, The Prince of Wales Business Leaders Forum in collaboration with The World Bank and The UNDP, 1998, p. 6.

Given on the following pages is the diagrammatic description of the five pillars and the key determinants of each pillar of performance. (Source: Jane Nelson, *Building Competitiveness and Communities*, 1998, pp. 7 and 33).

Virtuous cycles of shareholder and societal value creation

The relationship between a company and its key stakeholders, which is based on the exchange of different types of capital (financial, natural, human, social, political) and different types of product and service, can be mutually beneficial and reinforcing when the company is competitive, profitable and able to create shareholder value, as well as recognising the importance of societal value creation.

Flows of capital, products and services from the company

Flows of capital, products and services to the company

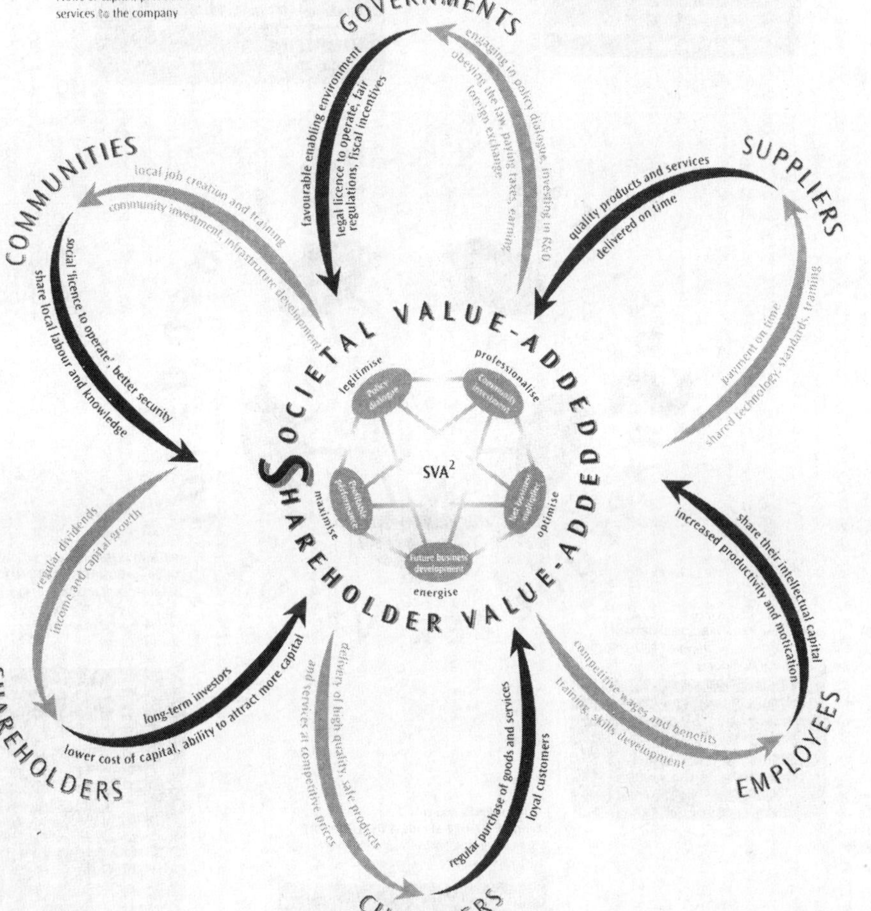

The Five Pillars of Performance in companies that are creating shareholder value-added and societal value-added

Pillar of Performance # 5
Legitimise POLICY DIALOGUE
at local, national and international levels

1. Promoting ethical business practices
2. Creating an enabling environment for private enterprise and investment
3. Supporting good governance
4. Contributing to economic, social, and environmental policies

Pillar of Performance # 4
Professionalise SOCIAL INVESTMENT AND PHILANTHROPY *in the following areas:*

1. Money: from cash donations to innovative funding mechanisms
2. In-kind support – from *ad hoc* approaches to mobilising core competencies
3. From philanthropy and public relations to partnership
4. From charity to community capacity building

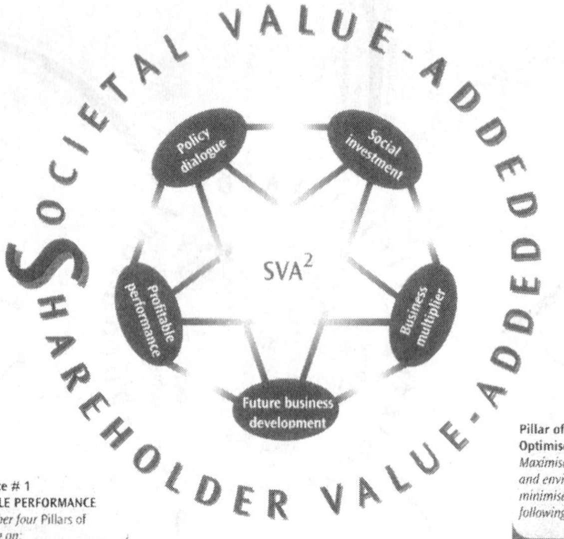

Pillar of Performance # 3
Optimise BUSINESS MULTIPLIERS
Maximise positive economic, social and environmental impacts and minimise negative ones in the following areas:

1. Generating investment and income
2. Creating jobs
3. Developing human resources
4. Providing goods and services
5. Building local business systems
6. Sharing international standards and business practices
7. Transferring technology
8. Establishing institutional and physical infrastructure

Pillar of Performance # 1
Maximise PROFITABLE PERFORMANCE
consistent with the other four Pillars of Performance, *focusing on:*

1. Resource efficiency and enhancement
2. Responsiveness to customer needs and opportunities
3. Relationship management
4. Reputation management (including brand equity management)
5. Risk management

Pillar of Performance # 2
Energise FUTURE BUSINESS DEVELOPMENT
by investing in distinctive assets and core competencies in the following areas:

1. People
2. Products and services
3. Processes
4. Places
5. Partners

London Benchmarking Group – LBG Model

This model seeks to develop and expand the reporting of company activities in the community so that they are more transparent and can be judged by the impact they achieve. Comprising of some of the leading companies in the UK, the London Benchmarking Group has devised this model to classify what companies do with the community on the basis of their motivation. This is illustrated in Fig. 1.

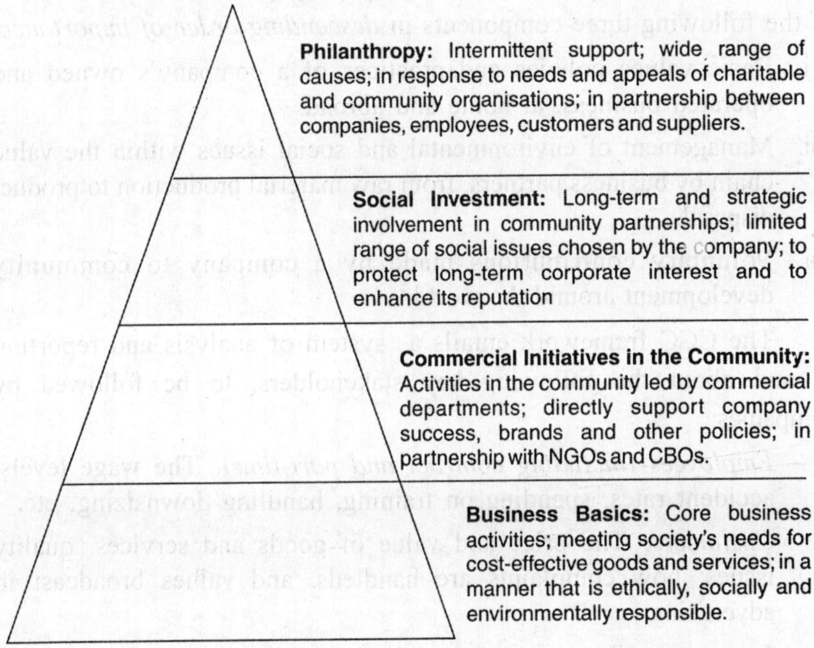

Fig. 1. London Benchmarking group Model for CSR Activities. (Source: Partners in Change, *Strategy Paper 2001–05*, p. 3).

The four components in the pyramid indicate the range of activities which companies undertake in society and the relative size of the components are meant to reflect their proportionate impact on society. In other words, a company's 'business basics' activities are expected to leave an impact on the society more than its 'philanthropic' activities. The LBG has also laid down a methodology to measure and report on inputs (cash, kind, and time) and outputs (classified as leverage, social impact, and business impact) of corporate community involvement.

Corporate Citizenship Company – CCC Framework

This framework has been developed by the Corporate Citizenship Company (Logan and Tuffrey, 1999), a UK based organisation, on the basis of its experience in the field. According to this framework, corporate citizenship (the term the company prefers to use) consists of the following three components in *descending order of importance*:

i. Basic values policies and practices of a company's owned and operated business, at home and abroad.
ii. Management of environmental and social issues within the value chain by business partners, from raw material production to product disposal.
iii. Voluntary contributions made by a company to community development around the world.

The CCC framework entails a system of analysis and reporting to and about the following key stakeholders, to be followed by companies:

- *Employees (including contract and part-time):* The wage levels, accident rates, spending on training, handling downsizing, etc.
- *Customers:* The price and value of goods and services, quality issues, how complaints are handleds, and values broadcast in advertising.
- *Investors:* The return on investment, corporate governance, directors' share dealings and transparency in financial information.
- *Business Partners:* The jobs sustained, the transfer of technology, and the timely payment of bills.
- *The Community:* Charitable gifts and community investment, the willingness to listen and engage in dialogue.
- *Government:* The payment of taxes, a fair transfer pricing policy, and compliance with financial and other laws and regulations.
- *The Environment* (or future generations and increasingly, other living things).

The CCC is also working on developing a Corporate Responsibility Index as a measure of corporate citizenship for companies.

Partners in Change Approach

While the previous frameworks have been developed in the context of Western businesses, Partners in Change, a Delhi based organisation, is active in promoting the concept of CSR in Indian businesses. They believe that a socially responsible company in India (and indeed in any developing country) must address three concerns – *how* it makes its profits, *what* it does with its profits, and *its influence on public policies.* Their model of a socially responsible business is given in Fig. 2.

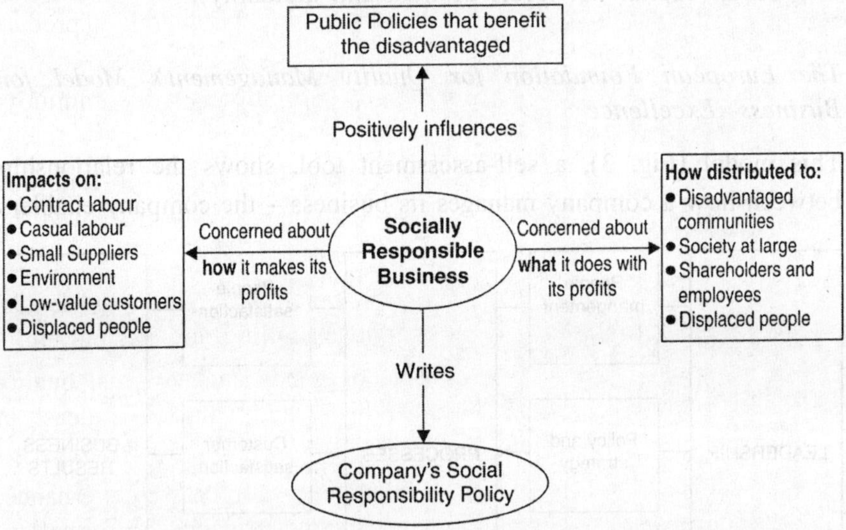

Fig. 2. Model of socially responsible business.
(Source: Partners in Change, *Strategy Paper 2001–05,* p. 22).

Measures for CSR Performance

Several approaches for measuring the performance of companies in the stakeholder value approach have also been developed. Some of them are mentioned here.

The Triple Bottom Line Performance Measure

Developed by John Elkington (1997) of SustainAbility Ltd., UK, it attempts to develop a range of metrics for the total net value added by a company. These metrics cover:

- **economic value** added or destroyed (focusing on the profits the company makes adjusted for the costs of capital employed);
- **environmental value** added or destroyed (adjusting measurements of profit with a charge on natural capital employed, and in the case of non-renewable resources, often consumed for a one-off benefit); and
- **social value** added or destroyed (accounting for knowledge and skills either developed or lost, and developing metrics to reflect social capital i.e. levels of trust and mutuality).

The European Foundation for Quality Management's Model for Business Excellence

This model (Fig. 3), a self-assessment tool, shows the relationship between how a company manages its business – the company enablers

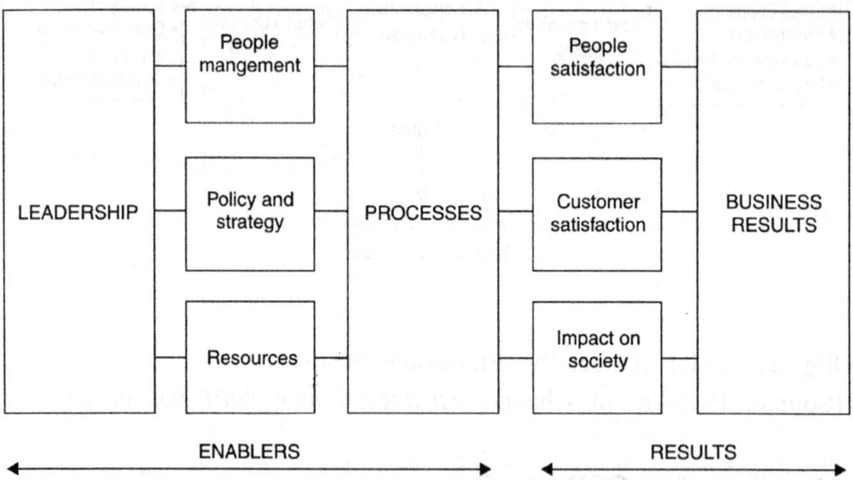

Fig. 3. The European Foundation for Quality Management Model for Business Excellence.

(Source: Jane Nelson, *Building Competitiveness and Communities*, p. 90).

– and the business results it achieves for its customers and other stakeholders. It offers a flexible but clear framework against which a company can evaluate its current performance, benchmark against best practice, and set targets for improvements.

The model consists of nine boxes, each of which has clear criteria and measures against which a company can evaluate its performance.

The key factors influencing the functioining of a business organisation are represented by the individual boxes in this model. The business 'Enablers' are identified as 'Leadership', which has to address 'People Management', 'Policy and Strategy', and 'Resources'. These together define the 'Processes' which a company adopts. The 'Enablers' are responsible for the business 'Results' which are achieved through 'People Satisfaction', 'Customer Satisfaction', and 'Impact on Society'.

Empowerment and CSR

Basically, the frameworks for understanding and measuring CSR described in this chapter are evolving ways of operationalising the stakeholder value approach to business in terms of its impact on society, reporting methodologies, and accountability to stakeholders. They provide a basis for understanding the interaction between the various stakeholders of business and how this redefines the relationship between business and society. The degree of emphasis on various stakeholders varies, but the focus is essentially on balancing the different interests they represent. Implicit in these frameworks is the concern for transparency and accountability in dealing with various stakeholders, which pave the way for democratic functioning of these organisations. This in turn unfolds the concern for empowerment in business.

Thus empowerment in business organisations is intricately tied up with its acceptance of the stakeholder value approach to business and its corporate social responsibility. The relationship between business and society is articulated in the self-concept of each business organisation and consequently defines how it can contribute to empowering society. Business is seen as an important actor in addressing the developmental challenges faced by any given country, both independently and in partnership with other actors in society. The self-concept of each business has a bearing on the manner in which it plays this role in the society.

References

Burns, Thomas G., 'Meeting the Emerging Social and Environmental Challenges –The Chevron Way' in Hazarika, Anjali (ed) *Corporate Social Responsibility and the Oil Industry – Global Experiences,* New Delhi: Tata McGraw-Hill, 1998, p. 20.

Dey, D. K., 'Partnership in Development: The Tata Experience' in Hazarika, Anjali (ed) *Corporate Social Responsibility and the Oil Industry – Global Experiences,* New Delhi: Tata McGraw-Hill, 1998, p. 119.

Diageo plc, *Global Brands Local Citizens – Corporate Citizenship Guidelines,* appendix, 1999, as quoted in Shrivastava, Harsh and Venkateswara, Shankar, *The Business of Social Responsibility,* Bangalore: Books for Change, 2000, p. 42.

Elkington, John, *Cannibals with Forks*, Capstone, 1997 as referred in Nelson, Jane *Building Competitiveness and Communities,* The Prince of Wales Business Leaders Forum in collaboration with The World Bank and The UNDP, London: 1998, p. 105.

Hazarika, Anjali (ed), *Corporate Social Responsibility and the Oil Industry – Global Experiences*, New Delhi: Tata McGraw-Hill, 1998, p. xix.

Lloyd, Bruce, 'Corporate Social Responsibility – Minimising the Abuse of Power' in Chakraborty S. K. and Bhattacharya, Pradip (eds) *Leadership and Power,* New Delhi: Oxford University Press, 2001, pp. 298–299.

Logan, David and Tuffrey, Michael *Companies in Communities: Valuing the Contribution,* London: Charities Aid Foundation, 1999, as quoted in Shrivastava, Harsh and Venkateswara, Shankar, *The Business of Social Responsibility,* Bangalore: Books for Change, 2000, p. 42.

Nelson, Jane, *Business as Partners in Development,* The Prince of Wales Business Leaders Forum in collaboration with The World Bank and The UNDP, London: 1996, p. 54.

Nelson, Jane, *Building Competitiveness and Communities,* The Prince of Wales Business Leaders Forum in collaboration with The World Bank and The UNDP, London: 1998, p. 31.

Partners in Change *Strategy Paper 2001–2005 – Putting Equitable Social Development at the Centre of Corporate Social Responsibility,* New Delhi, n.d. p. 22.

Pruzan, Peter, 'The Trajectory of Power' in Chakraborty S. K. and Bhattacharya, Pradip (eds) *Leadership and Power,* New Delhi: Oxford, 2001, pp. 170–176.

Scott, Ian, 'Multiple Stakeholders: Expectations and Response' in Hazarika, Anjali (ed) *Corporate Social Responsibility and the Oil Industry – Global Experiences,* New Delhi: Tata McGraw-Hill, 1998, p. 74.

Shields, Howard, 'The Petroleum Industry and Social Accountability' in Hazarika, Anjali (ed) *Corporate Social Responsibility and the Oil Industry – Global Experiences,* New Delhi:Tata McGraw-Hill, 1998, p. 5.

Sustainability and UNEP, *Engaging Stakeholders,* 1997 as referred in Nelson, Jane *Building Competitiveness and Communities,* The Prince of Wales Business Leaders Forum in collaboration with The World Bank and The UNDP, London: 1998, p. 105.

Watts, Phil, *Challenge to the International Petroleum Industry – Economic Actor or Social Activist?* London Group External Affairs, SI, Shell Centre, 1997 as quoted in Hazarika, Anjali (ed) *Corporate Social Responsibility and the Oil Industry – Global Experiences,* New Delhi: Tata McGraw-Hill, 1998, p. xvi.

XXIV Report of the Committee on Public Undertakings, 1993–94, New Delhi: Government of India as cited in Hazarika, Anjali (ed) *Corporate Social Responsibility and the Oil Industry – Global Experiences,* New Delhi: Tata McGraw-Hill, 1998, p. xiv.

Part II

Nature of Empowerment in Three Different Organisational Systems

Based on empirical data and published sources, the nature of empowerment in business, government, and social development organisational systems is described in this part with a separate chapter for each system.

4

Business Organisations

Indian businesses are increasingly adopting the stakeholder value approach as also specific frameworks for operationalising and measuring their corporate social responsibility. Accordingly, the focus on empowerment manifests itself in implicit and explicit ways in their functioning. Five case studies, specially prepared for the study, throw some light on how Indian businesses practice the stakeholder value approach to enhance their business interests and the nature of empowerment in their business operations. Their relationship with one particular stakeholder – the community – has been studied in greater detail to understand how these businesses view empowerment of the community. The empowerment approaches in the business operations and community development initiatives of these organisations are analysed to highlight how they are facilitating empowerment in society at large. The following abstracts of these case studies (full forms appear as Appendix III to this volume) provide valuable insights.

Excel Industries Ltd.

Excel Industries Ltd., a leading manufacturer and exporter of agro-chemicals and industrial chemicals, was established by C.C. Shroff in Mumbai in 1941. It started as a small laboratory in a kitchen at home. Today it has eight manufacturing plants in different parts of the country. It was the first agro-chemical company in India to get the ISO 9002 certification.

The Shroff family belonging to Kutch controls and manages Excel Industries Ltd. The Shroffs have been greatly influenced by Swami Vivekananda, Gandhiji, Vinobhaji, Jayaprakash Narayan and draw strength from the holy scriptures like the Gita and the Upanishads. They strongly believe in the values of equality and working and living together. The running of a business itself is a social activity in their view, because it enriches society, creates work opportunities, provides goods and services. In addition, they believe, business has to work directly for the benefit of the community. Community work is coterminus with the business at Excel where everyone is encouraged to get involved in community work. Kantisen Shroff, Chairman Emeritus of Excel, generally referred to as *Kaka*, says: 'Empowerment means treating everyone as equal and bringing out the potential in everyone by making it a part of one's way of thinking and functioning'. A sense of family belonging, easy work culture, free access to the promoter family members, an open system, and treating everyone as an equal are cherished organisational values at Excel. Excel tries to maintain a balance between equality and freedom in running the company. Empowerment is seen as freedom in the company, where a responsible leader assures freedom of choice to his members. As one senior manager puts it, 'At the AGM, the shareholders say that your real assets are not the Rs. 450 crore business but the good work you are doing in the rural areas for the farmers and others. *Kaka* says that the improvement in the number of farmers reached is far more important than the increase in the size of the business as per plan and targets. If you look after mother earth and the farmer the business will increase by itself'.

Community Development Initiatives

As Kutchis, the Shroff family feels that they owe a responsibility for the development of their motherland – the Kutch district of Gujarat. Since the mid-seventies Excel Industries has been investing directly in the development of Kutch through a cluster of sister organisations including Shrujan, Vivekanand Research and Training Institute, and Agrocel Service Centre.

Shrujan, an organisation setup to enhance the income of women artisans of Kutch engaged in hand embroidery work, provides income opportunities for 3,500 artisans (mainly women) in 120 villages. It was registered as a trust in 1981 and has a central office at Bhujodi, near Bhuj and seven centres in different parts of Kutch. The artisans earn up to Rs. 2,000 per month depending on the quality and quantity of work done. Confidence building, exposure programmes, skill base broadening are parts of an all round growth of women through the work of Shrujan.

Vivekananda Research and Training Institute (VRTI) was formed in 1979 and is registered as a trust in Mandvi. The initial years at VRTI were spent in developing the physical infrastructure for water harvesting such as check dams, storage tanks, and ponds. These activities paved the way for an integrated approach to rural development in the area such as water management, agricultural research and land management, composting, afforestation and horticulture, soil and water testing, bee keeping, animal husbandry and animal care, biogas, sanitation, conservation of energy, non-conventional energy resources and equipment. More than 550 water harvesting structures have been created and over 18,000 hectares of land has been covered in the watershed development programme in 33 villages in the different talukas of Kutch. Decentralised systems for planning and implementation have been established with people's involvement for economic development. VRTI believes that economic growth and resources in the hands of people leads to their empowerment. A *Gram Vikas Mandal* (Village Development Committee) is constituted in every village. The *Mandal* is active at the village level and implementation level, and VRTI is active at the policy influencing and advocacy level.

Agrocel Industries Ltd. Service Centre is a joint venture of the Gujarat Agro Industries Corporation and Agrocel Industries Ltd. to provide extension and physical services to farmers for increasing productivity and realising better prices. There are six such centers in Kutch, one in Gujarat outside Kutch, and two in other states. Ten thousand farmers benefit through these service centres.

Gujarat Ambuja Cements Ltd.

Gujarat Ambuja Cements Ltd. (GACL) was established in 1982 and is a major cement producer in the country. It is a family owned business but run on professional lines. Since its inception, GACL has followed a corporate philosophy of 'sustainable development'. Its plant at Ambujanagar near Kodinar (45 kms from Veraval town) in Gujarat is a good example of this commitment. GACL has been able to achieve a pollution free environment at its plant site by using state-of-art technology. The mined out areas of its captive limestone mines around Kodinar are reclaimed through afforestation and related activities. Domestic waste and sewage water from its colony is recycled and the treated water is used for various purposes such as cooling of process equipment, road dust suppression, and maintaining the gardens and trees on the campus. The company has developed and maintained a rose garden in the heart of the plant and changed the mindset of people to accept that cement can be produced without creating imbalance between the environment and development. GACL was the first cement company in Gujarat to receive ISO 14001 certification for excellence in environment management.

GACL pursues a value based approach to managing the business and relating with its stakeholders which is operationalised through seven *mantras* developed with the involvement of the employees. Empowerment at GACL is the open and transparent systems of work as well as the mutual support extended to each other. Stress free atmosphere, problem solving approach, fairness and honesty in dealings, encouragement to improve performance, freedom to work in your own way contribute to the positive feelings experienced by everyone. 'I can' is an inspirational and motivational *mantra* in GACL since inception. In the words of Narottam Seksaria, MD, GACL: 'These days its fashionable to talk of empowerment, but given our line of thinking, we had no choice. If costs had to be controlled, it seemed absurd for engineers to check back with their seniors for every little decision. The time lost would be far more expensive than any error they would make. It was much the same for controlling power consumption. Who better than our engineers to suggest ways to cut costs. They worked night and day on the plant. It made eminent sense to listen to them. Over time this has become a natural company culture: 'I can'. As a result, the standards our people have set for themselves are so high, the company is driven by fear of mediocrity'.

Ambuja Cement Foundation (ACF)

ACF was established in 1991 with the objective of improving the social and economic status of the community around the plant site through human, managerial, technical, and natural resources on a sustainable basis. It was registered in 1993 as an independent non-profit NGO under Section 25 of The Companies Act.

Saurashtra, where the GACL's Ambujanagar plant is located, and which is the source area for its mining operations, is a very water scarce region of Gujarat. The vision of ACF is to tap every drop of rainwater that falls and not allow it to be drained into the sea. Accordingly, its major programmes are Water Resources Development, Soil and Water Conservation, Agriculture Development, Farm Forestry and Afforestation, Animal Husbandry, Health Programme, Non-conventional Energy Sources, Children and Women Development, and Drinking Water Programme. ACF Kodinar work extends to 96 villages in its project area.

ACF believes that direct involvement of the community through building capacities is the only answer to sustainable development. Villagers have been mobilised and organised into groups, committees, and associations to manage their common assets. ACF facilitates the required technical and management inputs for these village institutions to carry out their tasks with confidence. The approach to empowering people is to facilitate the process for everybody to be incharge of their own lives and be able to address various situations they are faced with by themselves.

Tata Chemicals Ltd.

Tata Chemicals Ltd. (TCL) was incorporated in 1939 and began producing soda ash in 1944. Its inorganic chemicals complex in Mithapur,

Gujarat is the largest and most integrated plant in India. TCL is among the top 20 companies, constituting the core of the Tata Group, one of the oldest and highly respected industrial groups in India.

With liberalisation of the Indian economy, TCL is gearing itself to face global and local competition to retain its leadership position. It has become a flatter organisation to face the post World Trade Organisation (WTO) reality and prepare itself for the post 2005 reality. Consequently, restructuring the marketing function, improving operational efficiencies, and improving supply chain management are major initiatives. Similarly, there is strong emphasis on implementing the Safety, Health, and Environment Policy (SHE Policy). TCL seeks to increase shareholder value through SHE excellence. The Mithapur plant is a major employer in the area since its inception. ISO 14001 has been awarded to the Mithapur township – this is the first case of an industrial township being honoured with such a distinction.

TCL has started implementing an action plan for the Tata Business Excellence Model (TBEM), based on the Malcom Balridge Model, which will enable it to adopt world class business processes in all its functional areas. The TBEM has a methodology for scoring various activities of the company and recording progress made on various business processes. The activities of Tata Chemicals Society for Rural Development, a separate body setup for community development initiatives, also contribute to the total score achieved on the TBEM. The community development work of TCL is thus integrated completely with the business operations. As a key official in the company puts it: 'Empowerment is built into the design of the TBEM and its internalisation at every level'.

Tata Chemicals Society for Rural Development (TCSRD)

TCSRD was registered in 1991 as a trust. Its objectives are promotion and growth of the rural economy, development of facilities for public education, and upliftment of the people in the rural areas by becoming a catalyst in the socio-economic development of the region. The Okhamandal region of Jamnagar district, where TCL is located, is highly susceptible to natural calamities like drought and cyclones. TCSRD has been working in all the 42 villages of Okhamandal region. TCSRD is an integral part of the HR department of the company.

The main programmes of TCSRD in Mithapur area include Agriculture development, Watershed development, Health care, Women's programme, and Infrastructure projects. The interventions are operationalised through groups of people in the villages. The TCSRD team facilitates the formation of groups and helps in building their capacities to manage the activities themselves. The guiding principle is that eventually the people have to become self-reliant. As one member of the team says: 'Empowerment means more the community can do on its own without us, the more empowered it is'.

TCL is an active member of the Tata Council for Community Initiatives (TCCI) which has been formed as an umbrella support and integration mechanism for all the community initiatives of the Tata Group companies. An address to TCCI by Ratan N. Tata, Chairman of Tata Sons Ltd. and also Chairman of TCL, captures the significance of social responsibility and community involvement in the whole Group: '...the message we should leave with our CEOs is that there is an integrated approach – that we want them to be profit oriented, we want them to be cost effective, we want them to be quality conscious, and we want them to be good corporate citizens'. All Tata employees sign a Code of Conduct when they join a Tata Group company. Corporate Citizenship is enshrined as an important clause in this code, as a core value.

Gujarat Cooperative Milk Marketing Federation Ltd.

Gujarat Cooperative Milk Marketing Federation Ltd. (GCMMF), formed in 1973, is the state level Federation of twelve District Milk Unions in Gujarat. With 10,852 Dairy Cooperative Societies at the village level having 22.23 lakhs milk producers as members (2001–02 figures), it is the largest food products marketing organisation and also the largest exporter of dairy products in the country. This case relates to one District Union, The Kaira District Cooperative Milk Producers Union Ltd. better known as Amul Dairy, alongwith GCMMF. The unique structure of the cooperative dairy industry in Gujarat and India has developed from the concern to build member owned, democratic, economic institutions which can strengthen the position of the cooperative members in society. Social, economic, and political changes for the members have been made possible by the dairy cooperatives.

The cooperative dairy industry in Gujarat has a three-tier structure. The village level primary Dairy Cooperative Societies constitute the first tier while the District Milk Unions and the apex Milk Marketing Federation at the state level constitute the second and third tiers respectively. This whole integrated approach has come to be known as the Anand Pattern of dairy cooperatives. It has demonstrated that farmers cooperatives can employ professionals, make use of modern technology, and harness market forces to serve their interest. Information technology and communications technology have been deployed effectively to network all the dairy cooperative societies. The GCMMF is among the top 100 IT users in the country. The implication of this structure for empowerment of the people is aptly summed up in the words of one of its employees: 'The right to speak, to ask questions, to raise issues is empowerment at village society level. Plus the right to represent a group of people at the Union level and at the Federation level. Politically the elected leadership is powerful but in technical and managerial matters the professional management is very powerful'.

To face the challenges of liberalisation of the Indian economy, GCMMF decided to introduce the concept of Total Quality Management (TQM) in 1994, with its twin pillars of customer focus and continuous improvement. Six years down the line the organisation has been transformed and continues to improve itself to achieve ambitious growth targets. The TQM approach has been extended upto the individual members of the village Dairy Cooperative Society on the production side, and the whole distribution channel upto the salesmen on the marketing side. A concerted effort is also being made to include women as members of the cooperative structure at all levels. A target of 50 per cent membership of women in the dairy cooperatives by 2010 has been set and conscious steps are being taken to achieve this.

The meaning of Corporate Social Responsibility in the GCMMF context (vis-a-vis the community) becomes a little different from the meaning in the company context. The whole business intervention itself emerges as a response of members (the community) to help themselves – addressing the socio-economic concerns of the members leads to the development of the business venture.

Moreover, each village Dairy Cooperative Society invests in the development of its village from its profits and reserves. The District Union pools back the profits from the milk business to the members in the form of an integrated package of various services. Over and above this, the District Union in collaboration with GCMMF, sets up a special body like the Tribhuvandas Foundation to address a district wide social need such as health care.

Tribhuvandas Foundation (TF)

The late Tribhovandas Patel, after whom the Foundation is named, pioneered this cooperation movement. He was concerned about the health of the rural masses in Kaira district, particularly the women and children. A milk cooperative linked preventive human health care programme was framed as the objective of Tribhuvandas Foundation, which was registered in 1975 as a trust. It became functional in 1980. Over the last two decades the Tribhuvandas Foundation has extended its activities to 644 out of 950 villages in Kaira/Anand districts through its centre in Anand and four subcentres in the district. TF visualises a cooperative based health care delivery system model at the district level by covering all the villages in the district. The basic approach is to integrate economic and environmental aspects with health to focus on economic upliftment and a clean environment. The major programmes of TF are Maternal and Child Health/Primary Health Care, Pre-school Non Formal Education, Income Generating Activity for Women, and Environmental Sanitation. A unique hospitalisation expenses subsidy programme was initiated in 2001 for the milk producers in collaboration with the Sardar Patel Arogya Mandal which has been formed for this purpose.

Individuals pay an annual membership fee to TF to avail of the health services. The Dairy Cooperative Society pays annual contributions to TF to support the programme. The extension network of TF is built through the participating dairy cooperative societies at the village level.

Indian Farmers Fertiliser Cooperative Ltd.

Indian Farmers Fertiliser Cooperative Ltd. (IFFCO) is a unique venture in which farmers of the country, through their own cooperative societies, joined hands with the Government of India and created a new institution in 1967 to produce fertilisers and safeguard their interests. IFFCO is the largest producer of fertilisers in the country with 36,114 member societies which market the produce (2001–02 figures).

All cooperative societies associated with agricultural activities are eligible to be members of IFFCO which is a multi unit cooperative society registered under the Multi State Cooperative Societies Act. The rights of the members are related to specified basic minimum level of utilisation of the services/products or the business of IFFCO. The Representative General Body (RGB), which is the General Body, forms the supreme body that guides the various activities of IFFCO. An elected Board of Directors and a team of professional managers, who are experts in various fields, run the business operations of IFFCO.

IFFCO has plants at Kalol and Kandla in Gujarat, and at Phulpur and Aonla in Uttar Pradesh. The Kalol plant is the focus of this case. The culture of commitment to work is typical of the Kalol unit. A value system has been developed where management and workers both work together on the same side of the table rather than as antagonists. Both have a common stake in the plant running well, in increasing productivity, in achieving targets, in helping each other. The Kalol unit was the first plant of IFFCO, commissioned in 1975, and was the first in the fertiliser industry to receive ISO 9002 international certification for Quality Assurance in Production, Installation and Services in 1996. It has been awarded ISO 14001 certification in 2000 for its Environmental Systems. The employees at the Kalol unit like to refer to their unit as 'a plant in a garden' because of the clean and green plant site. The township of IFFCO Kalol unit is the first township in the country selected by the United States Agency for International Development (USAID) for ISO 14001 certification as a single identity. The experience of empowerment is reflected in the following words of one of the employees: 'Pooling of everyone's strength, unity of purpose, openness, fearlessness, trust, these are some of the processes which lead to empowerment. When the workers and management are both concerned about the well-being of the plant, then everyone's interest is met better'. IFFCO has been continuously improving its cost efficiencies particularly with the liberalisation of the Indian economy in the nineties. There has been consistent pressure to reduce the subsidy on fertilisers and IFFCO has been gearing itself up to face this challenge. Through plans called 'Vision 2000' and 'Mission 2005' it strives to become a leader in the field of fertiliser production and marketing.

Strengthening the nation's cooperative fabric has been IFFCO's principal concern. In the case of IFFCO too, the meaning of CSR is a little different than that in companies. The business of producing fertilisers itself is a member owned enterprise. The farmer's interests are looked after through the marketing function of IFFCO and also through the separate bodies created for specific purposes. It has set up a separate trust called Cooperative Rural Development Trust for further strengthening the farmers. A separate effort called the Integrated Rural Development Programme is also initiated. The Kisan Sewa Fund and the Insurance Facility through IFFCO-TOKIO are recent developments to provide a multi-faceted support to the farmers. A Group Personal Accident Insurance Scheme provides group insurance to any farmer buying a minimum of one bag of IFFCO fertiliser during the year. IFFCO is taking initiative to bring the benefits of Information Technology (IT) to the doorsteps of Indian farmers with specific focus on meeting the requirements of agriculture and cooperative sector.

Cooperative Rural Development Trust (CORDET)

Cooperative Rural Development Trust (CORDET) was promoted as a separate trust in 1979 to undertake integrated rural development programmes for the benefit of the farmers. The activities of Kalol CORDET include soil testing, production and supply of improved seeds, training camps to educate farmers and farm women in modern agriculture technology, dairy farming, animal husbandry, and home science, afforestation, rural development programme in the surrounding villages. A fund of Rs. 20 lakhs is allocated every year by IFFCO Kalol for assisting in the infrastructure development of the villages within a radius of 30 kms of the plant. A fixed amount is dedicated to CORDET for every tonne of fertiliser sold by IFFCO every year.

Empowerment in the Business Operations

In all these five cases the businesses have adopted a stakeholder approach. Employees, the community, and the environment are important stakeholders in addition to the shareholders. Concern for the community is a part of the business strategy in all the cases. In fact, enlightened self-interest has motivated the managements of all the five enterprises to integrate the community interest with the business interest. The extent of integration, admittedly, varies from case to case. The community itself emerges as a stakeholder of the business in these cases either as consumers or suppliers or both.

The employees in the business operations of these enterprises are part of a well-defined work system. They see their own empowerment in terms of the work culture and the scope for them to realise their own potential. Opportunities for personal and professional growth by fulfilling organisational goals are integral to this process. Women employees are in a minority in these businesses. The cooperative business organisations strive to achieve some measure of gender balance in their membership.

The nuances of their workplace dynamics which are perceived as conducive to empowerment have been highlighted by the employees of these five business organisations. These include a sense of belonging; stress free, family like work atmosphere; impartial and fair treatment for all; integrity in transactions; and striving for excellence. The freedom to define one's own way of work, freedom to make mistakes, matching authority and responsibility, systems based functioning, recognition of individual and group contributions to overall achievements of the business are also perceived as conducive to empowerment.

The employees feel that a sense of belonging and bonding with the business is consciously nurtured at all levels of the organisation. This is achieved by easy access to the organisation's leadership, open systems, hierarchy which is not intimidating, transparency, and good communication. These practices are reinforced by creating high trust levels, equality and dignity for all, a problem-solving approach, genuine support and help during personal crises. This bonding, in turn, leads to higher motivation and better performance by the employees. The personal and the organisational facets of the employees' lives are thus closely aligned. The individual goals of the employees are successfully met by achieving group goals.

This is reflected in the continuous increase in productivity in all the cases. The different forms of gearing up, undertaken in the 1990s, by these businesses to meet the challenges of globalisation, after the Indian economy has been liberalised, is a testimony to the commonality of interests between the organisation and the individual. These include getting ISO certification, adopting stringent quality improvement measures, and environment protection measures to become globally competitive. Achieving increases in productivity and energy efficiencies as well as in supply chain and distribution chain efficiencies have led to improved financial results. Together, these efforts have helped the businesses to retain their leadership position in the industry.

Well-defined business processes, targets for excellence, focused energies, are contributing to the high standards achieved by these business organisations. A declared value system, articulated vision and mission statements, and stated policies are contributing to clarity of direction for all. And of course success in business is feeding on itself to continuously reinforce all these processes within the work system as well as contributing to the sustained existence of the business itself. Thus, empowerment in the business operations is achieved by continued convergence of the individual and organisational objectives for improved performance.

Empowerment in the Community Development Initiatives

While the organisational environment and dynamics of the enterprises covered in our case studies contribute to the empowerment of their employees, the community development initiatives undertaken by them basically focus on economic empowerment of the people in the communities they work with. This is seen as the pre-requisite for other changes to happen. Self-reliance and building the all round capacities of people to manage and be incharge of their own economic resources and institutions is the thrust of empowerment in the community development work of these organisations.

Economic empowerment helps to integrate people in the economic mainstream and this is nurtured by encouraging them to value being independent instead of expecting doles from the government. This is very important and becomes the starting point for a continuous process of self-development as well as for improving their own quality of life. An integrated approach develops to address the related issues of education, water, health and sanitation, insurance, alongwith the economic interventions in a mutually beneficial way. Economic power helps the people to gain political power as well.

The infrastructure facilities and resources necessary for improving incomes have to be created and be placed in people's hands. The people get organised around the tasks of management of the infrastructure facilities and the resources. People grow as they gain experience and realise their own potential. The principle is to develop a stake for people in the infrastructure and resources being created, and economic growth of people will be taken care of by themselves. They will, thus, also be better integrated in the economic mainstream. Working together effectively will necessitate having trust in each other. Building trust and contributing to develop a high-trust society is another aspect which is implicit in the approach to empowerment in these cases.

The enterprises studied understand the term 'empowerment' more commonly as 'women's empowerment' even though men in the community are also being empowered by the various interventions. The influence of the women's movement as well as the emphasis on women's inclusion in the government programmes seems to have contributed to such an association. The interventions for helping women are separated as 'Women's Programmes' in all the cases. Very little effort is visible to integrate women and men in the same forums except in the dairy cooperatives.

The thrust of empowerment in the community development initiatives undertaken by the enterprises in our sample will be more clear if we look at some of their major elements as discussed below.

Organising Basis

People are organised around programme interventions such as watershed development, micro-credit, integrated agriculture development, afforestation, handicrafts production, etc. These lead to forming self-help institutions, which are limited to the village level at present. Federating these into larger forums has not yet happened on a sufficiently large scale.

The interventions by the cooperative institutions have organised people around specific occupations like dairy farming or agriculture to integrate them in the economic mainstream as well as in the political and social mainstream. The scale of operations of these interventions has become very large, and they have been able to tilt the terms of trade in favour of the producers/users.

Change Achieved

Change is visible in the regions where these organisations are functioning. Incomes of people have improved, difficulties such as lack of drinking water and irrigation facilities have become less acute, improved agricultural practices have been adopted, linkages with a range of expertise have been established, new markets have been accessed, self confidence of the people has increased, and health and nutrition levels have improved.

In some cases it is now possible to visualise large size economic ventures with a product focus such as date economy, cotton economy, groundnut economy, as a result of the infrastructure development undertaken so far. In the case of the cooperative institutions, large scale economic ventures have already been developed and they are growing. A sensitisation to the environmental concerns and need for a balanced use of natural resources for sustainable development has also begun. This can be seen in both the small size and large size institutions which have developed.

Changes in the economic situation of the people coupled with the design of the institutions that are promoted have led to noticeable social change in the communities where these initiatives have been implemented. Development of leadership qualities in the people, improvement in the status of the underprivileged and disadvantaged sections of the community, and hope for a better future are visible as a consequence. There are also signs of greater awareness of women's realities and better understanding of gender inequalities although gender integration in the economic mainstream is not so strong as yet.

Representativeness

There is a range of representativeness which is developing through these interventions. The role of the promoters of the business enterprises and the functionaries of the community development initiatives undertaken by them is interlinked with the role of the people themselves in the communities in building different types of representativeness.

The Shroff family, for instance, is acutely conscious of its responsibility to the people of Kutch and does not believe in abdicating it. They are at the helm of affairs in the community development initiatives of Excel Industries in Kutch, and intend to continue in that role. Being Kutchis themselves, they have adopted the locational (geographical) basis of representing the people of Kutch. People's capacities are also being developed on various facets and they do represent themselves at the village level. The full implications of people representing themselves on various facets of their lives at higher levels in society will unfold over time, as they become more capable.

A functional representation in society in terms of professional expertise seems to be emerging in the case of GACL and TCL. They seek to represent competence to address specific types of problems such as water scarcity, health care, livelihood options for deprived communities. These concerns of representativeness, however, are not yet articulated. The thrust of their interventions is that the people in the community have to represent themselves in their institutions and in their lives at the village level and at other levels also. Here too, the full implications of people representing themselves will unfold over time.

In the case of GCMMF, the professional staff in the whole structure of the dairy cooperatives are representing their expertise on a functional basis in the design of the institutions which have been established. Similarly, in the case of IFFCO the professional staff are representing their expertise on a functional basis with regard to the agricultural cooperative societies. People (men and women) are representing themselves in their occupation of dairy farming/agriculture and in their geographical areas through membership and leadership of their respective cooperatives at all levels ranging from the village to the nation. However, there is a very close interweaving of the people's power base and the professional's power base. There is a provision for professional expertise to be included in the decision making forums of the people. However, it is very clearly stated that the professional expertise is employed by the people to serve them. A balance is sought to be achieved between political power (of the people) and technical/ managerial power (of the professional expertise) to bring about social and economic change. The challenges to be faced in developing people's capacities to represent themselves in institutions of ever increasing economic size and scale are clearly highlighted in the history of GCMMF. In the case of IFFCO the challenges of working with the government as a shareholder are highlighted. If the efforts made by the other organisations included in this study, to facilitate people's own institutions are successful and develop in size and scale in the same way as in the case of GCMMF and IFFCO, then they will also face similar challenges.

Value for Empowerment

The Business Excellence Models (Malcom Balridge and Total Quality Management), used by TCL and GCMMF respectively, consider the community as an integral stakeholder of the business. Developing metrics for measuring empowerment of the community, and defining the exchange relationship of the business vis-a-vis the community is being pursued by TCL. This can provide direction and focus to the community development initiatives at a generic level.

Business organisations have to balance the interests of their various stakeholders, and this inevitably places a limit on their efforts at empowering the people in the communities they engage with. The amount of funds provided by the business operations for community development initiatives fluctuates with the fortunes of the business. And yet, having access to their own funds helps them to be rooted in their work independently of outside support. This can contribute to developing long term plans for change. Also, having one's own funds as the base, it becomes easier to access additional funds from elsewhere. All the cases in the study have been leveraging funds from government sources as well as from other funding sources on the strength of their own funds. The business organisations also bring to bear their managerial experience on the management of their community development initiatives. This is reflected in the emphasis on economic empowerment, self-reliance, and mainstreaming with the economy. This is also used to build partnerships, to facilitate cross sectoral learnings, and to develop a business like orientation in all interventions.

The value for empowerment thus gets reflected in the business strategy adopted by these enterprises. The better the integration of the community as a stakeholder of the business in the form of its consumers or suppliers or both, the greater the perceived value for empowerment of the community by the business.

5

Government and Governance

While empowerment is a relatively new mission with business organisations, it has always been regarded as an integral part of the functions of government. In recent times, however, the role of government and the quality of governance have become increasingly critical for improving the lives of the people they govern. Government initiatives to achieve this end constitute a principal road to empowerment as the *Human Development Report, 2002* rightly points out:

> Countries can promote human development for all only when they have governance systems that are fully accountable to all people – and when all people can participate in the debates and decisions that shape their lives.
>
> In an integrated world democratic principles have a global dimension because global rules and actors often affect people's lives as much as national ones.

This chapter describes some of the current frameworks for governance to understand the functions of the state and the changing role of government. The nature of empowerment through government action in the Indian context is presented later.

Functions of the State

The World Development Report, 1997 has presented a framework for the functions of the state as shown in Table 1.

Table 1. A Framework for the functions of the State.

Functions of the State

	Addressing market failure			**Improving equity**
Minimal functions	*Providing pure public goods:* Defence, Law and order, Property rights, Macroeconomic management, Public health			*Providing the poor:* Anti-poverty programs, Disaster relief
Intermediate functions	*Addressing externalities:* Basic education, Environmental protection	*Regulating monopoly:* Utility regulation, Antitrust policy	*Overcoming imperfect information:* Insurance (health, life, pensions), Financial regulation, Consumer protection	*Providing social insurance:* Redistributive pensions, Family allowances, Unemployment insurance
Activist functions	*Coordinating private activity:* Fostering markets, Cluster inititatives			*Redistribution:* Asset redistribution

(Source: *The World Development Report, 1997*, p. 27.)

The movement from Minimal functions to Intermediate functions to Activist functions in Table 1 is visualised as increasing degrees of state capability. The state can enhance its capability in this regard, according to this document, through a range of mechanisms categorised as three major clusters called effective rules and restraints, greater competitive pressures, and increased voice and partnership.

The Department for International Development (DFID, United Kingdom) (2000) stresses the same point when it lists out the key capabilities of the state to make government work better for poor people. These are:

- To operate political systems which provide opportunities for all people, including the poor and disadvantaged, to influence government policy and practice.
- To provide macro-economic stability and to facilitate private sector investment and trade so as to promote the growth necessary to reduce poverty.
- To develop a policy framework which can meet the poverty eradication targets and to raise, allocate and account for resources in accordance with those pro-poor policies.
- To guarantee the equitable and universal provision of effective basic services.
- To ensure personal safety and security with access to justice for all.
- To manage national security accountably and to resolve differences between communities before they develop into violent conflicts.
- To develop honest and accountable government that can combat corruption.

Some recent studies also focus on the role of government though with different emphasis. One of these is *Reinventing Government* by David Osborne and Ted Gaebler (Khandwala, 1999). It enunciates the following principles to create an entrepreneurial and businesslike state for effective governance:

- The government should concentrate on catalysing various social and economic activities. It should steer, that is, give broad support and direction, rather than get involved in rowing, that is, in actual operations.

- The government should empower communities to serve themselves rather than itself get involved in community service activities. The services in which community control can be especially beneficial may be health, schooling, and welfare related activities.
- The government should set out to create competition in public service delivery so that customers get the best value for money. For example, monolithic public sector organisations can be broken up into numerous units to foster competition; public services can be contracted out to the best bidder, and bidders can include public as well as private service agencies; and an option can be given to government agencies to buy from inside the public sector or outside it. Privatisation of a government activity or service can be done in such a way as to promote competition, for example, by handing it over to several parties rather than a single party.
- The government should be transformed from being rules-driven to being mission-driven, that is driven by a vision of excellence and a sense of mission.
- The government should be results-oriented, and fund outcomes rather than inputs. The tendency in democratic governments is to worry about whether the budgeted expenditure is incurred or not, and whether government rules have been followed or not in incurring it. Instead, the stress should be on getting results, even if it means liberalising the budgeting rules and regulations, such as by permitting agencies to reallocate money from one head to another freely, or to carry forward the unspent balance next year without prior government approval.
- The government should be customer-driven, meeting the needs of the citizen-customer rather than mainly the needs and requirements of the bureaucracy. This can be done through customer surveys and follow-up assessment of changes introduced as a result of such surveys, compulsory minimum contact of each staff member with the customers of the government agency or department, setting up of customer councils for feedback, of focus groups for dialogue on a new service or service modification, creating electronic facilities for customers to communicate directly with an agency, customer service training for agency staff, test marketing of new services, giving of quality guarantees to customers, use of undercover inspectors to monitor public services, the setting up

of efficient complaint registering and complaint tracking systems, etc.

- The government should become more business-like and try and earn what it spends on its various activities. Thus, its agencies should price their services rather than give them gratis, and price them to generate a surplus. Having to support activities on their own would make these agencies value efficiency much more.
- The government should concentrate on prevention rather than cure, and learn to anticipate problems. Often governments undertake activities without thinking through their wider implications for pollution, environmental degradation and effects on disadvantaged groups. Anticipation of these consequences can lead to more effective plans.
- The government should decentralise its operations and learn to get its work done through participative management and teamwork rather than hierarchically through the orders of bosses. For example, the bulk of authority over schools can be transferred from local government to teams of principals, teachers, and parents; a field laboratory to test creative policing ideas can be participatively set up; staff meetings can be held to brainstorm on how to rehabilitate a moribund sanitation department, etc.
- The government should harness incentives and markets rather than controls and regulations to bring about desired changes, such as by offering guarantees for educational loans by banks to students, by creating a secondary market for building loans, or by taxing pollution at punitive rates rather than banning it, or by providing tax credits or vouchers to low income families to get childcare from the market.

What the above prescriptions highlight is that instead of directing or controlling the people, the government should concentrate on 'enabling' them to achieve maximum impact. Nobel laureate Amartya Sen (1995) sees the role of government as promoting development for its people. He identifies five distinct types of instrumental freedoms which he regards as the end as well as the means to development, and which government has to ensure. These are Political Freedoms, Economic Facilities, Social Opportunities, Transparency Guarantees, and Protective Security. Sen's account of these freedoms is the following:

Political freedoms broadly conceived (including what are called civil rights), refer to the opportunities that people have to determine who should govern and on what principles, and also include the possibility to scrutinise and criticise authorities, to have freedom of political expression and an uncensored press, to enjoy the freedom to choose between different political parties, and so on. They include the political entitlements associated with democracies in the broadest sense (encompassing opportunities of political dialogue, dissent and critique as well as voting rights and participatory selection of legislators and executives).

Economic facilities refer to the opportunities that individuals respectively enjoy to utilise economic resources for the purpose of consumption, or production, or exchange. The economic entitlements that a person has will depend on the resources owned or available for use as well as on conditions of exchange, such as relative prices and the working of the markets. Insofar as the process of economic development increases the income and wealth of a country, they are reflected in corresponding enhancement of economic entitlements of the population. It should be obvious that in the relation between national income and wealth, on the one hand, and the economic entitlements of individuals (or families), on the other, distributional considerations are important, in addition to aggregative ones. How the additional incomes generated are distributed will clearly make a difference.

Social opportunities refer to the arrangements that society makes for education, healthcare and so on, which influence the individual's substantive freedom to live better. These facilities are important not only for the conduct of private lives (such as living a healthy life and avoiding preventable morbidity and premature mortality), but also for more effective participation in economic and political activities. For example, illiteracy can be a major barrier to participation in economic activities that require production according to specification or demand strict quality control (as globalised trade increasingly does). Similarly, political participation may be hindered by the inability to read newspapers, or to communicate in writing with others involved in political activities.

Transparency guarantees deal with the need for openness that people can expect: the freedom to deal with one another under guarantees of disclosure and lucidity. When that trust is seriously violated, the lives of many people – both direct parties and third parties – may be adversely affected by the lack of openness. Transparency guarantees (including the right to disclosure) can thus be an important category of instrumental freedom. These guarantees have a clear instrumental role in preventing corruption, financial irresponsibility, and underhand dealings.

Protective security is needed to provide a social safety net for preventing the affected population from being reduced to abject misery, and in some cases even starvation and death. The domain of social security includes fixed institutional arrangements such as unemployment benefits and statutory income supplements to the indigent as well as ad hoc arrangements such as famine relief or emergency public employment to generate income for destitutes.

According to Sen, all the five freedoms collectively contribute to an overall improvement in the quality of life of a people. The market mechanism alone will fail to deliver results unless these other freedoms are provided by the State. The task of the government is to ensure access for all its citizens to the facilities, environments, and freedoms which are needed to enable them to achieve their full potential.

Empowerment through Government Action – Concepts and Cases

Empowerment through government action basically takes the form of legislations, policies, and resolutions which define the powers of government vis-a-vis the people. Consequently, political, fiscal, and administrative powers of the State are defined and redefined continuously.

Government action has to address the needs of the total population. Hence government action adds to or takes away power from all sections of people. Selective empowerment by government action is possible by reservation policies for some castes or groups. Positive discrimination – pro-poor policies and programmes which address the reality of underprivileged and disadvantaged sections of the population – is no more regarded as discriminative.

The devolution of powers under the 73rd and 74th Amendments in the Indian Constitution is a good example of empowering people through government action. The 73rd Amendment passed in 1992 paved the way for the creation of statutory institutional structures for realising the goals of self governance under the Panchayati Raj system. The explicit objective of this initiative for democratic decentralisation of governance is to accelerate the socio-economic development of the rural areas within a participatory framework at the grassroots level. This Amendment has given statutory recognition to a three-tier system of governance through Panchayati Raj Institutions at the district (Zilla Panchayat), intermediary (Mandal Panchayats), and village levels (Gram Sabha/Panchayats). Similarly the 74th Amendment adopted in the same year has paved the way for creating statutory institutional structures for self governance in the urban areas through Municipalities and Municipal Corporations.

The scope of the Panchayati Raj Act has been extended to panchayats in the scheduled tribal areas of nine states. Under the provisions of the Panchayat (Extension to the Scheduled Areas) Act, 1996, power has been vested in the Gram Sabhas for controlling the institutions and functionaries in all social sectors including ownership of minor forest produce, selection of beneficiaries under various programmes, management of minor water bodies, and minor mineral leases.

The reservation for women in Panchayati Raj Institutions has opened the doors to political power for women in unprecedented ways. This is a step towards addressing the gender imbalance with regard to political power for women at the grassroots level.

The accent on empowerment through government action is also reflected in the renaming of the Ministry of Social Welfare of the Government of India as the Ministry for Social Justice and Empowerment. Welfare programmes for the scheduled castes, religious and linguistic minorities, socially and educationally backward classes, the aged, the physically handicapped as also the programmes for social defence and juvenile social maladjustment are undertaken by this Ministry. Economic empowerment of socially disadvantaged groups is a major area of concern for this Ministry. Five apex level finance corporations assist beneficiaries to launch self-employment ventures. These are National Scheduled Castes Finance and Development Corporation, National Backward Castes Finance Corporation, National Handicapped Finance and Development Corporation, National Safai Karamcharis Finance and Development Corporation, and National Minorities Development and Finance Corporation. These corporations also fund self-help groups for micro funding in order to expand the coverage of the target population.

These initiatives of the Government of India illustrate how a single government action can simultaneously affect the lives of millions of people either positively or negatively. Empowerment through government action is dependent on clarity of thought and political will on the part of government to define its role and powers vis-a-vis those of the people. The role of government is changing from that of provider and implementer to that of facilitator and supporter of development interventions. Consequently, new spaces emerge for other actors to take up the provider and implementer roles. Increasingly, a variety of public-private partnerships have been negotiated for implementing government policies and programmes such as building roads, running schools, hospitals, providing water facilities, housing for the poor, slum improvement. Another dimension of the shift in government roles is emphasised through privatisation of government functions as seen in the case of telecommunications, air transport and divestment of public sector units.

The government has launched a series of programmes to improve the facilities available to the people. Substantial amount of money is allocated to these programmes. This is clear from the following figures released by the Government of India in *The Economic* Survey, *2003–04*:

Central Government expenditure (Plan and Non Plan) on Social Services, Rural Development, Pradhan Mantri Gramodaya Yojana (PMGY) and Pradhan Mantri Gram Sadak Yojana (PMGSY) for 2002–03 was Rs 48,165 crores. Total Central Government expenditure as per cent of GDP at current prices was 16.2 per cent in 2002–03 and 15.9 per cent in 2001–02. Expenditure on Social Services, Rural Development, PMGY, PMGSY together as a per cent of GDP at market prices was 2.0 per cent in 2002–03 and 1.7 per cent in 2001–02. The quantum of funds spent on these programmes has not led to change in commensurate measure at the grassroots in the lives of the people for whom they are intended. Consequently, the government is continuously trying to find more effective ways of operationalising these programmes. The changes in the design and mode of implementation of these programmes are another manifestation of empowerment through government action. They reflect the realisation by government of the need to involve the people themselves in the implementation, for achieving better results.

Several recent programmes are illustrative of steps towards empowering people through government action. These are, to mention a few, Watershed Development Programme, Joint Forest Management Programme, Micro Credit Programme through self-help groups, Swarnajayanti Gram Swarozgar Yojana, Swarnajayanti Shahri Swarozgar Yojana, and Development of Women and Children in Urban Areas Programme. Sponsored by the Government of India, all these programmes are designed to encourage people to organise themselves. The groups that emerge from this process are visualised as direct counterparts to the government departments responsible for these programmes. Resources and rights are transferred to the groups to enable them to operationalise the programme according to specified guidelines. The results achieved and the benefits derived from these programmes are owned by the people involved.

With proper support and capacity building efforts these groups can become robust people's organisations which are defined as sets of people taking responsibility for improving their own life situation themselves. There are strong elements of empowerment in these programmes, which can be used to nurture the government organisation-people's organisation interface. (The concepts of people's organisations and their interface with government organisations as well as with other types of organisations are elaborated in the next chapter). The operationalisation of empowerment through government organisations, however, has proved to be a very complex and difficult process because vested interests have to be confronted in changing the status quo. That is where the role of a catalyst or change agent becomes important. The experiences of many state government sponsored programmes in healthcare, education, water and sanitation, agriculture and several other areas highlight a similar situation. Many government programmes increasingly feel the need for a catalyst or change agent for successful implementation, though some have been effective in reaching out to the people directly.

Several case studies illustrate the nature of empowerment possible through government action, both with and without the involvement of external catalysts or change agents. The **Swajal Project** in the state of Uttar Pradesh is a good example of integrating non-governmental organisations in the government-people interface for community empowerment through government action (Planning Commission, GOI and UNDP, 2003, pp. 4–14). This project has achieved a basic shift in the role of government from a provider of water supply and sanitation services in rural areas to that of a facilitator for the community to become a key player in service delivery. A partnership between the village communities, non-governmental organisations, and the government has been formed through a tripartite agreement which clearly defines the roles of each partner. The non-governmental organisation is designated as a Support Organisation and acts as a social intermediary to mobilise the community. The village community organises itself into a Village Water and Sanitation Committee and is responsible for building necessary infrastructure for water and sanitation services jointly with the other two partners. The government acts through the Project Support Unit created at the state level for the Department of Rural Development, Government of UP, and the District Project Management Units at the district level where the project is implemented. A cost sharing arrangement to cover capital costs and maintenance of the infrastructure created has been worked out between the three partners. At the village level the funds are handled through a joint bank account operated by the Village Water and Sanitation Committee and the concerned Support Organisation. The role of the Support Organisations is critical to the successful implementation of the project and they are seen as one of its major beneficiaries. The community is also empowered compared to its position before the project was initiated, but so is the Support Organisation.

The **Slum Networking Project** in Ahmedabad is another example of empowerment through cooperation between public and private agencies (Asnani, 2003). This project aims at transforming the physical environment of slums and *chawls* by providing physical and social infrastructure facilities to integrate them in the mainstream of the society. The project is being implemented with active participation of the slum and *chawl* dwellers, non-governmental organisations, industry, and the local city government. The physical infrastructure facilities to be provided include individual services of water supply, underground sewerage and toilets to each household along with total paving of internal roads and lanes, street lighting and storm water drainage and solid waste disposal facilities. Providing health services, primary education, opportunities for income, savings and credit facilities constitute the social infrastructure. The physical work is undertaken by the Ahmedabad Municipal Corporation on a cost sharing basis wherein the Corporation, private industry and the residents of the slum each contribute one-third of the total cost of physical infrastructure. The social infrastructure services are provided by a non-governmental organisation on a cost sharing basis with the Municipal Corporation on a 30/70% basis. The non-governmental organisation has to motivate the communities of slum residents to participate in the process and facilitate the formation of registered Residents Associations and help them build direct links with the Municipal Corporation and develop their capacities to maintain the newly created infrastructure. The experience of the upgraded slums shows that the Resident Associations are yet to become fully active as representative forums of the slum community though they do have a legal status and are recognised as such. The non-governmental organisations are quite visible in this project and they have a very active interface with the Municipal Corporation.

The National Bank for Agriculture and Rural Development (NABARD) has initiated a **microFinance Programme** since 1992 to provide access to banking services to the poor and marginalised (www.nabard.org and *NABARD Annual Report 2002–03*). The thrust of this programme is to organise self-help groups of 15–20 members, mainly women, who meet regularly for pooling their savings and building a common fund. This fund is leveraged by the group to link with nationalised banks for getting a group loan which it uses for lending to its individual members. NABARD encourages non-governmental organisations to facilitate the formation of such groups and bank staff can also play this role wherever possible. As on 31 March 2003, over 2,800 non-governmental organisations and 31,000 rural outlets of more than 500 banks with a loan portfolio of more than Rs. 2,000 crores are associated with the programme. Almost 116 lakhs households access banking services including micro-credit through 7.17 lakhs self-help groups spread over 488 districts in 30 states and union territories.

The **programme for transfer of canal management responsibilities** to the farmers for more effective use of water for irrigation in Gujarat, Maharashtra, and Andhra Pradesh in cooperation with the Water Resources Departments of the three State governments, envisages the creation of water user associations for 500 hectare blocks. All operations and maintenance responsibilities for minor and small channels within the blocks are transferred to the water users associations which are charged for the water on the basis of volumetric pricing. The collection of water charges from individual farmers is managed by the water users associations. They are also responsible for managing the interface with the government department for all issues concerning irrigation water from the channels. The Water Resources Department or non-governmental organisations or the Panchayati Raj Institutions can play the role of organising water users associations and provide the capacity building inputs to equip them for self management of the irrigation function. (Brewer et al, 1999)

The **Tamil Nadu Women in Agriculture (TANWA)** is a successful project where the Department of Agriculture of the Government of Tamil Nadu is engaged with the community directly to contribute to community empowerment (Planning Commission, GOI and UNDP, 2003, pp. 55–63). This is an example of effective government-people interface without the intermediation of a change agent or catalyst. Women Agricultural Officers of the Department train small and marginal farmers in skills relevant to manage some important crops. The women who receive this training, in turn, form a self-help group of 10 other non-trained, farm women and provide them training. This self-help group is called the TANWA Farm Women's Group and acts as a Village Focal Resource Centre for technical, economic, and social empowerment. Yield levels of crops are increased through this project to achieve overall improvements in the lives of the women farmers.

The experience of the **Kudumbashree Project** in Kerala highlights the process of successful community organisation achieved by the state government (Planning Commission, GOI and UNDP, 2003, pp. 64–75). This is a women oriented project which draws upon resources from the Union Government, National Bank for Agricultural and Rural Development, and UNICEF as well as bank linked poverty alleviation programmes of the government. This project is the state level scaling up of the experience with the Mallapuram Community Development Society, which was a pilot project where the refinement of interventions took place over a period of time. Essentially this is a networking effort to eradicate absolute poverty through the building blocks of Neighbourhood Groups (NHGs). A systematic approach to identify poor households and organise NHGs of 20–30 families each in rural and urban areas is operationalised through community-based, transparent mechanisms. The NHGs are networked into Area Development Societies (ADS) at the ward level, and into a registered Community Development Society (CDS) at the local government level. The CDS is co-terminus with the village Panchayat or Municipality. A development microplan is prepared by each NHG to cover income generation, health, and physical amenities requirements for its members. The development microplans of the NHGs are combined to form a mini plan at the ADS level, which in turn are consolidated by the CDS to form a development plan at the local government level, to be taken up for rigorous implementation. A democratically elected, representative forum at each level of the organisation is responsible for the overall functioning, monitoring, and continuous refining of the various processes put in place. The project operates by leveraging the savings of individual members at the NHG level to raise financial resources from commercial banks. These funds are available to the members for meeting their credit requirements for consumption and productive purposes. The Mallapuram CDS has achieved impressive results in meeting the environmental sanitation and drinking water, education, community health, and micro enterprise needs of its members and enable them to come out of poverty. The government has facilitated the emergence of an effective interest group of the community in the form of the Mallapuram CDS as the people's organisation. The government-people interface is thus managed directly by the two sides concerned and leads to creating political space for the community to effectively influence policy making.

The **Bhagidari Scheme** of the Government of Delhi is another case in point for direct engagement of government with the people. In this programme the Delhi government enters into a partnership with interested Resident Welfare Associations (RWA) in housing colonies to solve urban infrastructure related problems such as water, drainage, and electricity. The RWA is encouraged to represent the problems of its members and the government authorises it to implement the corrective actions. Various RWAs have come together to form a Joint Front of RWAs to deal more effectively with the government authorities. There is also a move to allow Bhagidari representatives to fill in one column of the Annual Confidential Report of the Municipal Corporation of Delhi and Delhi Jal Board officials with a view to making the government more accountable to its citizens. (Hindustan Times, Delhi edition, 16 September 2004).

E-governance experiments – the use of information technology for providing government services – are making it possible for government to reach all citizens directly and equally. They are proving very effective in helping common people to avail their entitlements without the intermediation of an apathetic bureaucracy or through clout and connections. Consequently, Government-to-Citizen (G2C) and Citizen-to-Government (C2G) linkages are being built as a new basis of empowerment through government action. The BHOOMI project in Karnataka for computerised land records, Computer-aided Administration of Registration Department (CARD) project as well as the Computerisation of *Mandal* Revenue Offices project in Andhra Pradesh for land records are providing easy access to the citizens for land records. The GYANDOOT project in Madhya Pradesh for providing intranet connectivity for villages with market information and some government services, the Community Information Centres (CIC)) project in the North Eastern states, the Fast Reliable Instant Efficient Network for Distribution of Services (FRIENDS) project in Kerala for providing government services to the people are making it easy for the citizens to avail various government information and services. These are some initiatives which are showing the way for fundamental changes in the relationship between government and citizens and leading to more effective governance.

The relationship of government with underprivileged and disadvantaged sections of the population is often established through social development partnership programmes with non-governmental organisations. More often than not, the government organisation-non-governmental organisation linkage gets stronger in such partnerships and mediates the government organisation-people's organisation interface. That there are more examples of successful government organisation-non-governmental organisation collaboration than there are of government organisation-people's organisation collaboration for empowerment of the poor and underprivileged only underscores this point. This is not the case in the relationship of government with other sections of society where the government organisation-people's organisation interface is strong and direct. When government deals with industry bodies like the Confederation of Indian Industry or the Federation of Indian Chambers of Commerce and Industry or other such forums, it does not feel the need for any intermediary non-governmental organisation to facilitate interaction with them. But when it deals with the poor and underprivileged sections of the population it encourages intermediaries in the form of non-governmental organisations through which it interacts with the concerned people. In the Joint Forest Management (JFM) programme in Gujarat, for instance, the Forest Department has constituted a State Level Working Group to address policy matters related to the effective operationalisation of the programme. There has been a continuous demand by the state level federated body of JFM communities to include its representatives as members of this forum, but without any success. Non-governmental organisations, academics, bureaucrats are represented in this forum but not the JFM communities themselves for whom this whole effort has been undertaken.

Similarly, the Karnataka Electricity Regulatory Commission (KERC) has constituted an Electricity Consumers Network (ECON) to develop a consumer network in Karnataka to ensure effective consumer participation in the electricity regulation process (www.kerc.org). Nine interested consumer advocacy organisations (non-governmental organisations) have been brought together by ECON, from the four electricity zones of Karnataka, to network amongst themselves and with technical and research organisations for this purpose. KERC will support ECON for a period of three years by helping it to access funds and providing it other secretarial and logistics assistance. Once ECON establishes itself as a credible and effective intervener on behalf of the general consumers, in the regulatory process, KERC may fund it through a charge included in the electricity tariff. Thus, self-appointed groups of people who take up consumer issues have become the official representatives of consumers of electricity (not necessarily with the knowledge or consent of the consumers) to negotiate electricity reforms with the state government.

Empowerment through government organisations for the underprivileged and disadvantaged has to transcend this intermediation and nurture the government organisation - people's organisation interface as is the case with other sections of the population.

References

Asnani, P.U., 'Slum Networking Project-Ahmedabad' in Jumani, Jyoti (ed), *Partnership for Poverty Alleviation,* New Delhi: Tata McGraw-Hill, 2003, pp. 1–22.

Brewer, J. et al., *Irrigation Management Transfer in India – Policies, Processes and Performance*, New Delhi: Oxford University Press and IBH Publishing, 1999, pp. 40 and 117–120.

Department for International Development (DFID, UK), *Strategies for Achieving the Millenium Development Targets – Making Government Work for Poor People,* Consultation Document, 2000, p. 2.

Hindustan Times, Delhi edition, 16 September 2004.

Human Development Report 2002, New York: UNDP, 2002, pp. 5 and 7.

Khandwala, Pradip, *Revitalising the State – A Menu of Options,* New Delhi: Sage, 1999, pp. 33–34, summarising Osborne, David and Gaebler, Ted *Reinventing Government: How the Entrepreneurial Spirit is Transforming the Public Sector from School House to State House, City Hall to Pentagon,* Reading, MA: Addison-Wesley, 1992.

Planning Commission, Government of India and UNDP, *Successful Governance Initiatives and Best Practices – Experiences from the States*, New Delhi: Academic Foundation, 2003, Swajal pp. 4–14, TANWA pp. 55–63, Kudambashree pp. 64–75 .

Sen, Amartya, *Development As Freedom,* New Delhi: Oxford University Press, 1995, pp. 38–40.

World Development Report, 1997 – The State in a Changing World, Washington DC: The World Bank, p. 27.

6

Social Development Organisations

The nature of empowerment through business organisations and government action has been described in the preceding chapters. Besides these two types of organisations, there are a large number of entities engaged in social development activities for different segments of the population. This category, called non-governmental organisations (NGOs), constitutes the third actor in our comparative framework for empowerment. The role of non-governmental organisations and the nature of empowerment emerging from their actions are discussed in this chapter.

What is an NGO?

At the generic level, every legal entity (whether commercial, educational, religious, social, political, charitable, not-for-profit, recreational, etc.) that is not a part of the state or government machinery comes under the umbrella of non-governmental organisation. At the specific level, however, self-appointed groups of people registered as a variety of legal entities, and engaged in development work for the deprived sections of people are included in this category. These are commonly referred to as NGOs. Over the last thirty years or so, NGOs have created a societal context to portray themselves and government as the key actors in improving the lives of deprived people. The societal function of governance is rightfully that of the State, but for various historical and ideological reasons, in many countries, the State has also taken upon itself the societal function of 'development' and 'development programme implementation'. The emergence of NGOs as vehicles of development is based on this reality.

Yet another type of system, concerned with the well-being of the deprived sections, has emerged in recent times. These are known as People's Organisations (POs). In contrast to the NGOs, which are run by people other than whose betterment they seek to achieve, the POs are run by the concerned people themselves. People's organisations are different from NGOs in the specific sense, but are one type of non-governmental organisation in the generic sense. Such institutions are an essential part of civil society.

NGOs and Civil Society

A few selected definitions may provide some idea of what the term 'civil society' stands for. Nicky May (1995) defines civil society as, 'an arena of conflict, with the goal of development being to organise an articulate and active citizenry'. According to Andre Beteille (2002) civil society has three basic components: '(a) state, (b) citizenship, and (c) mediating institutions. Each has certain distinctive features, although they are homologous with each other'. The state, the private sector, and civil society are posited as the three institutional anchors of society in the *World Development Report, 1997*. The private sector is referred to as market institutions and for-profit sector while the state is referred to as government or public sector in some other definitions.

V. Kurien (2002) views civil society as composed of voluntary action groups. According to him, 'Voluntary action springs from the spirit of self-help which is perhaps one of the noblest of traits. Voluntary action is perhaps the only alternative to the state. If we accept voluntary action to encompass every form of activity outside the state and profit-oriented organisations, the voluntary sector should include all the societies, NGOs, trusts, professional bodies and associations, trade unions, cooperative societies, and every conceivable organisation in the not-for-profit sector, the only motive of the organisation being self-help'.

As can be seen from these definitions, the terms civil society, not-for-profit sector, non-governmental organisations, voluntary organisations are very often used interchangeably even though each of them may have its own distinctive features. For the purposes of this study the term civil society subsumes the other three terms – not-for-profit, non-governmental, and voluntary. Civil society, therefore, is composed of several types of organisations and our focus is on the non-governmental organisations (NGOs) which are but one category of organisations in it. Ashis Nandy (2002) elaborates on the positioning of NGOs in civil society in the following words:

> The new interest in civil society is due to the collapse of the old interest in the state. Civil society is now expected to do what the states have not. At the same time, civil society is expected to contain the excesses of the state. I do see NGOs as a crucial part of civil society. At the same time, I don't think they are the only part of civil society, though many NGOs presume this. I think this idea of a civil society that consists solely of and survives by the merit of the NGOs, has in some sense done harm to the NGOs themselves. They have dropped their self-doubts and self-criticisms and become less modest. NGOs are neither elected nor do they enjoy public endorsement beyond a point. They also often lack a larger vision. These are not handicaps when an NGO sticks to issues it is concerned with and does not claim an overall democratic mandate. Its downfall begins the moment it thinks of itself as the voice of people and becomes self-righteous. You do not have the democratic right to speak on behalf of the people if people have not elected you to do so. And in the case of NGOs there is no proof that they enjoy the support of a majority.

The government itself has been promoting the importance of NGOs as its counterpart in implementing development programmes. A Planning Commission paper, 'Action Plan to Bring About a Collaborative Relationship Between Voluntary Organisations and Government' (1994), states that the objective of NGOs should be 'mobilisation and organisation of the poor…with a view to empowering them, breaking the culture of silence and dependence and…converting them (the lowest strata of society) from passive recipients of doles to active participants in the process of planned development'. No statement is made about the relationship of the government with the forums which will emerge when the poor are organised and empowered, what we have called as people's organisations (POs).

To appreciate the place of NGOs and POs in civil society, it is important to recognise that the social development process entails a relationship between five sets of actors – people, government, donors, experts, and NGOs. Within these, people and government are the two sets of actors which have an indefinite existence and a permanent on-going relationship with each other. The other three sets of actors must become increasingly redundant to a given set of people in the development process, if true empowerment of people is to happen. The following three interfaces between the actors therefore have to be understood in some detail to draw out the nuances of empowerment of people through NGOs:

- NGO — Government Organisation
- NGO — People's Organisation
- Government Organisation — People's Organisation

These three interfaces subsume the relationship with the experts and the donor agencies because their inputs are tied up with the other three actors in one way or the other.

Typology of NGOs – Concepts and Cases

Several typologies of NGOs have been put forth by various writers classifying them by size, area of operations, geographical coverage, functions and roles, origins, sources of funds, etc. A slightly different way of categorising NGOs is on the basis of their involvement with the people they seek to serve. Based on this criterion, the following typology of NGOs can be visualised for the purposes of understanding the process of empowerment of people. Drawing on published sources, a brief description of select NGOs is included to illustrate each category in the typology of NGOs.

Those working directly with poor people

These may be called direct action groups or organisations. They engage in struggle and/or constructive activities for the benefit of the people for whom they work. Some examples of this type are the following NGOs.

Gram Vikas in Berhampur, Orissa (Madiath and Jayapadma, 2002) has been active in improving the quality of life of tribal and other marginalised communities through various development interventions since the mid-seventies. Its Rural Health and Environment Programme is a comprehensive effort to utilise the physical, natural, social, and human capital in every village to provide various types of facilities to all families in the villages where Gram Vikas works. As many as 5070 families in 67 villages have been involved in this initiative. Sanitation and supply of piped drinking water are the focal points around which they facilitate community organisation. This, in turn, has led to other development activities such as common assets, irrigation infrastructure, livelihood diversification, savings and credit facilities, revitalisation of schools, better functioning of health centres, and involvement in the Panchayati Raj Institutions for local self-governance. A Village Corpus Fund is established by contribution from each family in a village. Gram Vikas staff facilitate the process of enabling the entire village to come to a consensus about contribution to the Village Corpus Fund and to participate in the Rural Health and Sanitation Programme. A village committee is elected from the community and this body implements the programme jointly with Gram Vikas functionaries.

The **Aga Khan Rural Support Programme (India), [AKRSP (I)]**, has been working in the rural areas of three districts of Gujarat since the mid-eighties. Its interventions are primarily through land and water conservation efforts to enhance agricultural productivity and income of the people. Sustainable management of natural resources is a central focus of the AKRSP(I) approach to livelihood enhancement. Simultaneous development of human resources also is implied in this approach to enable communities of people to take control over development processes along with project planning and implementation. Towards this end, AKRSP(I) facilitates the formation, development, and maturation of a range of institutions which are owned and managed by the community where it intervenes. These are called village institutions and include *Gram Vikas Mandals* (Village Development Committees), which work on issues of common interest to a village; *Mahila Vikas Mandals* which work on women's empowerment; Self Help Groups and Credit Management Groups which work on issues of economic empowerment; and theme based interest groups like Salinity Prevention Groups, Water Savings Groups, *Pani Samitis*, Watershed Associations, Water Resource Development User's Groups, Canal Irrigation Societies, etc. AKRSP(I) has been encouraging these various groups to federate at the taluka level for collective strength. These federations take on the role of marketing, procurement of inputs, training and capacity building, advocacy, building linkages with the government machinery and with the market as well as with other federations of people and with NGOs. AKRSP(I) has covered 528 villages in these three districts reaching out to nearly 23000 households as of 2003. In the initial stages the works are implemented more by AKRSP(I) staff in collaboration with the village community. Once a village forum evolves, funds for implementing works are transferred to this group through a bank account jointly operated by AKRSP(I) staff and the village community. As the group matures, the bank account is increasingly operated by the village community and eventually the AKRSP(I) functionary does not have any say in it. The same process is followed for the funds of the federations as they develop and mature. As the federations in Gujarat become more and more capable, AKRSP(I) has been initiating activities in the state of Madhya Pradesh and eventually plans to transform itself into a service provider to various organisations. (Underwood, 2002 and *AKRSP(I) Annual Report 2003*).

Pratham is a tripartite partnership which brings together the corporate sector, the voluntary sector, and the government to intervene in the field of primary education (Chavan, 2003). Registered as a trust in Mumbai in 1994, Pratham defines its primary goal as '*Every child in school and learning well*'. It believes that while government has both a right and a duty to provide funds for education, everyone in society has to be involved in creating systems which ensure proper delivery of educational inputs. Hence all segments of society must invest time, money, and skills and play an active role in making the government system more effective, more productive. Towards this purpose it began its work with the municipal schools in Mumbai and has developed pre-school programmes, remedial education programmes, bridge courses with the active involvement of the community. The basic thrust of these initiatives is to strengthen the educational foundation of children studying in municipal schools as well as of drop-outs. Processes to increase attendance in schools and improve performance have been put in place and are closely monitored. There has been a spontaneous replication of the programme in several cities of the country, with the result that Pratham has been able to reach out to about two lakh children in the municipal school system to help them to attend school and learn well.

Seva Mandir is engaged in rural development interventions in Udaipur in Rajasthan (Gulhati and Gulhati, 1995 and www.sevamandir.org). Formed in 1966, its initial activities centred around a literacy programme for tribals. Over the years it has evolved into a comprehensive rural development programme covering 583 villages in 6 blocks in and around Udaipur district and reaching out to more than 18000 families. The programmes include environmental improvement, water and vegetative conservation, wasteland reclamation, health and community welfare, non-formal and adult education, women's development and community action. Seva Mandir attempts to involve people in their own development. It helps them to recognise the benefit of community effort and to strive for sustainable long term goals. Its staff and functionaries work directly in the villages, through a team of paraworkers, with the people who benefit from their programmes. The paraworkers are drawn from the community and provide leadership to the programme at the village level. Village committees are formed with the paraworkers and other leaders as members for smooth implementation of programmes. Continuous interaction and dialogue with the beneficiaries precedes any implementation work so as to create awareness and facilitate informed decision making by the community. A people's management school has been set up to strengthen the people's capacity to manage their own development.

The **Mazdoor Kisan Sangathan Shakti (MKSS)** was set up in Devdungri village near Barar in Rajsammand district of Rajasthan in 1990 (Roy, 2002, Mander, 2003 and www.righttoinformation.info/rajasthan). It began by attempting to operationalise a non party political process for strengthening the hands of the poor. MKSS has developed the mechanism of *'jan sunwais'* (public hearings) wherein information about development programmes implemented by the government agencies is shared with a public audience of that region and complaints of the local people are addressed. This has been done to create accountability of the government functionaries to the people whom they serve. The initial struggles for land and minimum wages by MKSS later led to the pioneering work on the right to information for the citizens as the first step to participatory democracy. This struggle has spread across the country through the National Campaign for the People's Right to Information. It has been successful in embodying the right to information as a legal right through legislation enacted in Rajasthan and several other states of the country. The Government of India has passed the Right to Information Act in 2005.

Those working directly with poor people and/are also providing a variety of support activities to other groups and organisations

These may be called support-cum-action groups or organisations. They usually work in one field area and are engaged in struggle and/or constructive activities for the people to understand the issues and problems as well as to seek the relevant solutions for the people. Simultaneously they encourage and support other direct action groups to work better. The following cases illustrate this type of NGO.

Vikram Sarabhai Centre for Development Interaction (VIKSAT) has been functioning since 1977 in Gujarat. Through interaction with government organisations, NGOs, and people's institutions VIKSAT addresses the problems of natural resources degradation. It promotes and strengthens participatory resources management systems at the local level involving the communities and concerned government agencies. VIKSAT works at the grassroots level and as a resource centre in the area of forest and water management. Its activities include research, training, and networking. VIKSAT has two major programmes – Forestry and Land and Water Management – with community based field projects which serve as a learning ground. In the field areas VIKSAT facilitates the organisation of communities into cooperatives, provides training for cooperatives for institution building and strengthening technical capabilities, informs the cooperatives about various government programmes and schemes, and assists them in the implementation of various projects. In the field projects the focus is on widening the magnitude and quality of participation. VIKSAT has made pioneering efforts in setting up Tree Growers' Cooperative Societies to implement wasteland development through people's participation. Today there are more than fifty registered cooperatives involved in forest management and land and water management activities in Sabarkantha, Mehasana, and Kutch districts in north Gujarat. VIKSAT also provides conceptual and secretarial support to SAKSHAM – a state level network of people's institutions and federations working in the area of natural resource management. It assists NGOs and community based organisations to increase their involvement in natural resource management. (VIKSAT publications).

The **Society for Promotion of Area Resource Centres (SPARC)** is an NGO in Mumbai city, working directly with people in the field of housing and infrastructure for the urban poor since the mid-eighties (Burra, 2002 and Mohapatra, 2003). It organises the urban poor to enable them to address issues such as housing, basic services, credit, and livelihoods. Over the years, it has facilitated the emergence of Mahila Milan which is a network of savings and credit groups formed by pavement and slum dwellers in Mumbai and other cities. Simultaneously it has been an active member of the National Slum Dwellers Federation (NSDF) which represents the interests of pavement and slum dwellers from different cities of the country. This alliance of SPARC, Mahila, Milan and NSDF works collectively to address urban poverty through the intervention of housing and urban infrastructure for the poor. The strategy is to build the capacities of people's organisations to enable them to negotiate their own entitlements with local authorities. They believe that it is possible for the state to reach the poor only by linking up with NGOs and community based organisations. They also believe that the community based organisations can negotiate from a position of strength only when they are aligned with an NGO. By themselves they would find it difficult to develop a mutually beneficial relationship in the matrix of stakeholders – state, market, non-governmental organisation/community based organisation. SPARC has been active in implementing large housing and sanitation projects in partnership with the government and its agencies in several cities like Mumbai, Pune, Chennai to benefit several lakhs of poor people. SPARC also provides support to other NGOs in Maharashtra and other states of the country to enable them to strengthen their work by sharing its own experiences and practices with them

Cooperative Development Federation (CDF) is an NGO established in 1982 in Hyderabad city (Ray and Vasundhara, 1998 and *Sahavikasa Newsletter*, May 2003). It works to promote an environment for the cooperatives to flourish as decentralised, democratic, self-help, and mutual aid organisations. Paddy farmers cooperatives and thrift and credit groups of men and women in Andhra Pradesh have been the focus of promotional activities of CDF. The thrift and credit cooperatives are organised groups of people at the village level, who meet regularly to pool their savings and lend these funds to members of the group according to rules and procedures decided by them. CDF assists these groups to function along the principles of cooperation enunciated by the International Cooperative Alliance and encourages them to become self-reliant in managing their funds as well as in running their organisations. The thrift and credit cooperatives coalesce into associations of thrift and credit cooperatives at the cluster level. CDF works in its field area of four districts of Andhra Pradesh where, as of December 2002, it has promoted 400 thrift and credit cooperatives of men and women, which have formed 41 associations of thrift cooperatives with 87,671 members and Rs. 21.05 crores of own funds. CDF extends technical and financial support to other NGOs in Andhra Pradesh and other states of the country to promote similar thrift and credit cooperatives. It is also active in advocacy work with the government to bring about necessary changes in the legal framework of cooperatives to make them truly owned by their members.

Those providing a variety of support activities to other groups and organisations

These may be called support groups or organisations. They do not work directly with the people but with other direct actions groups and support cum-action groups engaged in struggle and/or constructive activities for the people. The **Centre for Health Education Training and Nutrition (CHETNA)** is an example of this type of NGO.

CHETNA is an Ahmedabad based organisation in Gujarat and has been active in the field of nutrition and health care since 1980. It started with a project aimed at improving the effectiveness of government implemented supplementary feeding programmes for mothers and children in the state of Gujarat. Over the years, the activities have broadened to include nutrition, health, education, and development from a 'Rights' perspective. CHETNA works to empower disadvantaged women and children by enabling them to gain control over their own health and that of their family and community. It is a support organisation which works to build the capacities of various NGOs active in the health care field with particular emphasis on Reproductive and Child Health. It addresses the health concerns of women from infancy to old age through its two resource centres – Child Resource Centre and Women's Health and Development Resource Centre. Its relationship with the community is clearly demarcated as it reaches them through other NGOs. Training, research, sensitization and awareness building of functionaries of government and non-governmental organisations in Gujarat and Rajasthan are the major activities of CHETNA. (Gulhati and Gulhati, 1995 and CHETNA brochure 2003).

Those providing funds to other groups and organisations as well as provide some types of support to these organisations

These may be called funding cum support groups or organisations. These are grant making organisations which provide funds to all the above three types of NGOs. They also provide support in the form of technical and organisational inputs, intended to enhance the performance of the groups they fund. This type also does not work directly with people.

The **National Foundation for India (NFI)** is a case in point (www.nfi.org.in and Maharishi and Dhillon, 2002). It is a grant making and fundraising body. Set up in 1992 in New Delhi, it operates at an all India level. NFI supports development activities focusing on issues of poverty, illiteracy, ill health, and the poor living conditions of millions in the country. It envisions people to be the driving force behind all developmental activity. Its major programmes include Gender Equality and Justice, Public Affairs and Urban Governance, Regional Imbalances-Northeast and East Initiatives, Development Communication, and Explorations and Innovations. It has raised funds to generate a corpus through which it provides grant support to NGOs all over the country active in its chosen spheres. Its programme staff interact with various organisations and provide any assistance required for successful implementation of projects it has funded.

An NGO's effectiveness in developing the capacities of a given set of people for self management and protecting their interests themselves makes its direct action role with the same people increasingly redundant. This implies that an NGO may move from being a 'direct action organisation' or 'direct action cum support organisation' to become a 'support organisation' as reflected in the case of AKRSP(I).

As can be seen from these examples of NGO activity, a variety of relationships are forged with the people they decide to serve, particularly in the case of 'direct action organisations' and 'direct action cum support organisations'. The boundary between these categories of NGOs and the people for whom they work (in the form of People's organisations – PO) characterises the relationship between them. The issues of membership, ownership and control of resources and assets, governing body, office bearers, leadership, authority, and representation define the nature of this boundary. Accordingly, the relationship between the NGO and the PO may have a clear cut, blurred, or non-existent boundary between them. In the case of the clearcut boundary, the NGO and the PO both have their separate norms and criteria for each of the boundary defining aspects. An autonomous status develops for both of them over time. A blurred boundary between the NGO and the people's organisation develops when there is a shifting of focus from the NGO to the PO and vice versa depending on the situation and the need of the moment, even though both may have separate legal status on several boundary defining aspects. When there is no boundary between them, the NGO and the people's organisation are interchangeable. The PO is usually subsumed in the NGO in this situation. Each of the boundary defining aspects are applicable primarily to the NGO and remain amorphous for the PO.

The relationship of the 'support organisations' and the 'funding cum-support organisations' with the agencies they work for (which are the 'direct action organisations' and 'support-cum-action organisations') has a clearcut boundary between them. As these organisations rarely work with people's organisations directly, they are not faced with the issue of defining the boundaries of their relationship with people's organisations.

There is increasing emphasis on forming federations and networks of NGOs at the state, regional, national, and international levels around specific issues or to facilitate sectoral interventions in development work. All the four types of NGOs described above join as members of these federations and networks. The people's organisations emerging from NGO interventions are also encouraged to federate, form associations and forums. The relationship of the NGOs with the federations and associations of the people's organisations often tends to be of the blurred boundary type even though the groupings of people's organisations may have a distinct legal status. The NGOs and their office bearers and functionaries are often quite central to many of the federated forums and alliances. They have become the representatives and spokespersons of the people for whom they work.

Approaches to Development

The approaches to development adopted by these organisations can be described as:

- a rights based approach
- a service delivery based approach
- a capacity building approach.

These three approaches can be viewed as pure types. In practice a mix of the three approaches in varying degrees gets adopted with a dominant thrust of any one approach as central to a given NGO.

The struggle/pressure group organisations (a type of 'direct action organisations') are generally engaged in a rights based approach to development. They focus on rights and entitlements of people from the state and the government. They campaign for enforcement of laws and policies, for changes in laws and in existing structures and for policies to ensure that people get their entitlements. The work of MKSS for the right to information is an illustration of a rights based approach to development.

The constructive action organisations (another type of 'direct action organisations') are usually engaged in a service delivery approach to development. They implement, organise, manage constructive activities for the poor and focus on building an alternative structure centred around NGOs in place of or parallel to government delivery systems. Gram Vikas, Sewa Mandir are examples of a service delivery approach to development.

The capacity building approach to development is typically followed by 'support cum action organisations'. They are engaged in conscientising, training, linking, sensitising poor people and government functionaries as well as providing technical support to people for capacity building efforts They act as catalysts to encourage and enable people to form and take responsibility for running their own organisations effectively. SPARC, VIKSAT demonstrate the capacity building approach to development.

The 'support organisations' and the 'funding-cum-support organisations' usually follow the capacity building approach to development. They are more commonly engaged with other NGOs than directly with people's organisations. Hence they are more active in developing the capacities of other NGOs. CHETNA and NFI are examples of this form of capacity building approach to development.

NGOs organise people on a basis consistent with their approach to development. They have been able to demonstrate results in the form of prototypes of social change through their interventions. But the scaling up of these prototypes of change has happened in a very limited way.

NGOs are projected as catalysts of social change to help to improve the lives of the poor and deprived. The term catalyst is drawn from Chemistry, meaning an agent that helps to initiate or hasten a chemical reaction but itself remains unchanged. In social change where NGOs are projected as catalysts, though they no doubt help bring about interactions between parties which would have otherwise found it difficult to interact, they themselves (the NGOs) also get changed in the process. The opening which gets created by bringing different parties together also provides a window of opportunity to the NGOs concerned to represent the interests of the people they work for. The space created in the power structures in the name of poor people can be, and often is, captured by the NGOs. Thus NGOs can become a self perpetuating force. The empowerment of poor and deprived people has to take this reality into account.

There are very few NGOs which are serious about not perpetuating their existence. GIVE Foundation is among the exceptions in India. Formed in 2000 for fundraising and connecting donors and recipients of funds for development works, it has set a time frame of 20 years to accomplish the task. In fact it has made a public declaration of its plan to wind itself up after 20 years of work, in its first annual report. Entitled as '*Give Foundation – Annual Report 2020 (what it should be...)*', this document addresses its 'stakeholders' in the following words:

> *We have great pleasure in informing you that your company has commenced winding-up operations. The last 5 years have seen the NGO sector increasingly able to sustain itself without external help. The charity 'marketplace' has reached high efficiency levels, there are a large number of players offering a variety of financial services to NGOs, transparency and accountability are no more questioned. Subsidiaries promoted by your company to provide services to the sector, have become self-sustaining.*

This kind of a self-liquidation perspective at the time of forming an NGO is very rare.

Empowerment Through NGO Action

There has been a marked shift in orientation over the years from welfare to empowerment in the area of social development work. Empowerment of people has become very current in the perspective on development and in the efforts for poverty alleviation. Consciousness raising of people and use of participatory methods to involve them in making their life better has become the thrust of empowerment in social development work.

Education, health, housing, savings and credit, income generation, skills development, childcare, access to resources and assets, natural resource management, legal frameworks, communication strategies, gender relations are some of the focal points where the empowerment orientation has been pursued in social development efforts. Gender and development interventions have been particularly advocating empowerment approaches to address the lower status of women in society vis-a-vis all these issues. These are also the issues around which NGOs work to improve the situation of deprived people and organise them in rural and urban areas.

A typical project design involving collaboration between government organisations and NGOs to improve the situation for people is shown in Table 1. This particular project named 'Rural Women's Development and Empowerment Project' is supported by international organisations and implemented by the government with the support of non-governmental organisations. It relates to micro-credit interventions through self-help groups of poor women in several states of the country. As can be seen in the annexure describing the institutional arrangements for project management (given in Table 1), the self-help groups are at the bottom rung of the whole design. The intense efforts required to facilitate empowerment of underprivileged and disadvantaged people vis-a-vis this larger institutional design can be imagined. To what extent they are successful in making such empowerment a reality is the real issue.

Table 1. Rural Women's Development and Empowerment Project.

Institutional Arrangements for Project Management

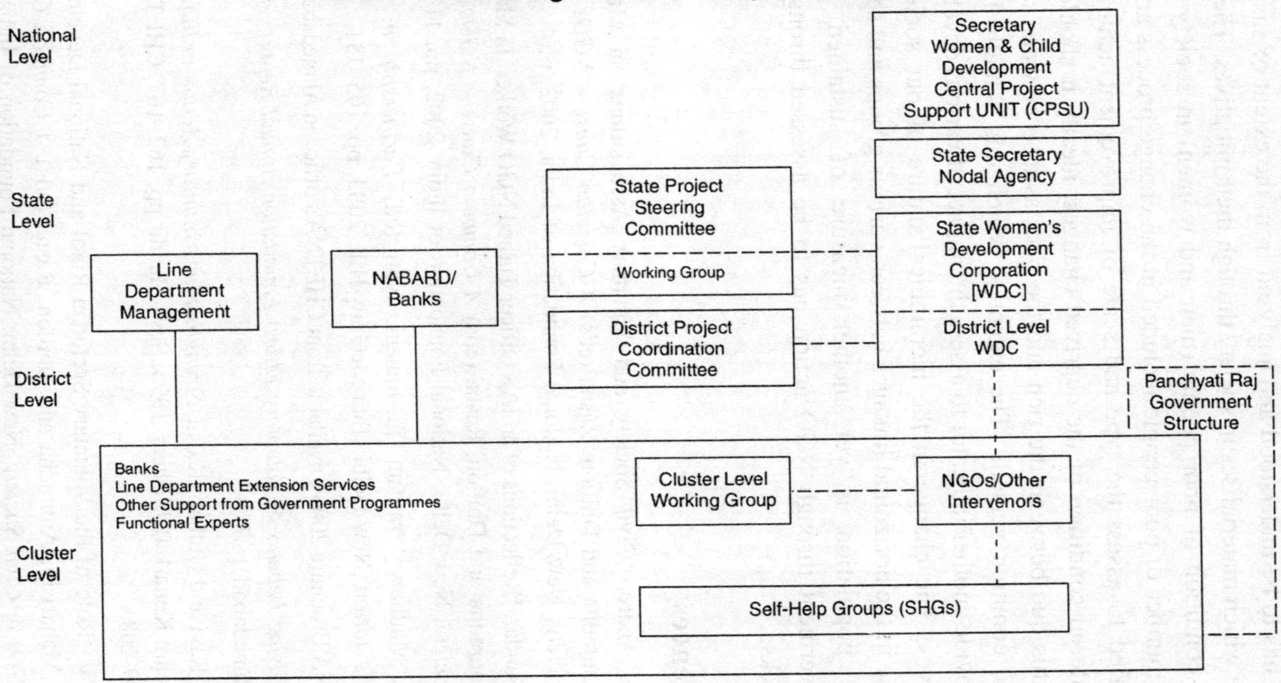

Source: *Project Proposal – 'Rural Women's Development and Empowerment Project', Government of Gujarat, Annexure 2*

The nature of empowerment of people witnessed in the work of NGOs has to be understood and analysed from the extent of sustainable change which materialises in society through their initiatives. The change in the condition of poor people (men and women) in society as well as the number of poor people included in the change process are easily quantified to assess the type and scale of improvement achieved. As the material condition of the deprived changes, ideally it should affect the status quo between the rich and the poor as also between the elite and the common person. The extent to which this actually happens can provide another indicator to assess the impact of various development initiatives. The change in the hierarchical nature of our society and increase in the horizontal linkages between various groups and segments of the population is yet another measure of sustained impact. Empowerment through NGO action has to be assessed through such yardsticks.

References

Beteille, Andre, 'Civil Society and Voluntary Associations' in Maharishi, Anuradha and Dhillon, Rasna (eds) *A Common Cause – NGOs & Civil Society*, New Delhi: National Foundation of India, 2002, p. 4.

Burra, Sundar, 'Reflections of an IAS Officer Turned NGO Worker' in Maharishi, Anuradha and Dhillon, Rasna (eds) *A Common Cause – NGOs & Civil Society*, New Delhi: National Foundation of India, 2002, pp. 117–122.

Chavan, Madhav, 'Pratham' in Jumani, Jyoti (ed) *Partnership in Poverty Alleviation,* New Delhi: Tata McGraw-Hill, 2003, pp. 105–131.

'CHETNA Brochure 2003', available from CHETNA's office in Ahmedabad, India

GIVE (Giving Impetus to Voluntary Effort) Foundation Annual Report, 2000–01, Ahmedabad, p. 7.

Gulhati, Ravi and Gulhati, Kaval, *Strengthening Voluntary Action in India,* New Delhi: Konark Publishers, 1995, Seva Mandir pp. 162–167, CHETNA pp. 199–208.

Kurien, V. 'Role of the Voluntary Sector in Rural and National Development' in Maharishi, Anuradha and Dhillon, Rasna (eds) *A Common Cause – NGOs & Civil Society,* New Delhi: National Foundation of India, 2002, p. 13.

Madiath, Joe and Jayapadma, R.V., 'Strengthening India's Villages the Sustainable Way' in Maharishi, Anuradha and Dhillon, Rasna (eds) *A Common Cause – NGOs & Civil Society*, New Delhi: National Foundation of India, 2002, pp. 167–172.

Maharishi, Anuradha and Dhillon, Rasna (eds), *A Common Cause – NGOs & Civil Society*, New Delhi: National Foundation of India, 2002.

Mander, Harsh, 'Corruption and the Right to Information' in Tandon, R. and Mohanty, R. (eds) *Does Civil Society Matter?,* New Delhi: Sage, 2003, pp. 145–163.

May, Nicky, 'Conference Report on Performance and Accountability in the New World Order', *Development in Practice,* Volume 5, Number 1, 1995, p. 72.

Mohapatra, B.M., 'A View From the Subalterns – The Pavement Dwellers of Mumbai' in Tandon, R. and Mohanty, R. (eds), *Does Civil Society Matter?,* New Delhi: Sage, 2003, pp. 285–313.

Nandy, Ashis, 'Countering Hegemonic Development: Dissent and the Voluntary Sector' in Maharishi, Anuradha and Dhillon, Rasna (eds), *A Common Cause – NGOs & Civil Society*, New Delhi: National Foundation of India, 2002, p. 36.

Planning Commission, Government of India, 'Action Plan to Bring About a Collaborative Relationship Between Voluntary Organisations and Government', New Delhi, 1994, para 4.1.1.

Ray, Nandita and Vasundhara, D. P. 'Like My Mother's House: Women's Thrift and Credit Co-operatives in South India' in Carr, Mariyln et al. (eds) *Speaking Out – Women's Economic Empowerment in South Asia*, New Delhi: Vistaar, 1997, pp. 85–101.

Roy, Aruna with the MKSS, 'Looking Ahead – The Crossing of Boundaries' in Maharishi, Anuradha and Dhillon, Rasna (eds), *A Common Cause – NGOs & Civil Society*, New Delhi: National Foundation of India, 2002, pp. 173–177.

Sahavikasa May 2003 – Newsletter published by Cooperative Development Foundation from Hyderabad, India .

Underwood, Barry, 'Village Institutions and Federations' Unpublished paper, AKRSP(I), Ahmedabad, 1997 and *AKRSP(I) Annual Report 2003* available from AKRSP(I) office in Ahmedabad, India.

VIKSAT Annual Report 2003–04 available from its office in Ahmedabad, India and *Joint Forest Management in Gujarat – A Status Report*, VIKSAT, Ahmedabad, 2002.

Part III

Towards a Framework for Empowerment

This part presents a framework for analysing the empowerment phenomenon. The suggested framework has five distinct strands which have to be woven together. These are – Process Orientation, Bases of Power, Organising and Organisation, Mainstreaming, and Representative Organisations. A separate chapter is devoted to each strand to analyse the approach of each of the three actors in the respective context of the concerned strand. The last chapter weaves these strands to present a framework for empowering society.

7

Strand 1: Process Orientation

In this chapter, the meaning of 'process' and its application in different types of organisations is elaborated to highlight its criticality to empowerment. The term 'process' is used extensively in business organisations as well as in social development organisations but with different connotations and end results. A common connotation of this term across different types of organisations adds rigour to its application.

What is a Process?

According to the dictionary, the term 'process' denotes 'a series of continuous actions that bring about a particular result, end or condition'. However, its specific meaning varies according to the context. In systems theory, for instance, 'the process element consists of technical and administrative activities which are brought to bear on inputs in order to transform them into outputs'. (Gibson et al, 1973). In the business context the term is described in a variety of ways as the following statements, drawn from a cross-section of sources, indicate:

> A business 'process is a series of steps designed to produce a product or service. Some processes (such as the programming process) may be contained wholly within a function. However, most processes (such as order processing) are cross-functional, spanning the white space between the boxes on the organisation chart'. 'Between every input and every output is a process'. (Hunt, 1996).

'A process is a sequence of steps which adds value by producing required outputs from a variety of inputs'. (*CII-EXIM Award for Business Excellence – Guidelines, 1998*).

'Process refers to linked activities with the purpose of producing a product or service for a customer (user) within or outside the organisation'. (*Tata Business Excellence Model – Criteria for 2001*).

'A process is any sequence of events which begins with an input and delivers an output'. (Kinlaw, 1995).

'Process is a complete end to end set of activities that together create value for a customer'. (Hammer, 1996).

In social development literature this term is referred to indicate a certain approach to project formulation and implementation. In the words of a competent authority, 'A process approach, as against a blue-print approach, is one where within agreed overall objectives for institutional change, outputs and the activities and inputs required to achieve them are defined only as the project develops. Such an approach requires particular attention to monitoring since this provides the framework for adapting the project to take account of the degree of progress and changing conditions'. (DFID Technical Note –14). For another scholar, 'Process suggests the notion of a series of activities or outcomes over a period of time and, as such, all projects can be seen as processes in that they usually seek to structure these activities towards a series of predetermined objectives'. (Oakley et al, 1991). Yet another source suggests:

A process approach puts a premium on active involvement and participation of the target group of any intervention in designing, planning, implementing, monitoring and evaluation of that intervention so as to develop a sense of ownership of the intervention, its outputs, and consequences by the target group. A process approach treats the target group as equal partners along with other actors engaged in any intervention and not as mere beneficiaries or recipients of deliverables. (*PAHAL Project Phase II, Reference Document*).

As suggested elsewhere, 'Process can be defined as who says and does what to whom, when, where, and how'. (Jumani, 1979).

It is clear from the above listed definitions that a process is a means to an end. Hence the use of the term is context specific – such as business process, organisational process, development process, democratic process, participatory process, technical process, legal process, funding process, organising process, management process, training process, learning process, decentralisation process, governance process, privatisation process, and so on.

In every context, however, the process mediates the relationship between inputs and outputs. Hence the results expected are as important as the means applied to achieve them. It also highlights the importance of appropriateness of means and ends; the results expected are dependent on the means applied. For example, to expect ownership of project interventions by its beneficiaries without using a participatory process is unrealistic. Likewise, to expect high motivation in an authoritarian context is unrealistic too. The importance attached to process is related to the importance attached to achieving results. This is the flux between process and product (the results).

Processes can be understood, analysed, mapped, redesigned, reengineered, to create a better match with the expected results. The understanding of process in business organisations is very critically related to performance and results. The broad thrust of Business Process Reengineering, as a body of knowledge and practice, focuses attention on improved performance in business organisations with the concommittant emphasis on cost and time considerations to achieve results. Process measurement is treated as equally important to know how well the processes are performing.

In social development organisations, however, this is not so obvious even though they use the word process quite extensively. The emphasis on process can also become an end in itself where the process becomes the product with minimal concern for the results to be achieved. It is not uncommon to come across many social development organisations (particularly NGOs) which present process as product. The considerations of time and cost for achieving results have very low priority in these situations. Consequently, process measurement is quite unimaginable as yet in social development organisations. Government organisations also, by and large, do not attach the same criticality for process as the business organisations do.

Given this differential emphasis on 'process' in business and social development organisations, it is important to develop a common understanding of this term in order to develop a process-orientation in all organisations. The operationalisation of process-orientation in business organisations provides a useful frame of reference which can be adapted appropriately by NGOs and other social development organisations as well as government organisations.

Developing a Process Orientation

Several scholars have elaborated on the centrality of process orientation in business organisations. Sumantra Ghoshal and Christopher Bartlett (1998) document the shift in understanding business organisations from a hierarchy of tasks to a portfolio of processes. They emphasise three core organisational processes that overlay and often dominate the vertical, authority based processes of the hierarchical structure. To quote them:

> The first is the *entrepreneurial process* which produces and supports the opportunity-seeking, externally focussed entrepreneurship of frontline managers. The second is the *integration process* which overlays the advantages of bigness – of size, scale, and diversity – on the advantages of smallness – flexibility, responsiveness, creativity – by linking the dispersed resources, competencies, and businesses of the company. And the third is the *renewal process* which creates and sustains the company's capacity to continuously challenge its own beliefs and practices, thereby, revitalising the strategies that drive the business.

They emphasise that by creating and managing these three processes a company is able to develop and sustain the three characteristics of the individualised corporation. This involves reorienting the self-concept and working of the business organisation from strategy, structure, and systems to purpose, process, and people. The focus is on developing and leveraging the individual's unique talents and skills to unleash the power of the individual as the driver of value creation in business organisations.

Michael Hammer (1996) provides a vivid description of how the process orientation in business organisations actually operates:

> In the old days, if someone approached a worker on Hill's manufacturing floor and asked what he did, the worker would have said that he was operating a machine. If the machine was running and he was meeting his daily quota, then he felt he was doing his job. If the output of his machine piled up, that wasn't his problem. If the product didn't get shipped, that wasn't his problem either.
>
> If you ask the same question today, the worker will say that he works in the production subprocess of the order fulfillment process. Is this just new corporate jargon? Not at all. It represents a refocusing of the individual and his activities from the small to the large.
>
> Now the worker realises that he is not there merely to do his own thing, to run his machine. He's there to contribute to the overall effort, namely to perform the process that leads to the result of shipped goods. Now, if his output piles up, he will take it upon himself to see what's happening further down the line. He will do this not out of company loyalty, but because his sense of who he is and what he does has been reshaped by the shift from a task to a process orientation. We have already remarked on the importance of language in any fundamental change in perspective. The Industrial Revolution not only turned peasants and artisans into factory workers, it practically coined the term 'workers'

> to describe them. Today this term, with its narrow task connotation, is dead language; it doesn't fit as we move to a process focus. Instead of (task) workers, we must speak of (process) performers, people who understand that in doing their work they are contributing to the performance of a process.

The centrality of process orientation in business organisations conveyed by these ideas can be applied to social development organisations and government organisations as well. This implies a big improvement in performance and results achieved by these organisations to become comparable to the process orientation of business organisations.

If societal empowerment has to be achieved, then all the three types of organisations – pertaining to business, government, and social development, have to reorient themselves. As discussed in earlier chapters, this process has begun. The role of business organisations is being redefined visibly from a shareholder to a stakeholder perspective. Business organisations increasingly view themselves as accountable to society and various other stakeholders. They make conscious efforts to balance the interests of various stakeholders and still run the business profitably. A great deal of discussion and some action is noticeable about changing the role of government from being a provider of services to a facilitator for ensuring that the various needs of its citizens are met satisfactorily. In the social sector, the lack of a results based process-orientation constrains the scaling up of projects. Government systems display a similar lack of proces-orientation in fulfilling commitments and achieving desired results. Also, there is increased emphasis to redefine the focus of social development organisations from process only to process-and-product, though the action towards this change is still very slow. An inherent factoring of process-orientation is visible in operationalising the governance function itself. Citizens and communities affected by the actions of government and social development organisations are increasingly underlining the importance of delivering on commitments made to them by these organisations.

These shifts highlight the importance of a process-orientation for empowering society. If social development organisations and government organisations also internalise the meaning of process, as the business organisations do, then it is more likely to lead to measurable results in societal empowerment. This calls for building appropriate means and mechanisms to enable the social development and government organisations to do so. Just as Business Process Reengineering (BPR) has become very important as a body of knowledge and practice for business organisations, so also Governance Process Reengineering (GPR), and Social Process Reengineering (SPR) or Civil Process Reengineering (CPR) can be visualised as corresponding bodies of knowledge and practice for government and social development organisations respectively, to develop a process-orientation. GPR and SPR/CPR need to be pursued systematically to bring about desired change in society as a whole.

A typical Process-Driven Improvement is shown in Fig. 1. This framework can be used effectively by social development organisations and government organisations as well to develop a process-orientation.

This framework essentially establishes the relationship between process reengineering and bottomline results. The inputs of vision, policy, and strategy; empowerment of individuals and teams; and integration of the enterprise provided by the top management leadership of an organisation help to understand, simplify and improve its processes which in turn leads to customer satisfaction; improved quality; and cheaper, better, faster ways of delivering results as the business outcomes. Government and social development organisations need to establish a similar relationship between their process reengineering efforts and their bottomline results. The first step in this effort is to have a consensus on what constitutes bottomline results in government and social development organisations. The successive steps follow by applying this framework in a logical manner.

Process Purity and Process Pollution

A process approach to change and empowerment emerges when people themselves are involved as active partners in bringing about desired

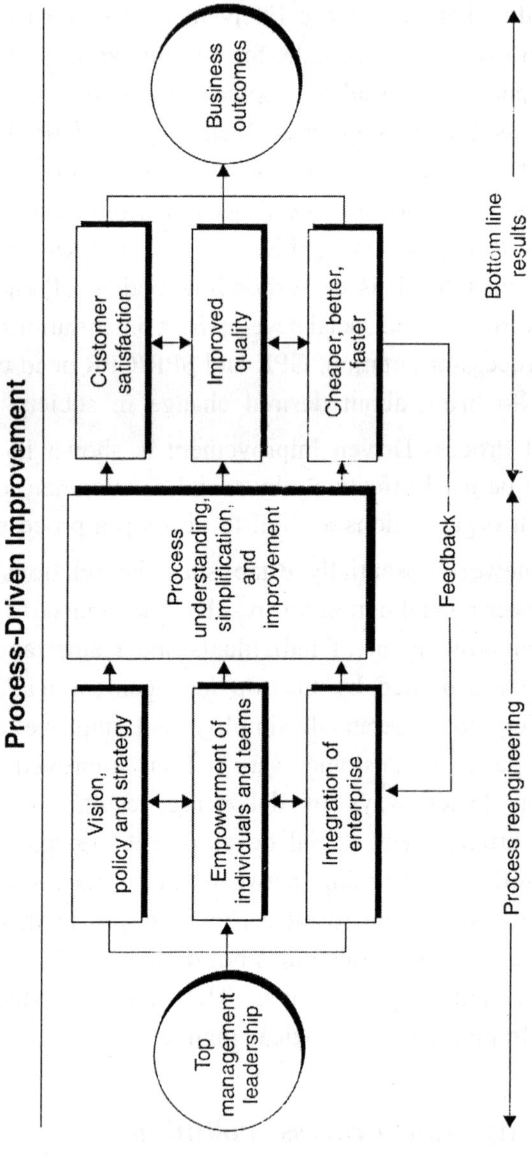

Fig. 1. Process–driven improvement.

(Source: Daniel V. Hunt *Process Mapping – How to Reengineer Your Business Processes* p. 31)

changes. The concept of process-orientation can be clarified with reference to process purity and process pollution as two ends of the empowerment continuum. The extent of process purity maintained in developing people's capacities connotes the extent of their empowerment. High levels of process purity lead to high levels of empowerment. Low levels of process purity indicate process pollution which blocks and compromises empowerment. This concept can be graphically presented as follows:

Process Purity ———————————————— Process Pollution

The concepts of process purity and process pollution can be used as a tool by the main actors in any programmatic intervention to constantly monitor the nature of change and the degree of empowerment that may come about as a result of the programme inputs. This concept can be applied to all programmatic interventions seeking to empower people – whether in business organisations, in communities, or in the citizenry of a state.

Serious debate and discussion is needed to analyse the reasons why process pollution creeps into the subsoil of social change being promoted by various actors. Is it possible to remove the elements of process pollution completely or does one have to live with the maximum acceptable levels of process pollution? Conversely, does one have to define minimum levels of acceptable process purity? Does the status quo at a societal level really undergo change when there is process pollution or is it reinforced under the guise of change? Does the gap between the powerful and the powerless at a societal level really reduce or increase in a sustained way, depending on the extent of purity of the process? These are some of the questions that can be answered by continuously measuring the levels of process purity and process pollution in programmatic interventions in society.

References

Confederation of Indian Industry, *CII – Exim Award for Business Excellence – Guidelines for Companies, Self Assessment 1998,* New Delhi, p. 35.

Department for International Development (DFID, UK), 'Institutional Development' Technical Note – 14, n.d., p. 12.

Ghoshal, Sumantra and Bartlett, Christopher A., *The Individualised Corporation,* London: Heinemann, 1998, p. 191.

Gibson, J. L., Ivancevich, J. M., and Donnelly, J. H. (Jr.), *Organisations: Structure, Processes, Behaviour,* Dallas: Business Publications Inc., 1973, p. 452.

Hammer, Michael, *Beyond Reengineering – How the Process-Centred Organisation is Changing Our Work and Our Lives,* London: HarperCollinsBusiness, 1996, pp. xii and 15.

Hunt, Daniel V., *Process Mapping – How to Reengineer Your Business Processes,* New York: John Wiley and Sons, Inc., 1996, p. 3.

Jumani, Usha, 'Process Lag and Individual Stress in Organisations: A Diagnostic Basis for OD', Doctoral Thesis, Indian Institute of Management, Ahmedabad, March 1979, p. 39.

Kinlaw, D. C., *The Practice of Empowerment,* Aldershot-Hampshire: Gower, 1995, p. 55.

Oakley, Peter et al., *Projects with People,* Geneva: International Labour Organisation, 1991, p. 173.

Government of India, Government of Sweden, Government of Rajasthan *Participatory Approach to Human and Land Resources Development (PAHAL) Project, Dungarpur – Phase II,* Reference Document, February 1998, p. 54.

Tata Quality Management Services, *Tata Business Excellence Model, Criteria for 2001,* Mumbai, p. 44.

8

Strand 2: Bases of Power

Having discussed process-orientation as the first strand in empowering society, we now move to the second strand in our conceptualisation of empowerment – the bases of power. Power with its varied nuances is an inherent part of empowerment. It is therefore important to understand the meaning and sources of power as well as the responsible use of power as an integral part of the empowerment process. The interventions aimed at empowerment have to be clear about what kind of power is being sought and how that power is to be used by the people who are empowered. The approaches to power and the various bases of power postulated by scholars is first described. This would lay down the spectrum of choice for empowerment by the three types of organisational systems.

Approaches to Power

Max Weber (1968) was perhaps the first one to attempt to define power. According to him, 'power is the probability that one actor within a social relationship will be in a position to carry out his own will despite resistance, regardless of the basis on which this probability rests'. Using this as the basic parameter for his conceptualisation, Milan Zafirovski (2001) has explained the notion of power as 'the potential (stochastic) or actual *(de facto)* individual and group capability, based on unequal positions in economy and society, i.e. in the economic system or social structure, to impose definite ideas, values, wishes, or interests on other individuals or groups, by overcoming the resistance of these individuals and groups'. Others have echoed the same ideas somewhat differently. For Hans Morgenthau (1967) for instance, 'Power is man's control over the minds and actions of other men'. Elaborating this concept J. K. Galbraith (1983) says that, 'the possession of "personality", property and organisation enables persons to dominate and exercise power'. As the economy grows and socio-economic life becomes complex, power moves into organisations and the individuals who control them. 'Decline in the power deriving from property, as also in that from personality, is most of all, to be attributed to the rise of organisation', he stresses.

Peter Pruzan (2001) traces the evolution of the concepts of power in Western societies since the Renaissance in a more or less chronological order, and visualises three kinds of power:

i. power for its own sake,

ii. power as a means of maintaining stable forms of societal governance, and

iii. power as a means of control in hierarchical organisations.

He says that a new concept of power is evolving within an organisational setting – 'power as the capability to serve others'. This, according to him, is 'spiritual power' which is based on a personal and organisational existential search of self-knowledge, meaning and wholeness leading to self-control.

He further focuses on three widely employed modern perspectives on power. The first is an outcome-oriented definition: 'the capacity to effect or affect organisational outcomes', enunciated by Henry Mintzberg. The second is a manipulative or behavioural perspective sugested by Robert Dahl: 'A has power over B to the extent that he can get B to do something that B would otherwise not do'. Both of these perspectives implicitly presume an individual as the wielder of power. The third perspective has been postulated by Talcot Parsons who considers power as a tool for collective action based on a system of reciprocal obligations. 'The primary functions of power', he says 'are to facilitate the mobilisation of instrumental resources like money and services...; this mobilisation occurs through the promotion of binding obligation...'. Parson's concept of power can be said to include both an outcome-oriented perspective as well as a behavioural perspective.

Pruzan then argues that these widely accepted perspectives on power are in the process of being supplemented by a spiritual perspective. In the spiritual perspective the notion of control is shifted from its subject-object perspective (control over nature, how to control events) and its subject-subject perspective (social control, how to control others) to a self-self perspective (self-control, how to control one's self so as to be able to serve others).

These approaches are operationalised in everyday life through different bases of power. Scholars have developed typologies of the bases of power and the way it manifests in different contexts. Griener and Schein (1988), for instance, categorise eight potential bases of individual power in organisations under three broad types as given below:

Knowledge – Expert, Information, Tradition

Personality – Charisma, Reputation, Professional credibility

Others' Support – Political access, Staff support

John Pen's (1971) classification is somewhat different but covers more or less similar ground. His seven categories of power include:

- Physical
- Personal
- Social
- Administrative/organisational
- State
- Legal
- Political

Yet another typology is provided by Suzanne Williams et al (1994). They refer to the following types of power, especially in the context of gender relations:

Power-over	This power is relationship of domination/subordination. Increasing his/her power comes at the expense of another.
Power-to	The power which is creative and enabling.
Power-with	Involves a sense of the whole being greater than the sum of individuals.

Power-within The spiritual sense and uniqueness that resides in each of us and makes us truly human. Its basis is self acceptance and self-respect which extend, in turn, to respect for and acceptance of others as equals.

These approaches to power and its typologies, which have emerged from essentially Western experiences and ethos, have been used extensively to understand individual and organisational power dynamics in the modern world. They are significantly based on a notion of control – control of outcomes and/or control of others. The recognition of the spiritual perspective to power by Western thinkers is of recent origin and is leading to a growing convergence between the Western and Indian approaches to power.

The Indian approaches to power have always highlighted the moral and spiritual dimension as the most critical in maintaining a balance between the forces of control and self-indulgence in the exercise of power. The ancient Indian authorities on polity define three types of powers centred around the institution of kingship (Bhatta, 2001). These are *prabhushakti* (the power of sovereignty), *mantrashakti* (the power of knowledge), and *utsahshakti* (the power of enthusiastic energy). To exercise the first type of power, a ruler needs a prosperous treasury and a strong army, but he can do so wisely only if he has the power of knowledge. He, however, can achieve little without *utsahshakti,* the power of energy. The power of valour depends on energetic action of the king and is necessary for the success of deliberations. These three powers of a king are inter-related and are of no use when isolated from each other. Power by itself is neither good nor evil; there is the *daivishakti* and there is the *asurishakti;* the benign power and the malign power. Characterising all power as poison, the Ramayana has the following advice for those who exercise power:

> We need the sovereign Grace of the
> Lord, both to exercise power and
> Be immune from its deadly poison;
> In our total submission to dharma,
> There's the sure promise of Grace, but
> Those that rely on power alone must
> Perish by its poison.

Bhatta interprets this advice through an analogy from modern times, 'Like those who handle electric power must wear rubber gloves for safety, those who exercise power must also wear the gloves of *dharma.* The consequence of exercise of power disregarding *dharma* is disastrous'.

Shekhar Sen (2001) on the other hand points out that, according to the ancient Indian scriptures, the sources of power are anchored in the interplay of *Dharma* (the spiritual), *Artha* (the material), and *Kama* (the sensual) – the *Trivarga* that constitute the three paramount objectives of life. The management of power, therefore, must be informed by a moral sense. This is also what the theory of triune *guna* dynamics (*triguna-tattva)* in Indian psychology emphasises. According to this theory, as S. K. Chakraborty (2001) has pointed out, human psychology as well as all manifestations in Nature is constituted of a blend of three fundamental psychological energy forces – *Sattva* (illumination), *Rajas* (activity), and *Tamas* (inertia).

About the essential working implication of this theory, Chakraborty says: 'The dynamic activism of *rajas,* indispensable as it is, must be subjected to the illuminated guidance of *sattva;* or the *rajas* turns wild, unethical, and destructive; the short-term successes of *rajasic* dynamism are wiped out by the irreparable long-term damages caused by its inherent blindness'.

Manoj Das (2001), a disciple of Sri Aurobindo, postulates two major approaches to power – impersonal and personal – which have to be managed by a ruler or king. He classifies 'Impersonal Power' (excluding Nature's powers) as Political Power (Monarchy or elected Parliament), Economic Power, Collective Power (Association, Trade Union, Party), and Scientific and Technological Power. Similarly, 'Personal Power' is classified as Physical Power, Vital Power, Mental Power, Psychic or Soul Power.

Das argues that power can be inherited, earned, or usurped and that power not earned can be dangerous. The interaction between 'Power Impersonal' and 'Power Personal' defines the use of power. The ways in which 'Impersonal Power' can be used depend on the 'Personal Power' available to a person – physical, vital, mental, and psychic. A harmony between the 'Impersonal Power' and 'Personal Power' is the way to ideally manage power. Higher levels of 'Personal Power' lead to a more constructive and fruitful application of 'Impersonal Power'.

The Indian theories of power basically emphasise the need to balance the various bases of power. The exercise of power is viewed as a means to an end and is always to be informed by high moral values. The spiritual dimension to power is continuously underlined to be able to adhere to the high moral values.

Government Power in a Parliamentary System

What has been discussed above are some abstract ideas related to the sources and exercise of power. Moving away from these abstractions, it will be instructive to have a synoptic view of the dynamics of power in the context of democratic governance, particularly under a parliamentary system that India has adopted. M. N. Buch (2001), an experienced bureaucrat, gives an elaborate yet succint description of it:

> If power is seen as authority to rule, or the right to command, then it immediately places one having power above the people over whom such power is to be exercised. If, however, power is viewed as the ability to do anything, as energy or a moving force, then power is something enjoyed only for the purpose of doing things for people for whose service one is employed. Seen from these two angles, power is either a means of exploitation or instrument of public welfare.
>
> Different political systems look upon power from different viewpoints and wield it differently. In a dictatorship, absolute..., or a weak and emasculated one..., power is seen as an object in itself, to be wielded for the personal aggrandisement of the dictator or ruler.
>
> Unlike as in a dictatorship, in a democracy power and sovereignty vest in the people, whereas functions are assigned to officials, whether elected or appointed. For example, the Preamble of the Constitution of India starts with the words,

> 'We, the people of India...' and goes on to state that the people have constituted India into a republic with the basic foundations of justice, liberty, equality and fraternity. The Preamble is the most important part of the Constitution because from it flows the rest of the Constitution, from Article 1 to Article 375. The Constitution is only the prescription of the rights of the people and the mandate given to various organisations and functionaries who are required to ensure that the people can enjoy these rights.

Buch further elaborates this point:

> At the macro level, then, power is shared between three and equal interactive constituents of the state – the executive, legislature, and the judiciary. Despite the fact that there have been demands by one or the other constituent to establish an overriding position for itself, the basic frame of the Constitution calls for each of these organs to act as a check on the others, but from a position of complete equality.

P. S. Appu (2001), another experienced bureaucrat, goes beyond the constitutional provision and provides a glimpse of how the government activity functions:

> In a parliamentary democracy all power vests in the council of ministers which is responsible to Parliament. The responsibility of the ministers is joint and several. Though all power vests in the council of ministers, in actual practice, there is a division of powers between ministers and bureaucrats. Ministers lay down policies and bureaucrats execute them. At the highest level, bureaucrats advise ministers in formulating policies and are also responsible for execution. At that level the exercise of power is a joint operation in which ministers and top civil servants are partners. The lower echelons of bureaucracy are concerned only with execution. It should, however, be pointed out that

in recent years ministers have generally shown greater interest in the details of execution than in the formulation of policy.

He then adds that bureaucrats derive their power from laws, the powers inherent in their respective offices, and powers delegated to them by their superiors.

Implications of Empowerment

All the interventions for empowerment re define the relationship between the various players in a given context. In India, socio-economic power is presently controlled by caste/class formations and business entities, while political power is controlled by government and political formations. As a consequence of empowerment, inroads are being made in the power bases of these conventional holders of power. Each base of power has a concomittant set of skills and capacities that enable the person holding that power to exercise it effectively. Empowering society means enabling every section of the population to access the different bases of power and develop appropriate capacities.

What kind of power is possible to get, and to what extent or degree it is possible to get any particular type of power has to be inherently defined in any intervention for empowerment. Whether any single power base is sufficient or a cluster of power bases is necessary for the desired changes has to be understood and analysed.

Social, economic, and political power is commonly sought in empowering underprivileged and marginalised sections of a population. Social development organisations and government organisations plan interventions for this type of empowerment.

Greater authority and matching responsibility with authority for everyone is the kind of empowerment sought in work organisations. Business organisations and other work organisations plan interventions for this type of empowerment which seeks to broaden the bases of power among a greater number of people within a work organisation.

Capacity building is important in all interventions seeking empowerment – whether in business, government, or social development organisations. Empowerment has to address the development of relevant capacities to equip the concerned people for actualising the particular base of power being sought. For example, the reservation for women in Panchayati Raj Institutions empowers women in the legal sense but unless women are equipped to function effectively as members of the Panchayat, they are not able to actualise the power base they have got.

In addition, capacity building for empowerment also has to address the various nuances of how to use power as well as the consequences of using power. Learning the ways to balance various power bases and the pitfalls involved in the exercise of power, understanding the resistance and opposition which get activated as a result, dealing with vested interests, and the ability to deliver results by being a part of the power network are some of the nuances which the capacity building efforts have to take into account. In effect, the learning legacy of the privileged and powerful has to become a reality for those sought to be empowered.

The effectiveness of various interventions for empowerment can be assessed by the clarity of purpose they display in identifying the base/s of power being sought; the extent to which that power is actually achieved by the concerned people to be empowered; and the ethical and moral values they uphold. The process of empowerment has to accomplish this complex objective. Empowering society, thus, becomes a challenge to create a society in which power is well dispersed across various sections of people and is exercised with high standards of moral and ethical principles.

References

Appu, P. S., 'Bureaucracy and Power' in Chakraborty S. K. and Bhattacharya, Pradip (eds), *Leadership and Power*, New Delhi: Oxford University Press, 2001, p. 284.

Bhatta, Panduranga C., 'Management of Power – Lessons from the Ramayana' in Chakraborty S. K. and Bhattacharya, Pradip (eds), *Leadership and Power,* New Delhi: Oxford University Press, 2001, p. 416.

Buch, M. N., 'Managing Power – A Bureaucrat's View' in Chakraborty S. K. and Bhattacharya, Pradip (eds) *Leadership and Power,* New Delhi: Oxford University Press, 2001, pp. 367–372.

Chakraborty S. K., 'Wisdom Power' in Chakraborty S. K. and Bhattacharya, Pradip (eds) *Leadership and Power,* New Delhi: Oxford University Press, 2001, pp. 191–192.

Das, Manoj, 'Management of Power in Sri Aurobindo – The Ascent from Self to SELF' in Chakraborty S. K. and Bhattacharya, Pradip (eds), *Leadership and Power,* New Delhi: Oxford University Press, 2001, p. 208.

Galbraith, J. K., *The Anatomy of Power,* Boston: Houghton Mifflin Co., 1983, p. 52.

Greiner, Larry E. and Schein, Virginia. E., *Power and Organisation Development,* Reading, MA.: Addison-Wesley Publishing Company, 1988, p. 27.

Morganthau, Hans, *Politics Among Nations,* 3rd ed., New York: Knopf, 1967, p. 31.

Pen, John, 'Bilateral Monopoly, Bargaining and the Concept of Economic Power', in Rothchild, K.W. (ed), *Power in Economic Selected Readings,* Harmondsworth: Penguin Books, 1971 as quoted in Chakraborty S. K. and Bhattacharya, Pradip (eds), *Leadership and Power,* New Delhi: Oxford University Press, 2001, p. 322.

Pruzan, Peter, 'The Trajectory of Power' in Chakraborty S. K. and Bhattacharya, Pradip (eds), *Leadership and Power,* New Delhi: Oxford University Press, 2001, pp. 166–167.

Sen, Shekhar, 'Management of Power in Ancient Indian Literature' in Chakraborty S. K. and Bhattacharya, Pradip (eds), *Leadership and Power,* New Delhi: Oxford University Press, 2001, p. 400.

Sen, Amartya, 'Goals, Commitment and Identity', *Journal of Law and Economic Organisation,* Vol. 1, no. 2, 1985, pp. 341–55.

Weber, Max, *Economy and Society: An Outline of Interpretative Sociology,* New York: Bedminister Press, 1968, p. 53.

Williams, Suzanne et al., *The Oxfam Gender Training Manual – Handout 33*, Oxfam (UK and Ireland), 1994, p. 233.

Zafirovski, Milan, 'The Nature and Operation of Power in Society and Organisations' in Chakraborty S. K. and Bhattacharya, Pradip (eds) *Leadership and Power,* New Delhi: Oxford University Press, 2001, p. 100.

9

Strand 3: Organising and Organisation

Empowerment can be an evolutionary or planned change. But the planned change is gaining centrality because the evolutionary change is not happening sufficiently fast. Organising as a process and the emergence of organisations as a structure is almost a precurser to empowerment as a part of planned change. This is what this chapter analyses as the third strand in our conceptualisation of empowerment.

The extensive literature on organisation theory and organisation management focuses on the dynamics and functioning of organisations once they have come into existence. There is very little emphasis on exploring the process of the formation of organisations. An attempt is being made here to explore the process of organising at the societal level in the context of organisation theory.

The Horizontal and Vertical Planes

There are three spheres of organising, which constantly interact with each other at the societal level. These are:

Organising people, groups, teams

Organising work, production, output

Organising ideas, concepts, knowledge

These three spheres can be viewed as concentric circles which may or may not be linked with each other. When concentric circles are linked with each other they can form a spiral (pila like) or a cylindrical shape. When they are not linked to each other they can be understood as spheres of influence impacting one another.

The spiral shape emerges from the conventional placing (visualisation) of concentric circles as one circle within another circle and so on with a common centre. The innermost circle has the smallest diameter and the outermost circle has the largest diameter. These circles can be linked to each other with connecting loops from the innermost to the outermost circle. In a three dimensional image this takes the form of a conical spiral with a base and a tip. Depending on which circle – innermost or outermost – is being pulled out from the two dimensional form, the tip of the spiral is above the base or vice versa. This can provide a way to understand what is more important – the values, forces, entities depicted by the innermost circle or by the outermost. The relationship between the circles in this juxtaposition can also be understood as a hierarchy or in the vertical plane. This is shown graphically in Fig. 1.

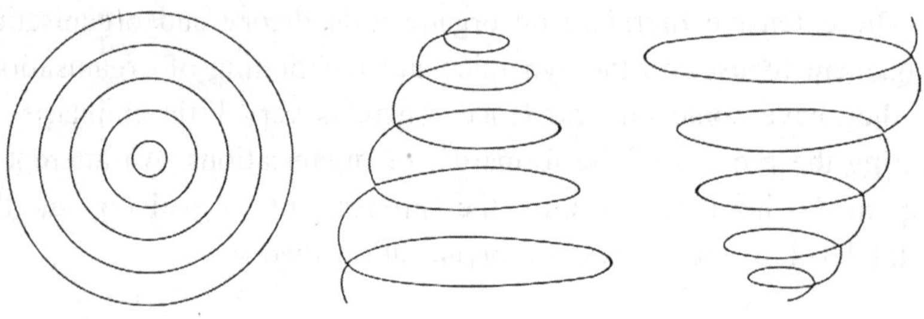

Fig. 1. The vertical plane.

The cylindrical shape emerges when the concentric circles are of the same size and superimposed on each other. When the circles in this arrangement are linked to each other and a three dimensional image is created it takes the form of a spring. In this imagery the values, forces, entities depicted by each circle are of the same importance. The relationship between the circles can be understood as equal or in the horizontal plane. A graphic representation of this is given in Fig. 2.

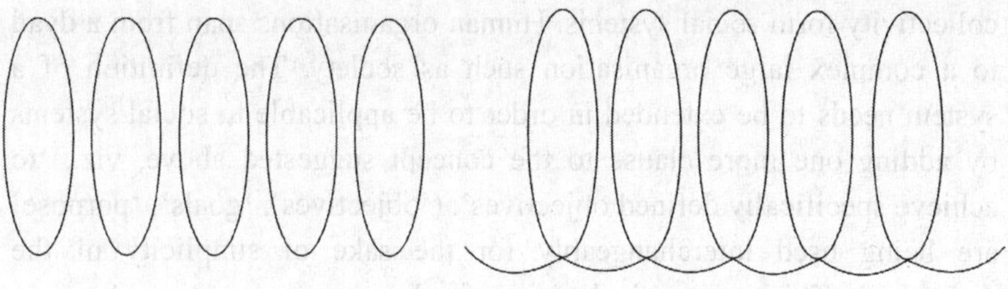

Fig. 2. The horizontal plane.

The horizontal and vertical planes constantly interact with each other and both are important in understanding the process of organising and organisations. Organising the three spheres of people, work, and ideas leads to the emergence of various types of organisations in society. The horizontal and vertical planes define the relationships between people within an organisation and the relationships between various types of organisations. The forces of equality and heirarchy, represented by the two planes, also define the basic structure of any society.

Human Organisations

The process of organising people, work, and ideas continues uninterrupted and leads to the emergence of various types of organisations. The largest form of organisation is society – national and global. An organisation is a structure where the relationship between the people it engages with, the work it engages in, and the ideas it engages for its purpose are defined. A fitting concept to define an organisation is contained in the 'systems approach' put forth by Bishoprick and Rice (1971). According to them, 'A system consists of a patterned functioning relationship between components'. Rephrasing this we can say a system is a set of mutually interactive elements functioning in a dynamically patterned relationship. The nature of the elements – either mechanical or organic – determines the nature of the system. All living systems, which include both biological and social organisations, constitute the organic systems. Human organisations are organic systems in this sense. The individual human body is a biological system but individuals in their collectivity form social systems. Human organisations span from a dyad to a complex large organisation such as society. The definition of a system needs to be extended in order to be applicable to social systems by adding one more clause to the concept suggested above, viz., 'to achieve specifically defined objectives'. ('objectives', 'goals', 'purpose' are being used interchangeably for the sake of simplicity of the definition). This is a critical clause for human organisations because the nature of objectives determines the various kinds of organisations that have been existing all through human history – family, work groups, clans, tribes, kinship groups, religious organisations, business organisations, educational and academic organisations, clubs, forums, associations, professional bodies, political parties, government organisations, defence organisations – in fact the whole panorama of human society.

All these, however, can be placed in three basic categories – social organisations, work organisations, and political organisations. Organisations emerge through the continuous process of organising. Organising, thus, can be defined as a slow continuous process of enabling a group of people to perceive common interests and act collectively to achieve social, economic, or political purposes (objectives, goals).

The reality of being organised and unorganised therefore constitutes two ends of a continuum which can be applied to people, work, ideas. When all three are at the organised end of the continuum, the organisation which emerges is vibrant and effective in achieving its objectives (goals, purpose). When all three are at the unorganised end of the continuum then no organisation emerges. At least one of these three spheres has to be well organised for an organisation to emerge which may then move towards the end of the continuum where all three spheres are well organised.

Seen in this fashion, the individual and the collective (collectivity of individuals) are the two foci which are relevant for understanding ourselves and the world around us. The collective takes the form of one or other kind of organisation – formal or informal; amorphous or morphous (crystallised); nascent or developed, transient or permanent; finite or infinite – engaged in some kind of societal transaction.

Societal Transactions

Societal transactions can be viewed in a mosaic of three interfaces:

i. Individual-to-individual transactions
ii. Individual-to-organisation transactions
iii. Organisation-to-organisation transactions.

In ancient times when technology and societal structures were simple, the social environment of human collectivity was stable and the pace of life was slow. The human population was smaller and the equilibrium of the field forces of society was anchored in stability. The individual-to-individual basis of interaction was manifested more visibly and obviously. Many individual needs were met in interacting with other individuals. The individual-to-organisation basis of interaction was manifested only in limited activities. Organisations being fewer, the organisation-to-organisation basis of interaction was very invisible. As such, individuals were the operational unit of society. Change as an evolutionary phenomenon occurred very slowly. At few and far apart junctures, change occurred suddenly and drastically as a revolutionary phenomenon. The limited and homogenous organisational forms of the earlier times, the comparative stability of societal processes, and the repetitiveness of modes of living provided individuals and organisations an opportunity to synchronise and stabilise the individual-organisation interface. The slower pace of life allowed integrating mechanisms to be instituted at the individual-organisation interface which were stable and had a built-in quality of endurance over a long period of time.

Over 4000 and more years of human transaction with the environment, human inputs have made technology more complex and have advanced the boundaries of society, making it more differentiated and heterogenous in the process. Science and technology, communication and transport, physical mobility, ecological resources, and political boundaries have all contributed to making life and society more complex and turbulent. The sheer increase of human population and consequent human interaction has generated forces of size, complexity, and growth in human organisations. Today, uncertainty and change have become the propelling forces in human existence. The multitudinous upheaval ushered in by the industrial revolution and urbanisation has shifted the field forces of society from stability towards transience and change. The communications and information technology revolution in the era of post-industrialisation has only reinforced the shift towards transience and change.

With the greater complexity and heterogeneity of societal structures prevalent today, individuals are increasingly interfacing with organisations for every facet of human existence. Now, organisations have become the operational unit of society and individuals, in turn, have become the unit of organisations. The focus of society has shifted from the individual-to-individual basis of interaction towards the individual-to-organisation and the organisation-to-organisation basis of interaction. Today, the individual-to-individual basis of interaction, though very important and necessary, has been relegated to the background of human existence.

The application of these concepts of organising and organisation to the Indian context is elaborated next to understand their linkage with the empowerment process.

The Indian Context

The Indian population is highly organised on social and religious lines in the form of caste/tribe associations, occupational guilds (often overlapping with caste/tribe), religious bodies, linguistic groups, and so on. However, a large proportion of the population in India (the poor, the underprivileged, the disadvantaged, the marginalised) is excluded from the organisational framework that characterises the modern world of work, finance, trade, communication, governance, education, health, insurance, etc. This world is typified by large sized, formal organisations that function within a written, legal, regulatory framework and are held accountable to designated authorities of the State. The modern world is conspicuous by its organisational fora and the predominance of individual-to-organisation as well as organisation-to-organisation transactions on practically all facets of life. These type of transactions vis-a-vis the modern world are thus a reality for a very small section of the population in India. It is the modern world which is defining the mainstream of progress and development globally and nationally. Individually and on their own, a large majority of the people in India are not able to be integrated in the larger development processes of the modern world unfolding around them. Their ability to improve their situation in life, consequently, is handicapped considerably.

Political parties in India are one modern organisational entity which effectively utilise the social and religious affiliations of the people on a large-scale for political mobilisation and vote bank calculations. Hence there is a very skewed scenario where the population is affiliated to political organisations of the modern world but is not yet able to deal with the handicaps arising from being underprivileged, disadvantaged, and marginalised because of lack of organisational affiliations with other modern organisational fora. What it means then is that all people and groups in the population need an organisational umbrella in the modern world to be able to interact as equals with other people in the world around them and to pursue, protect, and promote their interests. To create such an umbrella is a major societal need in India and also the major development challenge. The type of organisations which can meet this challenge become an important element of the empowerment process.

For computation of national accounts statistics and for describing the nature of the economy, the legal and regulatory frameworks in India draw an arbitrary, dividing line between the two ends of the organised – unorganised continuum. The result is that who or what is to be considered as the 'organised' segment on this contimuum is based on an arbitrary yardstick. The term 'unorganised sector' is used very loosely as an umbrella term to refer to the rest of the continuum. The majority of the population which is poor, underprivileged, disadvantaged, marginalised thus gets labelled as the 'unorganised sector'. The use of the term 'unorganised sector' to refer to a whole country or a whole economy is very misleading. It is possible to have unorganised workers in an economy, unorganised production, unorganised trade, unorganised services, unorganised markets vis-a-vis organised workers, organised production, organised trade, organised services, organised markets. It is difficult to visualise an 'unorganised sector' per se, that carries the connotation of being unorganised on every facet. As elaborated earlier, the collectivity of human existence is intricately woven into the fabric of organisation. Every collectivity of people has some basis and some form of organisation, though this may not be understood or valued by external interventions/interveners. The reality of any population of being organised on some basis does not get undermined because of the limited understanding of external forces themselves. The basis on which the majority of the population is organised has to be understood in greater detail by policy makers and the use of the term 'unorganised sector' has to be far more judicious to avoid such distortions.

This point becomes even more relevant in the Indian context when the organised-unorganised continuum interacts with the formal-semi formal-informal systems of work continuum based on the extent of written and verbal transactions. This gives rise to six types of combinations in which people in India can be classified. The informal system has organised and unorganised groups of people; the semi formal system has organised and unorganised groups of people; and the formal system has organised and unorganised groups of people. The ease with which government departments can collect data on employment status and other criteria for people in the formal system of work has created a situation where the organised groups in the formal system are referred to as 'organised sector' and all the rest get clubbed as 'unorganised sector'. This also leads to distortions in estimating the size of the different categories of people. The lack of adequate systems to estimate the size of the organised groups in the semiformal system and the organised groups in the informal system is the underlying cause of such clubbing and distortions. The proper estimation of the size of the different categories has relevance for the policies and measures initiated for improving the lives of the people.

In the Indian context, therefore, the combination of the traditional basis of organising and the informal systems of work create various categories of people with differential linkage to the modern world and with differential organisational strength to pursue, protect, and promote their interests. We take the concept of organising and organisation still further to understand the modern world, from which the majority of the people in India are excluded, as the corporate world.

The Corporate World

The term 'corporate' refers to that which is incorporated or a body incorporate. The literal meaning of the term is that which is combined as a whole or collective and relates to a corporation. The term 'corporation' in turn is defined as a body of persons recognised by law as an individual person or an entity having its own name and identity, and with rights, privileges, and liabilities distinct from those of its members and refers to any group of persons acting as one body.

Today, the world of large companies engaged in business is commonly referred to as the corporate sector. The fact is that companies constitute only the corporate world of business. There are bodies incorporated under legislations other than The Companies Act, in various fields such as health, education, entertainment, childcare, civic amenities and utilities, social work. All the registered bodies under various legislations are also part of the corporate world and constitute the corporate world of healthcare, education, entertainment, childcare, social work, etc. Viewed in this way, the corporate sector is very diverse and complex.

Corporate is the opposite of individual. The law recognises only two kinds of persons – natural persons and legal persons. All entities/bodies created under various legislations are legal persons and constitute the corporate sector in its totality. Companies are but one type of legal person. So to refer to the corporate sector as comprising of companies only is to take a very narrow and limited view of the term. When the corporate sector is understood in its broad view then performance norms, values, governance, codes of conduct are relevant to all the components of the corporate sector as much as they are to companies. Corporate power can be visualised in all these types of bodies/entities.

The corporate world is spread over all the three institutional anchors of society – the state, the private sector, and civil society – which have complementary roles to play to make the lives of the people better. Government organisations are the mainstay of the state, business organisations are the mainstay of the private sector. Various associations and forums, other than the government and business organisations, form the mainstay of civil society wherein NGOs constitute one component.

These three types of organisational systems also have relatively different capacities to organise people, work, and ideas. Social development organisations (a part of civil society) are more active in trying to organise people. They are not yet so effective in organising work or ideas. Business organisations are primarily active in organising work. Corporate forms of business organisations are able to organise their own workforce – i.e. people, on a limited scale – as well as organise work. Government organisations are active in organising work and their employees. They also have to organise people – the citizens whom they govern. Academic organisations are organising ideas and concepts – pushing the frontiers of knowledge. Thus all the three institutional anchors of society have mechanisms for providing an organisational umbrella to different sections of the population.

As discussed earlier, business organisations are expected to be socially responsible and a social audit is considered necessary for a business organisation to establish its social responsibility. The reverse can be made to apply to social organisations. They also need to stand on their own feet and establish a direct link with the economy for long term sustenance. Thus they have to be commercially responsible. A business audit can be applied to social organisations for them to establish their commercial responsibility. Over a period of time such a measure of performance will create a critical mass of organisations which are effective on the business front as well as on the social front – each such entity being commercially and socially relevant. The concepts of topline meaning revenue flows, middleline meaning expenditures, and bottomline meaning profits/surplus as a net of revenues and expenditures can apply to all such entities which are successful in organising people, work, and ideas in a direct interface with the economy and with society. Such an interpretation of the corporate world leads us to the concept of people's organisations.

People's Organisations

When a set of people form their own organisation to pursue, protect, and promote their interests in any sphere of life; manage their organisation themselves; and take responsibility for it; then a people's organisation comes into existence. There are traditional and modern people's organisations, there are spontaneous and induced people's organisations, there are voluntary and mandated people's organisations. The state, business, and civil society all have examples of people's organisations. They may emerge from people's own initiative, from state sponsored programmes, from donor funded development interventions, and from business funded development action, to mention only a few ways of their coming into being. The centrality of people's organisations is not yet fully acknowledged by any of the key players in the development process.

In an earlier chapter we have already indicated that people's organisations are not the same as NGOs. NGOs are self-appointed individuals or group of people working for the benefit of other deprived or disadvantaged groups of people. People's organisations work for improving the life situation of their own group members. Membership is a critical feature of people's organisations. The distinguishing factor is that people facing a particular issue come together as members of a group to solve the issue themselves. They may take the help of others outside their organisation but they themselves are in charge of their organisation. When leadership is from within the group itself, when resources and assets are owned by the group, when governance and office bearing is taken care of by the group, when management and responsibility of the organisation is taken by the group itself, then a genuine people's organisation emerges.

In some cases NGOs have a membership based structure by design, where the people they work for pay a membership subscription to qualify for receiving the support and assistance of the NGO. This membership basis is used as justification for calling such NGOs as people's organisations. The term 'membership organisation' is also prevalent to refer to such NGOs. It is important to differentiate between genuine people's organisations and NGOs projecting themselves as people's organisations. Whereas people's organisations are necessarily membership based, all membership organisations are not necessarily people's organisations. Holding elections for the positions of office bearers in such kind of membership based NGOs is also projected as a qualification for calling themselves people's organisations. Often, the

NGO representatives in these forums hold honorary but lifetime membership as a special category of members, whereas the people for whom the NGO works are time bound members. These are some of the pitfalls that the people's organisations have to recognise and insulate themselves against.

People's organisations are self-organising, self-governing, self-managing, self-regulating, self-controlled and self-led. When they become self-reliant in material terms also then their strength increases immensely. Community based organisations, youth clubs, cooperatives, self-help groups, professional associations, trade guilds, user groups, residents associations, panchayats, caste associations, chambers of commerce, industry associations are all examples of people's organisations. In the Indian context, empowerment which can be sustained is linked to the strength of the people's organisations which develop. People's organisations are the norm in a culture and economy where the majority of the population is self-employed and is engaged in informal systems of work. The following equation highlights the various strengths which people's organisations have to develop if they are to lead to sustained empowerment of their members.

Sustained Empowerment	=	Numerical Strength	+	Financial Strength	+	Organisational Strength

Empowerment and Organisations

It is possible to understand empowerment in the context of the interplay between the individual and the collectivity. True and sustained empowerment of people is directly related to the organisational strength of the organisations/agencies/forums they are a part of or are associated with. Strong and effective organisations therefore need to be built for all segments of the population. Empowerment interventions by all the three types of systems – business, government, and social development – visualise some form of organisation for improving the lives of people. The effectiveness of their interventions and the impact they achieve is related to the strength of the people's organisations which evolve from their efforts. Interventions which make it possible for people's organisations to develop all the three types of strengths listed above will be the ones which will have lasting impact. It takes time for these different strengths to develop and it is only the clarity of purpose of the empowerment intervention which can facilitate the growth of genuine people's organisations. The people's organisations emerging from the initiatives of social development organisations and NGOs are most vulnerable to being captured by forces outside the organisation. This is because the NGOs mediate the flow of funds and resources to the people's organisations.

There is a stratification of the grassroots, national, and international contexts of the world today where players at the grassroots level are organising people, players at the national level are organising work, and players at the international level are organising ideas and concepts. Such a stratification has encouraged a relationship between the three levels such that the international level is superior to the national level, and the national level is superior to the grassroots level. And there is an international context to every facet of life today. This is another manifestation of the spiral form, or the vertical plane, at the global level which reflects the hierarchy of relationships between the grassroots, national, and international levels. So the struggle for equality also has to deal with these forces of hierarchy.

If all organisations can be enabled to become skilled and effective in simultaneously organising people, work, and ideas then the relationship between the grassroots, national, and international levels can move towards a horizontal plane. This will be true empowerment at the societal level. Each organisation becomes strong and effective in its own right and can contribute to sustained change and sustained empowerment of its members. Organising and organisation thus are an important strand of empowerment to enable people to become more and more in charge of their own lives leading to sustained empowerment. Transient empowerment, which is quite visible in many developmental interventions, has to grow into sustained empowerment through organising and organisation.

Reference

Bishoprick, D. W. and Rice, G. H., *Conceptual Models of Organisation*, New York:Appleton-Century-Crofts, 1971, p. 163.

10

Strand 4: Mainstreaming

Mainstreaming is the fourth strand in our conceptualisation of empowerment. What constitutes the mainstream and the relationship of empowerment interventions with the mainstream is explored in this chapter to highlight the scope for sustainable results.

Unlike many other terms of social discourse, mainstreaming has not been properly defined. According to *The Chambers 21st Century Dictionary (1996),* the term means, 'The chief trend or direction of development in any activity, business, movement, etc'. *The New Oxford Dictionary of English (1998)* says the same thing about it, 'The ideas, attitudes, or activities that are regarded as normal or conventional; the dominant trend in opinion, fashion or the arts'. Mainstreaming, thus, can be interpreted to mean 'where the bulk or majority is'. Mainstreaming means enabling people to move from the fringes, peripheries, and margins towards the centre of social, economic, and political life of a community, region, state, or nation. In economic terms it can mean where the bulk of the money is; in sociological terms it can mean where the bulk of people are or the reality of the majority of people. In political terms it can mean where the dominant political forces are active.

Mainstreaming thus involves the convergence of the worlds of money, power, and people. In India these are yet two different worlds though with some overlap, often called India and Bharat. The category referred to as India has the bulk of the money and Bharat has the large proportion of the population which is underprivileged, disadvantaged, marginalised. Mainstreaming means enabling this majority of the population to overcome their handicap of being underprivileged, disadvantaged, marginalised. This will happen when each individual and group is able to interface directly with the economy for long term sustenance; each person has the capacity to access their basic rights of health, education, safe environment; and each one has an effective organisational affiliation for grievance redressal as well as for pursuing, protecting, and promoting his/her interests. In other words, mainstreaming will happen when income poverty, basic needs poverty, and capability poverty are removed from a given population. The extent to which this happens, the proportion of people who can reach and sustain this state, will signify the extent of mainstreaming.

While the business and government organisations are already a part of the mainstream, the same has to be achieved in the social development context as well. Pilot efforts in education, health care, child care have to scale up to cover more numbers and more geographical areas. Nascent organisational forms like savings and credit self-help groups have to graduate to manage more finances and offer more services, integrating with the mainstream world of banking and finance. Rights groups, like consumer action groups, have to expand the breadth and depth of their reach to protect all consumers. Environment protection groups have to address all the players involved in environmental degradation. Essentially, therefore, mainstreaming involves increasing scale of operations, developing integration mechanisms, and achieving depth of reach. This has to happen in a sustainable way which means the changes visualised in outlook, behaviour, and committment are internalised by the people. Civil society, business, and state all have to make efforts to facilitate the process of mainstreaming by inclusive efforts, enabling legislation, appropriate changes in rules and procedures, and capacity building at all levels.

Development and Commercial Phases

Mainstreaming implies moving from the development phase to the commercial phase in any intervention. A commercial phase starts when a direct interface with the economy is made for any particular intervention. The principle of 'user pays' becomes applicable to every intervention over a period of time. To begin with, external support in the form of grants, subsidies, capital investment, managerial and technical inputs, capacity building, et cetera are needed for a developmental intervention to take form and be able to address the issues it takes up. For instance, a primary education intervention must be able to address the issue of enrollment in schools and effective learning for the children. For this, development support is required and the intervention is considered to be in the development phase. Once it establishes the base for ongoing school enrollment, then it has to find ways of applying the 'user pays' principle to its activities to enter the commercial phase. The development intervention may itself take on the role of a regular school or it may make sure that the children attend the existing schools, or it may find some other ways of ensuring the continued availability of the school facility for children. This would be a shift to the commercial phase. Mainstreaming of the children into the schooling system would be the outcome.

The 'user pays' principle may ensure full cost recovery or partial cost recovery for any given intervention. The extent of cost recovery for different interventions will vary and has to be clarified. The greater the cost recovery the more the shift towards the commercial phase and consolidation of the move towards mainstreaming. Business organisations ensure full cost recovery and also a profit on their activities. They are referred to as commercial organisations. Mainstreaming increases the scope for social development and government organisations also to operate as commercial organisations.

Finite and Infinite Societal Functions

The development challenge of providing access to the whole population for a variety of services such as education, health, water, electricity, sanitation, housing, et cetera has a concept of finiteness of purpose inherent in it. Once a particular service is accessed by all, then the system created for that service is expected to cater to the needs of the people continually. To take the example of schooling again, once the 100 per cent enrollment is achieved, then the school system must ensure that 100 per cent enrollment happens year after year. It has to cater to the schooling requirements of the children and make sure that they are learning well. There is little need then for any external group of people to motivate parents to send their children to school or to run non-formal schools or to pressurise the school system to teach well. Till the value system of sending children to school gets internalised by the population, till the value system of teaching gets well internalised by the school system, and till there is a school available for every child, there will be a need for external agents. This time lag puts a finiteness on the need for external agents. Providing education to all children is the infinite societal function, whereas having an external agent to provide schooling to those deprieved of this facility is a finite societal function. Mainstreaming implies that the infinite societal functions take over when the finite goals are achieved. The setting of the Monitorable Targets for the Tenth Plan and Beyond by the Planning Commission of India illustrates a finite societal function. Likewise, the international organisations have set Millenium Development Goals for the world as a whole, to be achieved by 2015.

Mainstreaming highlights the indefinite existence of two sets of actors in the development proces – the people and the government. The two functions of the state–governance and development programme implementation – will also get polarised between these two sets of actors with governance being the mandate of government and development programme implementation being the responsibility of people and their organisations. The other actors, which are NGOs and the donor agencies, will have little or no role for a set of people for whom mainstreaming has been achieved in a sustainable way. The experts would be offering their expertise to whosoever needs it. The people would then be in a position to access whichever expert services they require by negotiating their own terms and conditions or by paying market prices. They would increasingly manage their lives themselves and look after their interests.

In this scenario, the role of the NGOs will be different from what it is at present if they also are to become part of the mainstream and have an indefinite existence. They could function as research organisations, training organisations, think tank organisations, standards and accreditation organisations, rating organisations, and so on. These organisations would have to establish a link with the economy and provide their services for a fee. Their on-going sustenance would be drawn from the economy. Consequently, they would represent their expertise, which becomes a function, rather than represent people, which they claim to do at present. The political space created for people will rightfully be taken by people's organisations.

The emergence, nurturing, and strengthening of people's organisations paves the way for this kind of mainstreaming and contributes to the empowerment of people.

11

Strand 5: Representative Organisations

Accessing a specific power base for a given set of people through a process-oriented, mainstream, organisational forum leads to the development of a representative organisation for that set of people. This is the fifth strand in our conceptualisation of empowerment. In this chapter we look at the issues involved in building representative organisations for all sets of people in a society and their relationship with empowerment.

A representative organisation necessarily represents people or interests. In a large democracy like India, there is a constant interplay between the forces of participative democracy and representative democracy. In a participative democracy all the eligible members of a system are directly involved in running it whereas in a representative democracy all the eligible members of a system elect their representatives for running it. The State in India is primarily a representative democracy except at the unit of the village where in the form of the Gram Sabha it becomes a participative democracy. All other manifestations of the State ranging from Gram Panchayat to Taluka Panchayat to Zilla Panchayat to State Assembly to Parliament are representative forums. Other organisational fora such as companies, cooperatives, societies have elements of both participative and representative democracy in their functioning.

Participative democracy by definition does not have to concern itself with who has the right to represent, but it is necessary to understand these nuances in a representative democracy. Who has the right to represent? Can people represent themselves at all levels ranging from grassroots to international levels? Can self-appointed individuals, forums, bodies, organisations appropriate the right to represent people? What are the bases for a representative organisation?

Location, occupation, and function can be visualised as the three bases for representative organisations. These three can be subsumed within each other to give centrality to any one base at a time. For instance, in a primary dairy cooperative at the village level only a person engaged in dairy farming as an occupation and belonging to a particular village can become a member. This cooperative represents the interests of dairy farmers (an occupation) belonging to a particular village (a location). When it coalesces with other dairy cooperatives to form district and state level organisations for dairy farming, it promotes the interests of dairy farming within a geographical area. The locational base gets subsumed in the occupational base. But when the village dairy cooperative comes together with the gram panchayat or the other cooperative organisations in the village to provide infrastructural facilities to the village, they together promote the locational interest. Here the occupational base is subsumed in the locational base. A similar process happens at the district, state and national levels.

A key functional base for representativeness is the governance function. Support services such as health care, education, banking, transportation, communication, water supply, power supply are functions. While these are material functions, religion in contrast is a societal function for spiritual care.

Caste, tribe, language are subsumed under function and location. Gender, today, is a strong contestant for a representative base for separate women's forums, but in fact when gender balanced mainstreaming happens, then women's forums and men's forums are included in the three bases of location, occupation and function. Class as a basis for representative forums also gets included in location, occupation, and function.

The Indian Context

Traditionally, in India, representative organisations of all occupations and activities have been established in the form of trade and artisan guilds to enable people to protect their work and social interests, to deal with conflicting situations, to set norms and standards of work, to ensure quality, to negotiate and bargain with other guilds and with the State, and finally to participate in public policy formulation. The social stratification of caste and tribe has been integrated with the occupations of different groups of people. The guilds, thus, integrated the social and economic interests of a group of people in the same forum. Religious bodies and cultural forums have included various occupational and caste groups. The result, in the words of Rajni Kothari (1998), was:

> Indian society for centuries survived the vicissitude of history without a centralised political system. Except for short periods, it lacked a clear centre. Even those short periods had a rather limited reach and proved to be transitions in the long march of Indian civilisation. The core of the civilisation was cultural rather than political. Its 'State' was intermittent, scattered and multipolar, an arena of conflicting claims of a large number of clans and regimes. The real 'action' was by voluntary entities representing trade and commerce and the 'mahajans' governing them, and cultural, religious and caste and caste-like organisations.

This form of representation, however, underwent a transformation, in the wake of industrialisation. The groups of workers with an established employer-employee relationship became more and more organised along the lines of trade unions developed in the industrialised countries. They have been able to bargain and negotiate for more and more economic strength for their members even though they constitute a minority of the workforce. The majority of the workforce, which is self-employed, has remained outside the fold of the representative forums called trade unions. This process of exclusion of the workers has continued to such an extent that the whole labour movement itself has become confined to those workers who have an established employer-employee relationship, and only these people are called 'workers' under labour laws. The labour movement, the labour laws and policies, the national and international labour organisations address themselves to the needs of those workers who have an established employer-employee relationship.

Today, there are very few representative forums of self-employed workers because they have not been organised as workers in the modern sense. The traditional representativeness of the poor self-employed, in the form of trade and artisan guilds, has been destroyed and has not been replaced by other forums. The rich self-employed have been able to metamorphose the guild form of representative forums into the present day version of trade and industry associations, chambers of commerce, professional councils, and societies, etc. They are able to protect their interests through these forums; they also exert various kinds of influence on policy formulation to suit their needs. But the rich and well-to-do constitute only a minority in terms of the total number of self-employed people. The vast majority of self-employed workers have yet to establish their representative forums to truly protect their interests. The cultural, social, religious organisations in India, however, continue to be very active and widespread.

What happens to the majority of the workforce then? Are they to remain excluded? Will they be able to change, under the present situation, the direction of the legal and policy framework in their favour? Will they be able to command the respect due to them by virtue of constituting the majority of the workforce in a democracy? This is possible if the reality of the self-employed workers is taken seriously by the policy makers, when the future envisaged for all these workers is seen within the perspective of strengthening self-employment in its own right, instead of replacing it with employer-employee relationships. This is possible by establishing representative forums of self-employed workers to protect their own interests.

How can representative forums for self-employed workers be built? The experiences of so many grassroots organisations, working with different occupational groups of the self-employed workers have shown that organising workers is the only way to strengthen the position of these workers in the overall socio-economic political context. Organising the self-employed is different from organising workers with an established employer-employee relationship. The conventional trade unions organise workers on the basis of collective bargaining and wage agreements with the employers. This basis of organising can be of very limited value for self-employed workers because there is no established employer-employee relationship in their case and hence, there is no particular employer with whom to bargain. The State and public policy are the main forces which determine the fate of the self-employed in any economy. So the focus of bargaining shifts from one employer to public policy. The direction, nature, and implementation of public policies and the responsibility of the State, affect the overall economic situation in a country. The economic atmosphere becomes either conducive to, or antagonistic to the survival and strengthening of the self-employed. The representative forums of the self-employed people therefore have essentially to bargain with the State for public policies favourable to their members so that their niches in the economy can move from strength to strength.

Development interventions over the years have led to organising these workers to some extent, particularly the Watershed Development Programme, the Micro Credit Programme, the Joint Forest Management Programme, the Participatory Irrigation Management Programme, and the Swarnajayanti Gram Swarozgar Programme. These programmes by design envisage groups of people to come together and organise themselves, if they have to realise concrete benefits. However, the population covered under these programmes as a per cent of the total population of the low income people is still very small. Besides, some of these programmes at present are directed at the community as a whole, i.e. all income groups, whilst some are exclusively directed at the population below the poverty line. The organising process initiated through these programmes, if nurtured carefully, does have the potential to develop representative organisations of the self-employed workers.

Building Representativeness

The process of building representativeness into a system by external agents can be visualised as a two-stage continuum as shown below.

The first stage can be depicted by 'no effort is put in for representativeness' at one end of the continuum to 'business represents the people', 'government represents the people', 'NGO represents the people' at the other end as shown below:

No effort put in for representativeness	__________	Business represents the people Government represents the people NGO represents the people

This process can be further developed into the second stage where 'business represents the people', 'government represents the people', and 'NGO represents the people' in different contexts is depicted at one end of the continuum and 'people represent themselves' at the other end of the continuum as shown below:

Business represents the people	_________	People represent themselves
Government represents the people	_______	People represent themselves
NGO represents the people	___________	People represent themselves.

Businessmen as residents/natives of a geographical area and investing in its development seek to represent the people of the area on the locational base. They also seek to represent people on the functional base.

Government as provider and facilitator seeks to represent the people on the occupational, locational, and functional base apart from being the elected representatives of the people.

NGOs having organised people on a variety of issues seek to represent people on the occupational, locational, and functional base.

Societal empowerment can be measured by the extent to which people represent themselves on different facets of life and the capacity of their organisations to pursue, protect, and promote their interests. People's organisations also become the representative organisations at all levels from grassroots to national to international.

At present, government deals with the people's organisations of the rich and well-to-do directly in the Government organisation - People's organisation interface without feeling the need for any intermediary. But when it has to deal with people's organisations of the underprivileged and disadvantaged, which come into existence through development interventions, the Government organisation - NGO relationship mediates. In this situation, the people's organisations, more often than not, become extensions of the NGO. Such people's organisations of the underprivileged and disadvantaged are very fragile and vulnerable and need to be strengthened the most as representative organisations. The underprivileged and disadvantaged have yet to stake their claim for representativeness through their own organisations. They have to empower themselves to become the rightful partners of government in development interventions in the same way as the people's organisations of the rich and well-to-do have already done.

Reference

Kothari, Rajni, 'The Future of Voluntarism' in Dantwala, M. L., Sethi, Harsh and Visaria, Pravin, *Social Change Through Voluntary Action*, New Delhi: Sage, 1998, p. 182.

12

Empowering Society

In order to understand how empowerment happens at the individual, organisational, and societal levels the five strands of empowerment have to be woven together. These three levels are iterative and continuously feed into each other to empower society as a whole. Individual change feeds into organisational change which feeds into societal change. Societal change influences organisations and individuals; organisational change in turn influences individuals and society.

At the societal level empowerment is a macro process, at the organisational level it is a micro process, and at the individual level it is a personal process. These three processes can be depicted as expansions of the word 'EMPOWER' as an acronym as elaborated below. The macro-micro-personal processes are operationalised through the five strands of empowerment. Empowered individuals in empowered organisations will be equipped to pursue, protect, and promote their interests effectively. An empowered society will be able to sustain this continually to ensure the greater good for all its people.

As a macro process, the thrust of empowerment at the societal level is to enable and mainstream people's organisations for wealth, equality, and representation. This is the main argument which has been developed in Part III of this book. The greater the number of people's organisations which are in the mainstream of the economy and polity of a given society, the greater will be the empowerment of that society. These people's organisations have to be wealth creators, they must be treated as equals, and they must be in a position to effectively represent the interests of their members. Empowerment at the societal level – a macro process – can be depicted as the expansion of the word 'EMPOWER' as follows:

E enable and
M mainstream
P people's
O organisations for
W wealth
E equality
R representation

At the organisational level empowerment becomes a micro process which individual organisations have to initiate and facilitate. Two types of organisations are visualised here for this purpose. One is those whose *raison d'etre* is to empower others – these are the NGOs. The other is those who seek to empower their members – these are the people's organisations, (POs).

When NGOs initiate empowerment efforts thc following steps are discernable. They begin *engaging* with a section of the population, then *mobilise* them for a specific activity (whether a rights struggle, or a service delivery, or both) and *promote* that activity which leads to *organising* the particular section of the population. Having organised a group of people, some kind of continuous *work* emerges which leads to *enrichment* of the people in some way or the other – either materially or psychologically. It is at this stage that true empowerment implies that the NGO *return* this whole initiative to the concerned group of people and let them run it themselves.

When people's organisations seek to empower their members, these organisations have to first *establish* themselves, then learn to *manage* their own affairs, and *provide* for the needs and requirements of their members. This leads to a sense of *ownership* of the organisation by the members. In continuing to provide for their members, the people's organisations have to *warrant* for the conduct and performance of their members as well as *excel* in whatever activities they undertake. The value they create for their members is *realised* as a result. This leads to sustained empowerment in people's organisations.

Empowerment at the organisational level – a micro process – can be depicted as the expansion of the word 'EMPOWER' as follows:

NGOs		**People's Organisations**	
E	engage	**E**	establish
M	mobilise	**M**	manage
P	promote	**P**	provide
O	organise	**O**	own
W	work	**W**	warrant
E	enrich	**E**	excel
R	return	**R**	realise

In the ultimate analysis, each individual empowers himself/herself with some help from others. For this, the individual has to *energise* himself/herself for empowerment. The *motivation* for being respected, treated as equal with others, living with dignity has to come from within the person. This leads to *pursuing* some purpose or path of action and *overcoming* various obstacles and difficulties to become *worthy* of the respect, equality, dignity which is sought by the person. He/she *earns* the right to *relate* to others as equal and continually improves his/her capacity to do so. This is the internal churning and learning within everyone seeking to empower himself/herself. Empowerment at the individual level – a personal process – can be depicted as the expansion of the word 'EMPOWER' as follows:

E energise

M motivate

P pursue

O overcome

W worthy

E earn

R relate

All the three processes have to happen simultaneously for societal empowerment to be achieved. The three levels of the macro-micro-personal simultaneity are constantly juxtaposed against each other. The forces of hierarchy and equality also continually interact at the three levels. The nature and extent of societal empowerment achieved derives from the state of flux between these forces.

Measuring Empowerment

The five strands of empowerment conceptualised in this study can also be used to assess the extent of empowerment achieved by the three organisational systems – business, government, and social development – as follows:

- What is the extent of process purity?
- What power bases are sought?
- What kind of organising process is initiated?
- What is the extent of mainstreaming?
- What kind of people's organisations/representative forums emerge?

Every organisation involved in empowerment of people can use these criteria to arrive at their own measures of empowerment. A ten point scoring system can be used to rank any intervention on each of these five criteria. Greater empowerment receives a higher score. The ranks on each criterion can be summed up to arrive at an overall score. The higher the overall score received, the greater the extent of empowerment achieved by any particular intervention. Comparison of scores for different interventions and different types of organisations can help in cross sectoral learnings for improving performance in each of the three types of organisations.

To illustrate, any empowerment intervention can receive a score from 0–50 by summing up the scores of 0–10 on each of the five criteria. The total score can be ranked as follows:

0–20 Low, 21–40 Medium, 41–50 High.

Empowerment Index

Another way of assessing the extent of empowerment is through an index of empowerment. Such an index should reflect the economic, social, and political dimensions of a person in the empowerment spectrum as well as capture the changes resulting from interventions to empower him/her.

Those who are to be empowered suffer from economic, social, and political deprivation. Economic deprivation can be expressed by poverty oppression, social deprivation by caste and gender oppression, and political deprivation by marginalisation in society.

A three-stage model is used to reflect the changes which lead to empowerment as follows:

i. When a person's income increases then his/her bargaining position with others increases. This leads to a decrease in discrimination and consequent increase in equality. Any other sequence dwelling on the interplay between income, bargaining position, and discrimination is valid in this configuration if it results in an increase in equality for the concerned person.
ii. When there is an increase in equality, the gap between the *de jure* and the *de facto* reality of a person reduces i.e. the legal rights conferred on all citizens become actual rights realised by him/her.
iii. When the gap between the *de jure* and *de facto* reality of a person reduces there is a change in the status quo.

Together the three stages reflect empowerment, each successive stage indicating a greater degree of empowerment. The index of empowerment can be computed by giving weights to each of these three stages as follows:

Stage I	Stage II	Stage III
30%	30%	40%

Stage III is given a higher weight because the sustainability of empowerment depends on a sustained change in the status quo.

A rank from zero to ten can be given for any empowerment intervention on each of these three stages. After adjusting for the respective weight of that stage the rank will get converted to a decimal number. Summing up the weighted ranks of the three stages will lead to a maximum total of one. The index will range from zero to one. The degree of empowerment achieved by a particular intervention can be measured as follows:

0–0.40 Low 0.41–0.70 Medium 0.71–1.00 High

To illustrate, suppose a particular empowerment intervention is given a rank of 7 for stage I, a rank of 5 for stage II, and a rank of 4 for stage III. This converts to a score of 0.21, 0.15, and 0.16 for each stage. Summing these scores we arrive at the total of 0.52. This score falls in medium empowerment on the index.

This index can be useful for gauging the degree of empowerment achieved by the three organisational systems and thus to assess the level of empowerment in society as a whole.

Comparative Analysis

A comparative framework of analysis to understand the relative strengths and limitations of the three organisational systems of business, government, and social development vis-a-vis empowerment is presented below in terms of the similarities and differences between them.

Similarities

The similarities between the three organisational systems point to a convergence in their efforts to empower society as seen in the following points:

- Business organisations have promoters, social development organisations have promoters, and government has a promoter role. Empowerment interventions by all the three types of organisational systems are critically dependent on the promoters.
- Business, government, and social development organisations have developed a stakeholder focus in their functioning. The concepts of primary, secondary, and tertiary stakeholders are used to differentiate between various stakeholders based on the extent of their stake in the particular organisation as well as their capacity to influence its functioning. Balancing the interests of the various

stakeholders has become the norm for all three types of organisational systems and this also sets the limits to empowerment possible by each type of organisation.

- Business, government, and social development organisations have an increasingly process-oriented focus in their work. This has a direct bearing on the type of results they achieve in general and the quality of empowerment they achieve in particular.
- Business and government organisations have a public accountability in their design. Social development organisations do not have a public accountability in their design. There is a great deal of concern about creating public accountability for social development organisations.
- In business organisations, management and leaders become facilitators when organisational teams are empowered. In government organisations, governments become facilitators when citizens are empowered. In social development organisations, NGOs become facilitators when people are empowered.

Differences

The following criteria are useful in understanding the differences across the three types of organisations in the context of empowering society.

- ➢ Who takes the initiative?
- ➢ Who is being empowered?
- ➢ What is the primary concern?
- ➢ What changes are expected as a result?
- ➢ What activities are undertaken?
- ➢ What is the cost structure?
- ➢ What is the sustainability of the results?
- ➢ What is the nature of gender balance achieved?

- In business organisations management takes the initiative for empowerment interventions. In government organisations government takes the initiative and in social development organisations the NGO takes the initiative for empowerment interventions.
- Business organisations empower their employees. Government empowers citizens and institutions. Social development organisations seek to empower the people they work with.
- The primary concern of business organisations is to increase their

market share. Government is concerned about increasing its vote share. Social development organisations are concerned about increasing their grant share from development assistance.

- Business organisations seek higher motivation and better performance from employees as a result of empowerment. Government organisations seek decentralised systems of governance and of service delivery as a result of empowerment. Social development organisations seek to redistribute power relations in society as a result of empowerment.
- Delayering, process centring, team building, performance and results orientation are some of the actions/activities undertaken by business organisations for empowerment. Service delivery, devolution of powers, instituting accountability to citizens are the type of actions taken up by government organisations for empowerment. Social development organisations take up rights based struggles, service delivery, capacity building as activities for empowerment.
- Business organisations function on the basis of full cost recovery in their operations. The costs involved in building capacities are also recovered through better business performance. Government organisations depend on revenues raised through taxes and duties and other sources. Some element of cost recovery is built into the interventions. Social development organisations are highly dependent on grants for the interventions they undertake. The cost recovery is practically negligible in most of their operations. Increasingly though, both government organisations and social development organisations have to think in terms of cost recovery for their operations.
- The sustainability of empowerment initiatives is usually high in business organisations because they are mainstream activities. Government organisations have medium to high levels of sustainability for their empowerment initiatives. Social development organisations demonstrate medium to low levels of sustainability of the empowerment initiatives.
- The gender balance achieved in business organisations is low. In government organisations it is medium and in social development organisations it is high.

The similarities and differences between the three organisational systems are summarised in Tables 1 and 2.

Table 1. Comparative framework – similarities.

Criterion / Organisation	Business	Business Supported NGO	NGO Independent of Business	Government
What is the critical factor for empowerment?	Empowerment is critically dependent on the promoters of the business	Empowerment is critically dependent on the promoters of the business	Empowerment is critically dependent on the promoters of the NGO	Empowerment is critically dependent on the promotion efforts of the government
What is the approach to empowerment?	Stakeholder approach is adopted for empowerment	Stakeholder approach is adopted for empowerment	Stakeholder approach is adopted for empowerment	Stakeholder approach is adopted for empowerment
What is the focus of empowerment?	Process-oriented focus recognised as essential for empowerment	Process-oriented focus recognised as essential for empowerment	Increasingly having to develop a process-oriented focus as essential for empowerment	Increasingly having to develop a process-oriented focus as essential for empowerment
What is the role change for the leadership as a consequence of empowerment?	Management and leaders become facilitators when employee teams are empowered	Management and leaders as well as NGOs become facilitators when people are empowered	NGOs become facilitators when people are empowered	Government becomes facilitator when citizens are empowered
What is the public accountability?	Public accountability in their organisational design is helpful for empowerment	No public accountability in their organisational design–need to develop it	No public accountability in their organisational design–need to develop it	Public accountabliity in their organisational design is helpful for empowerment

Table 2. Comparative framework – differences.

Criterion / Organisation	Business	Business Supported NGO	NGO Independent of Business	Government
Who takes the initiative for empowerment?	Management	Management	NGO	Government
Who is sought to be empowered?	Employees	Community	Community	Citizens
What is the primary concern?	Increasing market share	Increasing image share	Increasing grant share	Increasing vote share
What changes are expected as a result of empowerment?	Higher commitment, better performance from employees	Greater self-reliance for community	Redistribution of power relations in society	Decentralised systems of governance and of service delivery
What activities are undertaken for empowerment?	Delayering, process centring, team building, performance orientation	Service delivery, capacity building, move towards self-reliance	Rights based struggles, service delivery, capacity building	Service delivery, devolution of powers, instituting accountability to citizens
What is the cost structure?	Topline minus middleline equals a positive bottomline	Topline linked to the fortunes of the business for the NGO	Topline equals middleline for the NGO	Topline equals middleline Or

[Table 2. Contd.

Contd. Table 2.]

		Strive for topline greater than middleline for the interventions	Topline equals bottom line for the interventions	Topline less than middleline
What is the sustainability of the results of empowerment?	High	Medium	Medium to low	Medium to high
What is the nature of gender balance in empowerment?	Low	Medium	High	Medium

Cross Sectoral Learnings and CSR

The relative strengths and limitations of each of the three organisational systems provide the basis for cross sectoral learnings which can strengthen all of them.

Business organisations are good at creating material wealth, systems functioning, process-oriented focus, and sustainable results. But they are not so strong on taking up rights based struggles on behalf of communities of people, or on gender balanced interventions.

Social development organisations are strong on rights based struggles, on gender issues, on developing prototypes of alternative models of service delivery, and people's participation. They are not so strong on scaling up, on creating material wealth, on deriving sustenance from the economy, on systems functioning, and on process-orientation.

Government organisations are strong on reach and coverage, on large scale operations, and on systems of collection. They are not strong on coordination between departments, on innovative approaches to problem solving, on facilitating participatory approaches and involving people in decision making.

Given these various combinations of strengths and limitations, it is imperative that the three organisational systems develop mechanisms of learning from each other. Each of the three actors figure as stakeholders for each other with the community and society being common to all of them. The increasing number of public-private partnerships being promoted to address various problems facing the people also increases the common ground between these three organisational systems. CSR as a function offers considerable opportunities for delineating this common ground. It can become a meeting point for reconciling divergent approaches and experiences of the different actors. It can take the lead in analysing the different approaches for their relative merit and provide support in scaling up efforts by different actors. It can take on an educational role to sensitise various actors on the need for increasing the common ground and developing organisational synergies to take on the development challenges faced by the country.

Appendix I

Cross-section of Views on Empowerment from Practitioners and Academics

To provide an additional dimension of empiricism to the understanding gained from the case studies, a cross-section of people involved in business, academic organisations, and social development interventions were interviewed to understand how they define empowerment. These are listed here.

M. S. Swaminathan, renowned agricultural scientist and policy maker:

'Context and content are important in empowerment. Our perception and the other side's perception of empowerment have to be understood – the other side should feel he/she is empowered through whatever intervention is undertaken.'

Vinay Bharat-Ram, well-known industrialist:

'Empowerment is the freedom to take risks, make mistakes, and come out with a plus at the end of it.'

Kameshwar Choudhary, faculty member, Institute of Rural Management, Anand:

'Redistribution of power relations in all aspects at societal level is empowerment, which means eliminate the gap between people and move towards an egalitarian society. Whatever be your potential the system allows you opportunities to actualise it.'

Chandi Prasad Bhatt, social activist:

'The capacity of people on a large scale to understand their own interests and are able to pursue them'.

Madhu Sarin, independent researcher and social activist:

'The ability to make informed choices, the ability to participate in informed decision making. Create spaces for empowerment of people through people centric intervention and people's strategies for management.'

Pushpa Sundar, Executive Director, Indian Centre for Philanthropy:

'Empowerment is rights and duties and a set of entitlements which everyone is assured of alongwith a set of responsibilities.

Responsible behaviour and freedom to access my rights without undermining somebody else's right.

My "good" and others "good" are interrelated.'

V. B. Eswaran, senior retired IAS officer and policy maker: 'Political empowerment and economic empowerment.

Political empowerment is when my basic rights to vote, to safety, freedom from fear, oppression due to caste and poverty are taken care of.

My right to access facilities and services in the interim period between elections has to be assured.

My rights as a citizen. We see two types of citizens in our country

- First class citizens and
- Second class citizens

Empowerment is enabling everyone to be first class citizens.

Economic empowerment can help to fight oppression. Capacity building can be collapsed into a shorter time span to compensate for the learning legacy of the privileged.

Shift from less power to more power, and from none to some power. How much of oppression is due to lower caste and how much due to poverty. Conversely, when a group/person gets empowered how much is countering caste and how much is countering poverty.

If enough economic stakes have been created for the group members, they will continue and stay together even without the NGO – they will develop their own clout and linkages.'

CHETNA, well known NGO in the field of health care:

'To develop my own space within a power structure based on my values and choice but in collective effort with the other actors in the power structure.

In health interventions it means well-being at the

- physical
- emotional
- spiritual levels

and all the three influence one another and there has to be a balance between them.

Emphasis on the indicators of physical health is high presently but the balance between the three has to be also brought about. Emphasis on the indicators of emotional and spiritual health is increasing slowly. Physical health is a necessary condition for the other two types of well-being.'

Ajay Mehta, Director, National Foundation for India:

'Democratic values being internalised by everyone and reducing/eliminating the vitiating forces which do not allow democratic forces to have a free and fair play. Transparency and accountability to be the key indicators of a functioning democracy.'

Narayan Sheth, well known industrial sociologist:

'Empowerment is a continuous effort to reduce inequalities between people and groups. Some hierarchy is always there whether in organisations or in society – you do not find complete equality. Empowerment addresses these inequalities and attempts to reduce them.'

Sushma Iyengar, social activist:

'The ability to access and the ability to intervene/influence/get things done. Take responsibility for my own actions and be accountable.'

Meenakshi Nayar, company executive:

'Empowerment in the organisational context means having the authority i.e. the freedom, skills and competence to do whatever one is accountable for.

You have to empower yourself – empowerment has to come from within'.

G. Raju, social activist:

'To be able to take my own decisions is empowerment. I may not always be able to do what I wish, that kind of empowerment perhaps only the President of USA can have – he can do whatever he wishes. But in the context of ordinary people it means I must be able to take my own decisions'.

Kiran Karnik, President, National Association for Software Services Companies:

'Empowerment is economic sustainability with education and health as prerequisites to achieving it. One of the factors is, access to information is power. Literacy can help to access information. Information from all sources is necessary to negotiate, to bargain, and to protect and promote your interests. So access to information to all in important in the process of empowerment. The electronic media has a lot to offer in this regard – market information, land records information, et cetera for instance can become accessible equally to all'.

Manju Raju, independent researcher:

'Empowerment means being able to do whatever I want to do'.

Sara Ahmed, faculty member, Institute of Rural Management, Anand:

'Empowerment is a very relative term. I may feel very empowered in class but very disempowered in the presence of Chairman.

Women's empowerment, economic empowerment, the work of NGOs is empowerment'.

Viraf Mehta, Chief Executive, Partners in Change:

'Empowerment is from within – nobody can empower you – you have to feel and experience and want to be equal and you will set yourself on the path to empowerment'.

Sharda Jain, social activist:

'Empowerment has to be understood in the context of powerlessness. There are various types, categories and levels, degrees of powerlessness hence empowerment is in correspondence to the powerlessness.

Class and gender have to be disaggregated for understanding powerlessness.

Women's empowerment has to understand the other side of situation – men also have to be involved – otherwise it leads to violence and complications.

Look at the power relations, limits of empowerment, and the modes of empowerment.

Gender equity is possible, other things are not.'

C. N. Pandey, Director, GEER Foundation:

'Empowerment is a form of capacity building which develops the capacity of the person to participate in decision making and influence decision making.'

P.V. Narsimharao, company executive:

'Empowerment is releasing people's potential to do their best and help them to realise their potential by reducing fears – real or imaginary. To push people to higher levels of performance and thus increase the sense of achievement and competence in people.'

Katar Singh, Director, Institute of Rural Management, Anand:

'The weak – physically, socially, economically and politically – need empowerment.

All rounded approach, holistic intervention. The problem is multi-faceted so the solution also has to be multi-faceted.

Economic powers attract political power.

Politically strong are also able to influence the economic power.

Bureaucracy controls the policy making.

Organising leads to empowerment.

Education, good education for all is the key for empowerment'.

The limits to empowerment come from human nature and bad design of institutions.

In the design, the domain of ownership and management is kept separate. Both should not unsurp each other's spaces.'

Anil Nayar, management consultant:

'Empowerment is the authority to do what is right.'

Anant Nadkarni, GM, Tata Council for Community Initiatives

'Empowerment is within you – an outsider cannot empower you. You have to empower yourself. An outsider can only facilitate the process.'

Dhiraj Bhalani, social activist:

'Empowerment is a process of enabling people to be in control of their lives.'

Arvind Gupta, faculty member, Institute of Rural Management, Anand:

'The peception of what one can do is empowerment.'

Debashis Bhattacharya, consultant (SDCA), Confederation of Indian Industry

'Empowerment is one of the links in operationalising a vision into a sustainable reality. Vision, broad objective, immediate objective, empowerment, sustainability is the sequence of these links visualised as concentric circles. The social development organisations are mainly building advocacy networks to come closer to the sources of power.'

Appendix II

Perceptions of Empowerment

The Economic Times, Ahmedabad Edition, 15 August 2001

The Economic Times, Ahmedabad Edition, 1 November 2001

Vision of Andhra Government

Development of Women & Children for a better tomorrow

CM's Vision 2020 — Empowering Women & Children.

"Empowerment of Women & Child through proactive measures"
— Nara Chandrababu Naidu
(Hon'ble Chief Minister of A.P.)

Goals under Vision 2020 Empowering Women

- Increasing gender sensitisation through training.
- Address gender inequalities in education, employment and nutrition.
- Increasing gender sensitivity in Health, Welfare and Economic Programmes.
- Prevent atrocities against Women.
- Launching social security schemes for aged, disabled and widowed.

POLICIES

Women empowerment policy.

INSTITUTIONS

For orphan children & destitute women:

- Shishuvihars • Children Homes • Collegiate Home • Working Women Hostels • Service Homes • State Homes • Old Age Homes • Rescue Homes

Goals under Vision 2020 Development of Children

- Protecting child rights.
- Safeguarding child health.
- Ensuring maternal health.
- Eradicating Malnutrition.
- Expanding early childhood care & education.
- Ensuring education for every child.
- Eliminating child labour.
- Special protection to girl child and adolescent.
- Caring for disabled children and children in difficult circumstances.

SCHEMES

Girl Child Protection Scheme:
To remove prejudices against the girl child by helping parents in ensuring proper education and prevention of early marriage.
Number of beneficiaries for 2001 - 2002 : 50,000.
Budget Allocated
Rs. 30 crore.

Integrated Child Development Services-
Worlds largest network of Integrated Family & Community Services.
Number of beneficiaries : 82,51,757
Budget Allocated
Rs. 142.89 crore

Balika Samrudhi Yojana-
To remove the negative attitude of family and community towards a girl child.
Number of beneficiaries for 2001 - 2002 : 54,000.
Budget Allocated
Rs. 3.45 crore

Pradhan Mantri Gramodaya Yojana-
To eradicate malnutrition amongst 0-3 yr children by adding nutritional coverage through ICDS. The scheme has excellent acceptance from children and beneficiaries.
Number of beneficiaries for 2001 - 2002 : 4,52,744
Budget Allocated
Rs. 42.62 crore

ADOPTION

The government has taken comprehensive measures to strengthen & regulate the system of adoption.

- Adoption cell opened in the Directorate
- District level workshops conducted
- VCA reconstituted with a view to effectively facilitate incountry adoption.
- Active software to monitor adoption cases
- Existing rules and regulations are being studied to bring out a comprehensive legislation on child adoption
- The necessary rules are being enforced to streamline the adoption process.

Supplementary Nutrition programme at Anganwadi

Training Programme of Mothers Committee

36877 ANGANWADI NETWORKS

Operating as a village resource centre, Anganwadi aims to lay the foundation for integrated development of women and children. It is a unique concept that had been incorporated as one of the earliest among the states, in A.P. It also seeks to improve the conditions of children and offers a host of services.

Health: Immunization, Health check ups, Primary Health care, Treatment of minor illnesses.

Nutrition: Supplementary feeding, Growth monitoring, Health education.

Convergence: Environmental sanitation, Women welfare, Adolescent girls scheme.

HOLISTIC DEVELOPMENT OF CHILDREN

2,95,016 MOTHERS COMMITTEE, A DYNAMIC CHANGE AGENT

They are the catalysts, participants and recipients who -

- Promote sense of ownership.
- Ensure contextuality and sustainability of the initiative.
- Mobilize community involvement.
- Change social attitude and community practices.
- Bring about advancement, development and empowerment of women.

Department of Women Development & Child Welfare

Government of Andhra Pradesh

8-3-222, Vengal Rao Nagar, Ameerpet, Hyderabad - 500 038.

Frontline, 1 February 2002

The Economic Times, Ahmedabad Edition, 20 April 2002

A Performance That's EMPOWERING...

Provisional Profit After Tax around Rs.754 crores. An increase of 25% over last year

Profit Before Tax rises by 22% at Rs.945 crores

Sanctions reach an all time high of Rs.8,506 crores. Up by 11%

Disbursements reach an all time high of Rs.5,168 crores. Up by 60%

Recovery rate at 99% - Nil NPAs

Resource Mobilization at Rs. 4,398 crores. Up by 37%

Paid all time high dividend of Rs.150 crores

...And a Result That's ELECTRIFYING!

UNAUDITED FINANCIAL RESULTS (PROVISIONAL)
FOR THE QUARTER ENDED 31.03.2002

(Rs. in Lacs, Except EPS)

Sl. No.	Particulars	Quarter ended 31.03.2002 (Unaudited)	Quarter ended 31.03.2001 (Unaudited)	12 Months ended 31.03.2002 (Unaudited)	12 Months ended 31.03.2001 (Audited)
1.	Income from Operations	45782.85	33847.71	208396.88	189829.19
2.	Other Income	28.12	50.13	81.59	1168.13
3.	Total Expenditure				
	a) Staff Cost	400.31	626.23	1373.48	1729.66
	b) Exchange Loss	1176.49	-3152.34	4749.21	7748.32
	c) Other Expenditure	1488.32	973.67	3072.51	3627.58
4.	Interest	25169.15	27554.64	100644.87	96552.27
5.	Depreciation	1039.83	1043.19	4151.31	4164.25
6.	Profit (+)/Loss (-) before Tax (1+2-3-4-5)	20536.87	6852.45	94487.89	77193.24
7.	(a) Provision for Taxation-Current	1857.97	2083.44	18673.00	14183.44
	(b) Deferred Tax Asset	-502.10	0.00	1655.63	0.00
	(c) Add/Less Provision of Income Tax for previous years	2035.22	2596.00	2035.22	2596.00
8.	Net Profit (+)/Loss (-)	18141.58	2172.35	75435.30	60413.14
9.	Paid up equity share capital	103045.00	103045.00	103045.00	103045.00
10.	Reserves excluding revaluation reserves (As per Balance Sheet of Previous Accounting Year)				277913.83
11.	EPS for the period (per share Rs. 1000)	160.37	44.94	736.39	616.14

Note :

1. The Company has adopted the new Accounting Standard 'AS 22' relating to "Accounting for Taxes on Income" from the current year. The deferred tax asset has been created to the extent of Rs. 1655.63 Lakhs net of deferred tax liability of Rs. 581.38 Lakhs created upto 31.03.2001 by debiting general reserve.
2. The above financial results were taken on record by the Board of Directors in the meeting held on **18 April, 2002**.

Date : 18.04.2002
Place : New Delhi

Sd/-
(A.A. KHAN)
CHAIRMAN AND MANAGING DIRECTOR

POWER FINANCE CORPORATION LTD.
(A Govt. of India Undertaking)
Regd. Office : Chandra Lok, 36, Janpath, New Delhi-110 001
Tel. No. (91) (11) 373-2301 to 08 Fax : (91) (11) 331-6802
Website : http://www.pfcindia.com

Funding for a Brighter Tomorrow

MISSION 2012 : POWER FOR ALL

ICICI Annual Report, 2000-01

The Indian Express, Ahmedabad Edition, 1 May 2002

GIPCL – *Empowering Gujarat*

Gujarat Industries Power Company Limited (GIPCL) is a public limited company promoted by the Government of Gujarat. Gujarat Electricity Board, Gujarat State Fertilizers Co. Ltd., Gujarat Alkalies & Chemicals Ltd. and Petrofils Cooperative Ltd. The company had an innovative structure wherein the Government and industry jointly promoted a power company to meet the specific demands of each participating unit due to the acute power shortage in the State.

Baroda Station-I

The company has installed Gas Turbine & Steam Turbine having a generation capacity of 145 MW, supplied by BHEL. The feedstock for this plant is Natural Gas, and GIPCL has entered into a contractual arrangement with Gas Authority of India Ltd. (GAIL) for the supply of natural gas. This plant has been achieving high PLF right from commencement of generation.

Baroda Station-II

The company also has another plant of 160MW of capacity adjacent to the existing plant. This plant is a multi-fuel, combined cycle plant with a 106 MW gas turbine generator and a 54 MW heat recovery steam generator. This plant operates in the status of a 'Generating Company'.

The power is being evacuated and supplied to GEB. The plants operation has been greatly hampered due to high cost of Naptha and is being operated only on gas at around 60-65% PLF.

Surat Lignite Power Plant (SLPP)

This 2 x 125 MW lignite based power plant is located at Mangrol, near Surat. It is based on Circulating Fluidized Bed Combustion (CFBC) technology, which is environment friendly. The company has acquired necessary mining land for lignite required for this plant. One of the main advantages of SLPP is its proximity to this captive mine situated approximately 2 Km from the power plant. Even though this plant had initial teething problems, operation has stabilized from October 2001 after all necessary modifications and repairs have been carried out.

The company is embarking on an expansion programme of setting up additional 250 MW, similar to the existing power plant at Mangrol. This plant will have the same configuration as the present one.

The company has been making consistent profit right from the commencement of commercial operation and has also declared dividends till the financial year 1999-2000. With the stabilization of operation of all three plants and SLPP achieving higher generation, the profit for the current financial year is likely to be higher than the previous years. The company also expects a quantum jump in the profit generation in the years to come.

The Indian Express, Ahmedabad Edition, 17 August 2002

Providing connectivity with the world

- **Set up in every block of Assam, Arunachal Pradesh, Meghalaya, Manipur, Mizoram, Tripura, Nagaland and Sikkim**
- **Taken up as a Mission by the Ministry of Communications & Information Technology. Completed in record time bringing in new hope; new cheer for the citizens of North East**

CIC - Towards Empowerment

- Internet centre, e-mail facility etc.
- Information centre - for getting news, government gazettes & service rules, employment news & job opportunities, CBSE/ICSE results, college courses, admissions & results
- Access to data bases of social interest for public created by various public departments
- Road, rail & air reservation & status
- Health care & telemedicine
- e-Governance centres for friendlier interface between Government & citizens
- e-Education including facilities for distance learning
- e-Commerce centres to get news on latest farming methods & prevailing purchase & sale prices of agricultural commodities
- Entertainment Centre

Department of Information Technology
Ministry of Communications and Information Technology
Government of India

The Economic Times, Ahmedabad Edition, 18 February 2002

Will electricity Bill empower the sector?

The Economic Times, Ahmedabad Edition, 8 March 2002

Annual ritual of empowering women

The Economic Times, Ahmedabad Edition, 31 August 2002

'Emphasis is on empowerment'

The Economic Times, Ahmedabad Edition, 14 September 2002

Panicky Depositors Withdraw Rs 5,000 Cr From Scam-Hit Banks

State to empower co-ops to recover dues directly

The Indian Express, Ahmedabad Edition, 18 September 2002

Re-empower reformers

With Vajpayee's job secure, he must put prime ministerial authority to better use

The Economic Times, Ahmedabad Edition, 21 September 2002

Panchayats: Empowered, but funds-starved

Appendix III

Case Studies

Methodology

These case studies relate to the following five organisations selected out of a list of the corporate businesses in Gujarat which met our criteria for a purposive sample as detailed in Chapter 1, and which agreed to participate in the study. The field work for developing these case studies was carried out between July 2001 and June 2002.

- Excel Industries Ltd.
- Gujarat Ambuja Cements Ltd.
- Tata Chemicals Ltd.
- Gujarat Cooperative Milk Marketing Federation Ltd. (GCMMF Ltd.)
- Indian Farmers Fertiliser Cooperative Ltd. (IFFCO Ltd.)

These business organisations have plants and facilities in several states of the country. Visits were made to the offices and plant facilities of these organisations at the sites indicated below:

- Excel Industries Ltd. in Mumbai, and Bhujodi and Mandvi, Kutch district
- Gujarat Ambuja Cements Ltd. in Kodinar, Junagadh district
- Tata Chemicals Ltd. in Mithapur, Jamnagar district
- GCMMF Ltd. in Anand, Kheda district
- IFFCO Ltd. in Kalol, Gandhinagar district.

The community development initiatives of Gujarat Ambuja Cements Ltd., Tata Chemicals Ltd., and IFFCO Ltd. are coordinated from the same premises as the plant facilities. The special community development interventions of GCMMF Ltd. are coordinated from premises different from their plant and offices in Anand. The head office of Excel Industries is in Mumbai, but their focused community development initiatives are coordinated from Bhujodi and Mandvi in Kutch.

Meetings and discussions were held with key persons in the business operations as well as in the separate community development organisations set up by the above listed enterprises. People interviewed were asked to define empowerment from their own life and work experiences. Field visits to the programme areas of the community development work were made. Annual reports and other published documents provided by the organisations were studied to glean additional information.

The following key questions guided the data collection from these organisations:

- How does empowerment constitute 'value' in corporate social responsibility – of the inputs/resources spent, of the results achieved, of the sustainable change visualised? How does the impact assessment process of corporate involvement in community development take into account empowerment of the people/ communities?
- What is the extent of empowerment possible through corporate social responsibility efforts? Are there any limits to the nature of empowerment which can be achieved through this route?
- Which approaches adopted by the business organisations as part of their corporate social responsibility result in higher/greater empowerment of people? Which approaches result in sustainable empowerment?
- How is it possible to create a mutually reinforcing loop between the business interests and corporate social responsibility interests of a business organisation?
- How is the empowerment process adopted by business organisations as part of corporate social responsibility helping the communities/ people to develop representative forums of their own?

The case studies of these five business organisations, describing their business and social development activities follow. They have been prepared to highlight how each of these business organisations visualise and understand the process of empowerment in their own work. Hence, the literature they publish about themselves has been an important source of information in preparing these case studies. The purpose is not to evaluate the performance of these organisations but to capture their self-concept and statement of purpose vis-à-vis empowerment.*

The interviews with a cross section of the employees in each business are a reflection of how these individuals experience empowerment in their work in these organisations and what it means to them personally. This is the crux of how each of these organisations operationalises empowerment. The employees' views have been stated in their own words to provide a flavour of each person's experience of empowerment in his/her workplace.

---

* The reality of these business organisations at the time of the field work is described here. The changes which may have occurred in the interim period between the field work and the publication of this book have not been included in these case studies.

Case Study 1

Excel Industries Ltd.

Excel Industries Ltd. is one of India's leading manufacturers and exporters of agro-chemicals and industrial chemicals. Established by C.C. Shroff in Mumbai in 1941, it has pioneered the production of many chemicals which were not manufactured in India. It has developed new chemical processes and challenged foreign monopolies in the chemicals industry. Excel Industries has received several awards, both in recognition of its contribution to the chemical industry and for being a responsible corporate citizen.

Beginning from a small laboratory in a kitchen at home, Excel is a leading manufacturer today with eight manufacturing plants in different parts of thè country. Its turnover was Rs. 497.46 crores in 2001–2002. It was the first agro-chemical company in India to get the ISO 9002 certification in 1994.

Excel believes that 'if the chemistry is right, everything else will follow'. This has been a guiding principle for its business operations and for its dealings with all its stakeholders.

The Shroff family controls and manages Excel Industries. They belong to Kutch and their ancestors moved to Mumbai prior to the First World War. C.C. Shroff and two of his brothers after him have been at the helm of affairs. The second generation of the promoters family are now in charge of the business. The Shroff family has been greatly influenced by Swami Vivekananda, Gandhiji, and Vinobhaji. The personal values and beliefs of the Shroff family about concern for society, their sense of patriotism, and outlook on life have greatly influenced the character of the company. The mother of the Shroff brothers – *Ma* – has been the strongest influence for inculcating in them the values of equality and working and living together.

Excel sees the running of a business itself as a social activity, because it enriches society, creates work opportunities, provides goods and services. In addition, they believe, business has to work directly for the benefit of the community.

The sense of belonging, easy work culture, free access to the promoter family members for grievance redressal, problem solving or sharing ideas, the lack of stress at work due to open systems, and the importance of treating everyone as an equal are some of the organisational values at Excel. Even when it was a small unit in a cowshed, the Shroff family and the workers used to eat together – their mother cooked for all of them and the same food was served to everybody. This value system has continued till today and is reflected in a common canteen run for everybody – workers, officers, and promoter family members.

Even though Excel is not the best paymaster, their people prefer to work here. Nobody really leaves Excel – a few who have left have come back after experiencing the culture in other workplaces.

Kantisen Shroff – Chairman Emeritus of the company, referred to as *Kaka* by all – speaks of empowerment in the following words:

> Empowerment is treating everyone as equal and bringing out the potential in everyone. It is possible only when this is a value system for a person and becomes a part of your way of thinking and functioning.
>
> The concept of high and low, and less and more for the qualities of a person vis-a-vis others cannot be permitted. Everybody has something to give and do – it has to be nurtured and brought out by appropriate support and opportunities.
>
> Your business will also not be able to prosper if you alienate yourself from the community responsibility.

Concern for environment, concern for the community and always engaging in business ventures that are relevant to the community needs will enable the business to prosper and be sustainable.

Since the mid-seventies, Excel Industries has been investing directly in the development of Kutch district in Gujarat, their homeland, through the Vivekananda Research and Training Institute, Shrujan, and other sister organisations set up by them. The company spent Rs. 81.24 lacs in 2001–2002 to support various developmental and charitable activities for the community.

At Excel the community work is coterminus with business. Everyone in the company is encouraged to get involved, and is given exposure and opportunities to utilise his/her skills for community work too. Community work is regarded as 'on the job work'. The employees are paid for it as part of their job at Excel and it is not treated as extra work. However, people are expected to fulfil their job responsibilities also. This kind of opportunity creates an emotional attachment to the company. Full support is given to every volunteer.

Empowerment in the business context at Excel is the increase in sense of belonging and motivation created by equality, freedom, family atmosphere, growth of the person, realisation of potential, and opportunity for community work.

A vision statement, prepared for the next fifty years on the occasion of the fiftieth year celebrations of Excel Industries in 1990, reads:

> We, the members of Excel family, pay our respects to the memory of our founder Late Shri C.C. Shroff, our dear Pappa, on this 19th November, 1990, marking the commencement of the 50th year of what is now Excel and rededicate ourselves to further fulfill the vision of our founder to make humble contributions to Country, industry, rural society and our Company through technology, innovation and through individual and collective endeavour.

Satisfaction of our shareholders, customers, our own people, suppliers, institutions, investors, society and community is paramount to us. We will make whole hearted efforts for the fulfillment of this objective through our interactions and interdependence with them.

India, our country is blessed with abundant natural resources in terms of soil, sunlight, rain, ocean, rivers, minerals, underground resources, forests, mountains and snow. We are fortunate to have a background of thousands of years of culture and civilisation where values, principles and respect for nature are key factors. We the members of Excel family will follow the path of imbibing our cultural spirit, harmoniously working to preserve, utilise and protect our natural resources and to continue to base our practices on values and principles.

We have a responsibility towards industry and community. Rural community is heart of India. We will be friends and contributors to well being of both industrial and rural community. Not only through our products and services, but also through our knowledge and expertise, we will be of assistance to community and industry.

Company is togetherness. We will work and contribute, learn and grow together in the spirit of *'Saha Viryam'*. This is our resolution and we resolve so. We pray to the Almighty that we be granted the strength to fulfill our this mission.

Excel Industries sees its involvement in all these activities and forums as part of its corporate social responsibility. As Kutchis, the Shroff family feels that they owe a responsibility for the development of their motherland. Kantisen Shroff reminisces about when they set out for direct community work in the mid-seventies:

> In the year 1973 Jayaprakash Narayan invited a few industrialists to have a fresh look at Gandhiji's ideas on trusteeship. We were amongst them. He was clear that the world now needs a better system than what capitalism or communism can offer. Both are based only on material wealth while society is much much beyond just materialism.

It was then decided that we meet Vinobhaji and get his guidance on the issues related to trusteeship in the present context. Vinobhaji compared trusteeship to our old *Mahajan* traditions that kept our society intact inspite of bad or incompetent rulers also.

He explained the role of the Indian industrialist as the middle finger of our hand. He (Indian industrialist) uses his organisation skills to have the best of the experts and social activists around him to work with and for the community.

He (Vinobhaji) advised me to go to Kutch, see the district as a whole, and be there for years to come. He had assured me that within about 25 years the true impact of trusteeship, the *Mahajan* system, will be clearly visible. He said: 'Don't go with a programme or scheme but with a goal. Don't go with a fixed budget – identify work, understand the situation, and respond accordingly. Have the bigger picture in mind even if you are working in a small area.'

The five partners – government, society, financier, producer, customer – should share the benefits of production equally. They have to work together and so cultivate trust among all the five forces.

Now I can certainly say that Vinobhaji's advice has made sense. We in Kutch have created the impact that neither the government nor any other agency could have done. This togetherness seems to be the most practical way to build a healthy, sustainable, and non-exploitative civilisation.

Excel has tried to put this advice into practice. The younger generation of the Shroff family continues this tradition. In the words of Ashwin Shroff – MD, Excel Industries:

> We try to maintain a balance between equality and freedom in running our company. Freedom to make mistakes is there. If the concern and intention was genuine, then if a mistake is made it is pardoned. Even when freedom is given, internal checks and balances are there, so freedom is not misused.

> Equality means everybody is treated equally as a human being, nevertheless there is a hierarchy which is not intimidating.
>
> The younger generation of the Shroff family does not have to make any effort to convince the people in the company about the importance and need for community work because it has always been done like that by the founders. We have to balance the investment of our efforts and energy between running the business and community development work.

Dipesh Shroff, Jt. MD, Excel Industries, further explains this aspect:

> We see running an industry itself as community development work in which profit is a by-product. The simple logic which inspires our efforts in community development work is: 'If Kutchis will not invest in the development of Kutch, then who else will?'
>
> We try and create convergence of community work interests and business interests. The company deputes people full time for community development work, for varying lengths of time, at its cost. Managerial support and office infrastructure is provided by Excel Industries for the community development work in Kutch. The activities have to run on their own strength. No *a priori* limits are fixed for the financial support from Excel Industries. Whatever financial assistance is needed is provided based on proper planning and budget estimates.

Drawing strength from the holy scriptures such as the Gita and the Upanishads is very integral to the value system at Excel. The influence of G. Narayana, Executive Chairman of Excel, has also been very valuable. He sees empowerment as freedom. He has elaborated this by interpreting the following verse of the Gita in his publication *The Responsible Leader – A Journey through Gita:*

> *Ite Te Gnaanam Aakhyaatam*
> *Guhyaad Guhya Taram Maya*
> *Vimrishyaitad Asheshena*
> *Yathechchhasi Tathaa Kurul*

Which he translates in the following words:

This knowledge was declared to you
secret of secrets by me to you
reflection upon if now fully do you
as per your choice may act you.

He elaborates on the theme as follows:

Empowering Freedom

A responsible leader assures freedom of choice to his members.

Though he gives full knowledge, information and ideas about what is to be done and how, he finally leaves the options to the implementor himself.

He advises the member to do his own thinking, to consider all alternatives and choose the best one as per his own conclusion. Thus the real leader does not impose decisions on his team, but after exposing various angles of the situation, leaves them to act as they choose. Empowerment is ensuring freedom to select 'what' is to be done.

Delegation is the right to decide about how to complete an assigned work.

Empowerment is the right to choose the work itself along with the right to decide how to do it.

A responsible leader empowers freedom. The empowered team members then choose the right work and the right way. When the empowered members of a team choose the right work and the right way they themselves become responsible leaders. Then there is no difference between the leader and his team.

Empowerment transforms dedicated team members to responsible leaders.

The Excel management has adopted this approach in its business operations and also in its community development work.

Cross-section of Views on Empowerment

A cross-section of views on empowerment by the employees of Excel is as follows:

'There is lot of opportunity given here, you also need people who are willing to take the opportunity given. If I can grow from a peon to an officer you can understand how much effort and recognition of potential is there in this place – I am a non-matriculate but I am an executive. We try to live like a family here.'

'Stress is reduced because of the family like atmosphere – the decision making is slow because a lot of effort and time is spent on thinking, taking inputs, and thrashing out. Therefore it may look like a lot of cost but the implementation is very fast so we have savings later on. Also low stress reduces costs in terms of people's health and better performance.'

'Empowerment means – Tell me your final goal, tell me your immediate goal, give me responsibility and authority to do the job, and then give me the freedom to do it.'

'Equality means treating everybody as equal – it does not mean everyone is the same in skills, competence, qualities.

Give the same opportunity to all – equality of opportunity.

Equality and freedom can be reconciled.

The freedom to act responsibly, the freedom to learn, the freedom to achieve, the freedom to not act.'

'This place is different from other places where there is a lot of tension and stress all the time, where you are called up for everything and are expected to be responsible for everything even if you do not have the power to take action for every problem.

But there is also a downside because of the historical way of functioning, the family culture, the closeness of employees to the members of the Shroff family.

How can I wield authority over my department/team/group/ subordinates if there is open/direct access for everyone to the owners? This becomes an issue in developing a disciplined group. How can I work as per targets if the owners take a lenient view of targets not reached?

If a team member makes a mistake then the MD will hit himself on the back and say that we have made a mistake – we should be careful in the future – this kind of culture is good for a sense of belonging but not for a performance driven, target oriented work organisation.

Still people have a very strong bonding with the organisation. Empowerment is the work itself – there is freedom to work, to improve, to develop new things and methods.

At the AGM, the shareholders say that your real assets are not the Rs. 450 crore business but the good work you are doing in the rural areas for the farmers and others.

Kaka says that the improvement in the number of farmers reached is far more important than the increase in the size of the business as per plan and targets.

If farmers reached increases from 1 lakh to 1.5 lakh then the business base has been increased and business will grow even if there is a drop in a particular year.

How to manage a Rs. 450 crore business – this is the real question – we are in a phase of transition from family managed to professionally managed company, hence all these processes are evolving.'

Community Development Initiatives

Excel Industries has been active in community and relief work since many years, even when the businesss volumes were small. There are community development activities near all its plants and several institutes for training, research, and self-help set up by Excel industries. It also assists other organisations engaged in development work if they seek help.

The focused community development work initiated by Excel Industries in Kutch district of Gujarat is described here. Kutch is the second largest district in the country. It is largely desert area with a long coastline. Salinity in the soil, scarcity of water, and harsh weather make it a difficult terrain to work. Natural calamities like drought and cyclones occur frequently. It is located in a seismically active zone thus predisposing it to earthquakes. Excel Industries has set up a cluster of organisations for development work in the community. Those decribed here, among these, are Shrujan, Vivekananda Research and Training Institute, and Agrocel Farmers Service Centre.

Shrujan

Kutch witnessed a severe famine in 1969. In response to this natural calamity, some members of the Shroff family accompanied the Ramkrishna Mission team to help the people there. At this time Chandaben and Ranjanben Shroff saw the possibility of income coming to the families through the sale of the exquisite embroidery work that the women of Kutch were skilled at. This was the beginning of Shrujan. From an initial personal investment of Rs. 5,000 made by these two members of the Shroff family, and with five artisans in one village, the organisation has grown to become a source of income for 3500 artisans (mainly women) in 120 villages in 2001–02. Work is given to the artisans on piece rates and Shrujan takes the responsibility for marketing the products. Sales of Rs. 148.62 lakhs were achieved in 2001–02.

Shrujan was registered as a trust in 1981. It has a central office at Bhujodi, near Bhuj and seven centres in different parts of the district. The production team at Bhujodi visits all the centres as per a fixed schedule. The artisans come to these centres, completed work is returned to the Shrujan team, fresh raw materials are given to the artisans, payment is made, problems are discussed and sorted out. The artisans work at home according to their convenience. The artisans earn up to Rs. 2000 per month depending on the quality and quantity of work done. The piece rates are worked out after estimating the time it would take for embroidering a particular design.

The embroidered pieces are then washed, dyed, stitched at the head office depending on the product to be made from it. Finishing, packing, despatch are also handled here. Apparel, furnishings, utility and decorative finished items are made. There is a workshed and a design studio at the head office where all this work is coordinated.

Shrujan procures the raw materials and plans and also prints the designs on the fabric and cuts it before giving it to the artisans for embroidery work. The finished goods are marketed by Shrujan through its sales emporia in several cities as well as at Bhujodi. It also works against orders. The export market and the domestic market are tapped for selling the finished goods produced.

Confidence building, exposure programmes, skill base broadening are part of an all rounded growth for the women through the work of Shrujan. They are able to run their households with the income from embroidery, thus enhancing their status at home and in society.

In the recent past Shrujan has been focusing on developing entrepreneurs from among the artisans by providing them intensive training. These entrepreneurs develop a group of artisans around them for work and take responsibility for managing the planning, procuring the raw materials, and getting the work done. Marketing is done by the entrepreneurs and Shrujan.

There are also plans to develop worksheds at each of the centres to further decentralise the work. Some villages of Banaskantha district and Chhota Udepur region in Vadodara district have also been covered by the activities of Shrujan in the past couple of years.

Shrujan believes that this activity should be self-reliant and sustainable so it has to be run on commercial terms. All the running costs are met from the business itself. Only capital costs help has been taken from Excel.

Vivekananda Research and Training Institute (VRTI)

VRTI was formed in 1979 and is registered as a trust. It began with a study team in mid-seventies to understand the reality of Kutch, its issues, and what needs to be done. Water was identified as a major issue to be addressed. VRTI has a large campus and offices in Mandvi.

The views of some of the Trustees and office bearers indicate the approach of VRTI to community development.

'VRTI is a response to the impoverisation of Kutch. Over the last 25 years, a multipronged effort around natural resource conservation, management and development has been taken up with people's involvement, and the results are there for all to see. The main purpose of this effort is to improve the lives of the people in Kutch. Decentralised systems, people's involvement, and economic development lead to empowerment of people.'

'The whole economic landscape of Kutch can be changed if water and agricultural practices are addressed. The date plantations and its economy is an example of how the landscape can be changed.

VRTI is actively pursuing the path of revolutionising the date economy in the Mandvi side of Kutch. Working simultaneously on improving agricultural practices of date plantations, the genetic stock of the date palms by tissue culture, product development to absorb the increased yield of dates, and market studies for commercial viability of the venture, VRTI has a vision of organising the date farmers into cooperatives on the lines of the dairy cooperatives by having decentralised production of dates and centralised processing facilities. Dates are to be processed into pulp and then into products like biscuits, toffee, etc. depending on the market. The incomes of the farmers will increase substantially. A beginning has been made, and the numbers of farmers adopting improved practices are increasing. Prices of superior quality dates are much higher than those for traditional varieties.

Economic growth leads to empowerment of the people.'

'Resources in the hands of people is empowerment. This is what VRTI tries to do.'

The initial years at VRTI were spent in developing the physical infrastructure for water harvesting such as check dams, storage tanks, and ponds. Over a period of time, the availability of water in villages which faced great difficulties established the credibility of these methods. It also paved the way for an integrated approach to rural development in the area such as water management, agricultural research and land management, composting, afforestation and horticulture, soil and water testing, bee keeping, animal husbandry and animal care, biogas, sanitation, conservation of energy, non-conventional energy resources, and equipment.

VRTI has a team of over 84 professionals who work with the village people. More than 550 water harvesting structures have been created, to date, in the different talukas of Kutch. The village people have been active in the work of putting up these structures and they also take responsibility for the maintenance of these structures. Over 18000 hectares of land has been covered in the watershed development programme in 33 villages with a human population of over 32000 people and a cattle population of nearly 25000 animals.

Decentralised systems for planning and implementation have been established with people's involvement. A *Gram Vikas Mandal* (Village Development Committee) is constituted in every village – it is active at the village level and implementation level, and VRTI is active at the policy influencing and advocacy level.

Kutch has also witnessed many natural calamities which has necessitated relief measures to be taken up during the crisis periods. VRTI reaches out to people and teaches them ways of overcoming natural and man-made calamities.

Table 1 gives details about the cummulative achievements of VRTI over 27 years, from its inception upto 2001–02.

Agrocel Farmers Service Centre

Agrocel Industries Ltd., Service Centre is a joint venture of the Gujarat Agro Industries Corporation and Agrocel Industries Ltd. to provide extension and physical services to farmers for increasing productivity and realising better prices. There are six such centres in Kutch, one in Gujarat outside Kutch, and two in other states. 10000 farmers are reached through these service centres.

The major activities of the Agrocel Farmers Service Centre include soil testing, farm visit, door delivery service for reaching inputs, sale of bio fertilisers, distribution of chemical fertiliser, promoting the production of Indian Organic Cotton, integrated crop management advise and guidance, assured price mechanism for cotton and groundnut for selected farmers, and promoting farmers clubs. Mediating to reach the benefits of government schemes to the farmer, drip irrigation equipment distribution, after care services, certified seeds distribution, sale of pesticides, oil extraction services are also undertaken by the Agrocel Farmers Service Centre.

Considerable effort has been made to increase the productivity of cotton and groundnut crops. As Kutch is a rainfed area, there is very little use of chemical fertiliser. Organic farming of cotton and

Table 1. Achievements of VRTI from 1975 to 2001–02 (including Bhavnagar Centre).

Sr. No.	Activities	Number	Storage Capacity (Mcft)	Benefits
1	**Watershed Development Programme including Rainwater Harvesting**			
	a. Dams	554	733.00	12529.90 hectares
	b. R.T. Wells	111	–	–
	c. Farm Ponds	461	40.40	1220 hectares
	d Individual Wells Recharged	1019	–	1019 farmers
	e. Nala Plugs	236	37.70	582 hectares
	f. Embankments	103	–	569.14 hectares
	g. Tank Renovation	20	75.00	320 hectares
	h. Gully Plugs	43	–	47 hectares
	i. Land Levelling (Farmers)	42	–	74 hectares
	j. Loose Boulders	231	–	135.60 hectares
	k. Staggered Trenches	96481	–	306.90 hectares
	l. Field Bunding	432	–	500.32 hectares
	m. Soak Pits	333	–	333 families
	n. Agro Forestry Plantation	–	–	4 hectares
	o. Waste Weirs in Farmers' Fields	53	–	298 hectares
	p. Overhead Tanks (Nari)	1	–	13000 people
	q. Installation of Pipeline for Drinking Water	2	–	1 village and 1 hospital
	r. Compound Wall for Community Polytechnic	1	–	–
	s. Checkdam Repairing	1	0.40	4.85 hectares
	t. Contour Trenches	7000	–	131 hectares
	u. Protection Bunds	10	–	20 hectares
2	**Agriculture**			
	a. Kisan Nurseries	10	–	10 villages
	b. Bee Keeping Colonies	426	–	43 farmers
	c. Bullock Cart	1	–	Whole village
	d. Horticulture Plantation	1613	–	1100 hectares

[*Table 1. Contd.*

Contd. Table 1.]

	e. Crop Demonstration Plots	145	–	98.36 hectares
	f. Kitchen Garden Kits	1276	–	1276 families
	g. Teak Plantations (Trees)	72285	–	208 farmers
	h. Dusting Machines	174	–	174 families
	i. Afforestation Plants	37344	–	955 farmers
	j. Farmers Tours	7	–	269 farmers
	k. Live Hedge RMT	390	–	2 villages
	l. Water Tank for Plantation	1	–	1 village
	m. Community Lift Irrigation Schemes	3	–	74 farmers
	n. Drip Irrigation	102	–	166 farmers
	o. Celrich Demonstration Plots with Guar	152	–	152 farmers
	p. Silvipasture Development	8	–	8 villages
3	**Animal Husbandry**			
	a. Bull Houses	1	–	Whole village
	b. Fodder Banks	2	–	Whole villages
	c. Deworming Camps (Sheep, Goats, Cattle)	52	–	32466 animals
	d Vaccination Camps	58	–	12969 animals
	e. Cattle Camps	71	–	4211 animals
	f. Grass Demonstration Plots	46	–	46 farmers
	g. Drinking Water Tanks for Cattle (Aveda)	7	–	7 villages
	h. Travis Crates	16	–	16 villages
	i. Chaff Cutters	980	–	980 farmers
	j. Bull Distribution	1	–	Whole village
	k. Cattle Fair	1	–	15 villages
	l. Cattle Troughs	10	–	10 villages
	m. Compound Wall for Cattle Yard	1	–	Whole village
	n. Niran Kendras (Cattle Feeding Centre)	134	–	59520 cattle
4	**Health and Hygiene**			
	a. Rural Latrines	3533	–	3533 families
	b. School Sanitation Complexes	109	–	109 schools
	c. Ambulatory Service Units (Naliya)	2	–	880 patients
	d. Medical Camps	2	–	503 patients
5	**Biogas Plants**	111	–	111 families

[*Table 1. Contd.*

Contd. Table 1.]

6	**Employment Generation Programme**	76	–	1519 trainees
7	**Cyclone and Earthquake Relief Work**	–	–	Kutch and Orissa
8.	**Training Programmes for watershed villages, various NGOs, honeybee farmers, village artisans and water supply workers**	34	–	787 trainees
9	**Dairy Demonstration Project**	1	–	31 villages
10	**Cattle Feed Unit**	1	–	73745 mandays
11	**Gaushala Unit (Dairy Unit)**	2	–	Demonstration
12	**Energy Development Programme**			
	a. Smokeless Chullahs	22128	–	22128 families
	b. Portable Chullahs	6239	–	6239 families
	c. Solar Cookers	351	–	351 families
	d. Tube Lights (Solar)	24	–	24 families
	e. Small Pressure Cookers	10	–	10 families
	f. Stoves Distributed	67	–	67 families
	g. Big Pressure Cookers	3	–	3 hostels
13	**Computers for School**	112	–	8 schools
14	**Production of Endogram Cards**	788	–	–
15	**Construction of Houses Under Cyclone Relief Programme**	52	–	52 families
16	**Construction of Houses Under Indira Awas and Sardar Awas Yojana**	371	–	371 families
17	**Construction of Houses under Rehabilitation Programme**	1084		1084 families
	a. Temporary Shelters	921		921 families
18	**Construction of School Under Rehabilitation Programme**	1	–	1 village
19	**Public Awareness Programme**	85	–	85 villages
20	**Education**			
	a. Teachers Training Shibirs	3	–	93 teachers
	b. Publications	6	–	–
	c. Bal Mela	1	–	96 students
	d. Music Teachers Training	1	–	18 teachers

groundnut crop is being promoted by training the farmers and getting certification as organic produce to realise higher prices.

Growing cotton is being seen as the starting point for the whole chain of forward linkages till the stage of ready to wear branded garments for the customer. The international market is being tapped for this purpose.

Networking

This cluster of sister organisations – Shrujan, VRTI, Agrocel Service Centre – alongwith Vivekanand Gramodyog Society and Krishi Vigyan Kendra, Mundra have evolved over the years. They work in close coordination to provide a variety of services to the farmers and enable them to improve their life situation in a sustainable way. They are committed to serve and guide the inhabitants of Kutch, farmers and others alike, around one goal – to bring about rural development by making them aware of the hidden potentials of their land, utilise whatever meagre resources are available, and work towards building a prosperous Kutch.

VRTI and Kutch Mahila Vikas Sangathan (another NGO active in Kutch) have spearheaded the formation of Kutch Nav Nirman Abhiyan in response to the devastating cyclone in 1998 to undertake the large scale relief and rehabilitation operations in Kutch in collaboration with the DRDA, donor agencies, local agencies, NGOs, and the villagers. Since then it has emerged as a network of voluntary organisations in Kutch undertaking coordinated planning and capacity building activities on a range of development concerns. The massive earthquake on 26 January 2001 provided further impetus to the collaborating voluntary organisations to develop Abhiyan as an on-going network for rehabilitation and development work in Kutch. The major programmes undertaken by Abhiyan are Shelter, Health, Handicrafts, Dams, Information, Setu.

Case Study 2

Gujarat Ambuja Cements Ltd.

Gujarat Ambuja Cements Ltd. (GACL) was established in 1982 and is a major cement producer in the country. It is a professionally run, family owned business. The company has grown to reach revenues of Rs. 1,583 crores in 2001–02. It has units in Gujarat (Kodinar), Himachal Pradesh, Punjab, Madhya Pradesh, Maharashtra, Chhatisgarh, Rajasthan and West Bengal with the head office in Mumbai. Since its inception, GACL has followed a corporate philosophy of 'sustainable development' and has taken conscious decisions to reflect this commitment.

The plant at Ambujanagar near Kodinar (45 kms from Veraval town) in Gujarat is a good example of this commitment. GACL has been able to achieve a pollution free environment at its plant site by using state-of-art pollution control equipment like Glass Bag Houses and Electrostatic precipitators, to prevent dust emissions which are routinely associated with cement plants. The company operates captive limestone mines around Kodinar for its entire production requirement. It uses eco-friendly machines called Surface Miners which require no blasting. Mined areas are reclaimed through afforestation, developing orchards, pasturelands, artificial lakes, water harvesting structures, et cetera in them.

GACL uses a dry process of cement manufacturing which neither consumes water nor generates any industrial effluents from the processing plant. Water is required only for cooling purposes. The water needed for this purpose is made available by recycling domestic waste and sewage water from its colony through a Sewage Water Reclamation Plant with a capacity to treat 15 lakh litres per day. The treated water is used for various purposes such as cooling of process equipment, road dust suppression, and maintaining the gardens and trees on the campus. This has been done to conserve water which is very precious in the Saurashtra region, where the plant is located.

A well developed Environmental Management Division has been established with properly equipped laboratories and equipment as well as a mobile van for monitoring air, water and soil quality as well as for a complete check on the quality of raw materials, fuel, and finished goods.

GACL has achieved world class standards in production technologies and quality. It has been lauded as India's most modern energy efficient plant and is famous for production of cement with a rose touch. They have been able to grow and maintain a rose garden in the heart of the plant and changed the mindset of people to accept that cement can be produced without creating imbalance between the environment and development. GACL was the first cement company in Gujarat to receive ISO 14001 certification for excellence in environment management. It has also received several national and industry awards for its environmental management practices.

The plant at Ambujanagar has a large colony where most of the staff and workers live. The plant premises is the antithesis of a cement plant with no dust and other emissions hanging in the air. Well laid out gardens, trees, lawns contribute to the clean and green atmosphere of the plant and colony. The colony is more like a self contained township having a school, medical facilities, recreation facilities, place of worship, shopping, transport facilities, etc.

GACL pursues a value based approach to managing the business and relating with its stakeholders. Seven *mantras* which have been developed with the involvement of the employees reflect this value based approach at GACL. These are:

- we shall improve the quality of life around us
- we shall excel in everything we do
- we shall be committed to learning and growth
- we will do everything with a human touch
- we will enable our people to have the highest productivity
- we shall be known for our integrity
- we will ensure effective communication.

These *mantras* are internalised in the company culture and are practiced by all in their day-to-day work.

Empowerment at GACL is the open and transparent systems of work as well as the mutual support which is extended to each other. Stress free atmosphere, problem solving approach, fairness and honesty in dealings, encouragement to improve performance, freedom to work in one's own way contribute to the positive feelings which are experienced by everyone.

The 1995–1996 Annual Report of GACL quotes the Managing Director, Narottam Sekhsaria, on the work culture of the company:

> I have a confession to make. I do not like complicated things. 10 years ago as an established cotton trader I decided to enter an industry I knew nothing about. And I approached it with the open mind of a beginner. Some things immediately appealed to me.
>
> Cement is a capital intensive industry, and that is good. This meant limited competition from a small group of large industrial houses, all ethical players.
>
> Secondly, cement is not a high technology area where obsolescence is a way of life, like Information Technology.
>
> Thirdly, it is a basic industry, one that is critical to any growing country where infrastructure has yet to be developed.
>
> So there it was: limited competition, low obsolescence and a growing market. I couldn't have asked for a better industry to work in.
>
> Cement is 40% capital cost and another 40% is energy cost. If we had to succeed, the company would have to focus on these

two issues. If we had to compete with older established companies that had already written off their plant cost, it was important to have the lowest capital cost per ton of cement. Our plants would have to be set up in record time. Our capacity utilisation would have to be 100%.

Our power consumption would have to set a record low.

We achieved them all.

These days it's fashionable to talk of empowerment, but given our line of thinking, we had no choice. If costs had to be controlled, it seemed absurd for engineers to check back with their seniors for every little decision. The time lost would be far more expensive than any error they would make.

It was much the same for controlling power consumption. Who would be better than our engineers to suggest ways to cut costs. They worked night and day on the plant. It made eminent sense to listen to them. Over time this has become a natural company culture: 'I can'. As a result, the standards our people have set for themselves are so high, the company is driven by fear of mediocrity.

Not everything works out as planned, though. In the very first year of the company's existence, we hit an over-supply market. Prices were down.

It was the best thing that could happen to us. To survive, we had to offer a product of a consistent and higher quality than the markets were used to. Again our approach paid-off.

For the next logical step from consistent quality was to push a commodity into a brand. And we were ready.

The thinking is simple once again. With a brand, we could command a premium.

All such increments would go directly to the company's bottom line. The increased marketing costs would be a mere fraction of the revenue gained.

As the company grows bigger and the problems it faces turn far more complex, I spend time trying to keep things simple.

I worry about losing sight of the simple objectives we started out with. Even as I am gladdened that the inventive 'I can' spirit continues to thrive.

Writing this hasn't come easily to me, for I am not much of a public man. But the greater difficulty is, I find, there are no great strategies to declare.

10 years on and I have no wisdom to pass on. No formulas to share. No management theory. For the future will bring its own share of problems and opportunities.

If we can continue to reduce each new problem down to its basics with clarity of thought, we will spot the opportunities. Its that simple, really.

As the 2000–01 Annual Report of GACL says on its opening page:

Give a man orders
And he will do the task
Reasonably well
But let him set his own targets,
Give him freedom
And authority
And his task becomes
A personal mission:
'I can'.

'I can' is an inspirational and motivational mantra in GACL since inception and this is what they practice.

The Ambuja Cement Foundation (ACF), set up in 1993, is an independent non-profit NGO working in collaboration with local, national, and international development agencies. ACF has dedicated itself to community development and over the last ten years it has achieved encouraging results in all the programmes it has implemented, especially in its integrated efforts to develop natural and human resources for sustainable agriculture and rural livelihoods. GACL and ACF are kept separate so that no misperception develops in the minds of the people in the villages that ACF is set up to make purchase of land easier for GACL. Both teams are separate, both have their own work, and responsibilities of both are separate. ACF has been provided separate office space on the company premises.

Shri A.C. Karnik, Joint President, Commercial at Ambujanagar, explains at some length how the work culture visualised by the MD gets operationalised.

Empowerment is delegation mainly with a matching of authority and responsibility.

Most people in the company have been with us for many years. They have grown with the company.

Ours is a value based company. When I joined, the MD gave me two parameters – one is integrity and the second is that you should never be in a position where you have to tell any government officer that you have done something wrong so please condone this mistake. Between these two parameters you have the full freedom to work out your own methods and systems to achieve your plans and targets. This percolates down the whole organisation. Everybody knows his responsibility and he is given the authority to do it. So only when someone has a problem he comes to the superior. Hence, here the work flow is from bottom to top and not from top to bottom. There is very little stress because it is a value based system; no tension of getting unfair and wrong things done.

We insist on quality, the same quality every time throughout. So we buy the best raw materials and use the best inputs to give the customer the best quality throughout.

A person should be happy here; we take care of that. If a person gets a good environment and his needs are well taken care of, then he will not cheat. The same principle applies to the suppliers. He must get his fair return, then he will not cheat.

The *mantras* are very important, the MD himself believes in them.

We do everything with a human touch. If anyone has a personal problem we always find a way of helping and solving the problem. We do not make his life difficult by putting more pressure of work on him at that time but let the situation ease out. The person compensates for such consideration by himself.

Communication is very important. We meet every Tuesday and these meetings are very important for the senior management, as we thrash out all problems in these meetings. Earlier when the plant was newly commissioned we used to meet everyday; now it is a weekly meeting.

Everybody's energies are channelised into productive work and not in politics and game playing. That is why we have a work culture of openness and value based management. Hierarchy does not become a constraint; anyone can walk into my office and talk to me.

I am the common link between GACL and ACF. The work of ACF is very important – it is the conduit through which we can reach out to the community to change the image 'that cement company does damage and goes away'. We believe in protecting the environment even though we do mining activity. By reaching out to the community we are building a bond, a relationship with them; it is enlightened self-interest. When there are camps, special programmes, we all join the work of ACF as volunteers. We believe in two-way traffic and would like that ACF also is able to know and discuss how the business is being run.

ACF activities are an extension of the same value system vis-a-vis the community.

Cross-section of Views on Empowerment

A cross-section of views on empowerment from the employees of GACL is as follows:

'Work culture is high in Gujarat. Because of ACF our image is good. I do a lot of liasoning work with excise, with government. It helps me because the officers say, "You are doing good work – we should also support you".

There is clarity in everyone's mind about the *mantras* of the company. They were discussed with the team and then the MD finalised them. If we don't believe in these *mantras* then we will not fit in well here. Peer pressure works to ensure that everyone follows the *mantras.*'

'Freedom and flexibility are practiced here. Anyone can knock on the Director's door and go to meet him.'

'Transparency is high. *Kathni* (profession) and *Karni* (action) are the same here (We walk the talk here).'

'I am given my job and then I am expected to do it. No one asks me whether I have finished my job or not. The culture is such that everyone does his job on time and completes it.'

The MD says, 'Try out things, conduct experiments and don't be afraid of failures. The failures are mine, successes are yours. So even if things go wrong continue with experiments for improving things. Give me half baked findings also'.

'Hierarchy levels are there but it is not used to discriminate between people at work. Everyone is treated well and with respect, everyone is valued.'

'Promotions are only once in the year based on performance. There is no reward in between in the form of promotions or pay rise.'

'There is a very high sense of responsibility towards one's work.'

'Environment and safety area is one place where you can test whether management is walking its talk because if you know your job well, you can find out how much is actually being done in this field.'

'We are encouraged to interact and mix with everyone – attend social functions and events whenever invited, and create an open atmosphere.'

'We work as a well-knit team here and don't underline the hierarchy. Workers and officers are all treated well and valued. If there is a crisis at work everyone pitches in to set it right immediately. If anyone has a personal problem them that is also addressed to help the person deal with it. Detailed planning, monitoring, and reporting ensure that all the work is done on time and is of specified quality. Hence it is a very tension free atmosphere.'

'I wish and I get it from the management. My problems don't remain a problem because they are addressed in earnest by all concerned. There is a very high degree of support and openness which makes it very easy to work here.'

'We develop the capacity here for people to achieve their potential. Everyone is given opportunity to experiment, improve, and learn more. We keep in touch with the world outside even though we are in a faraway place. Continuous exposure to new developments is very important and valued by all.'

'A system is created here for giving everybody the freedom to work in his own way. Checks and balances are established and followed to ensure that the system works. Budgeting, reporting, accounting, and cost comparision are done on a continuous basis. Everyone appreciates the importance of filing reports in time so that variances are captured very quickly. Continuous feedback in the form of data based reports is very helpful in monitoring and improving performance. Advice on cost-cutting and performance monitoring is also made available. The systems designed are put into practice very meticulously; so subjective judgements or personal biases do not affect decisions negatively'.

Encouraging everyone to get involved in the community initiatives is aptly expressed in the following lines on the first page of a report on Ambuja Cement Foundation:

What if you helped people see a solution,
instead of a problem?

What if you gave meaning to somebody's life,
instead of living yours?

What if you started serving the mankind,
instead of serving the industry?

What if, in the process you built a country,
instead of building a company?

What if you got up and announced, 'I can, I will'.
instead of just sitting on your chair?

Just what if...

Ambuja Cement Foundation (ACF)

The Saurashtra region where the GACL Ambujanagar plant is located, and the source area for its mining operations, is a very water scarce area of Gujarat. Several districts are included in the Saurashtra region. The terrain is stony and rocky with a large coastal belt and salinity ingress. ACF activities were started in Kodinar block of Junagadh district around the Ambujanagar plant and have extended to Jafrabad block of neighbouring Amreli district.

Subsequently ACF activities have been initiated around all the plant sites in other states, but are coordinated from its office at Ambujanagar. The Senior Manager/Programme Coordinator of ACF, supported by a multi disciplinary team at each plant site, manages the community development programmes. They have quarterly meetings for planning, review and coordination. Exposure programmes are organised to visit the various field areas for mutual benefit. The details presented here cover the ACF activities around the Ambujanagar plant.

The Mission Statement of ACF entitled 'Our Way of Life with Society' reads:

We shall improve the quality of life around us:
for this we shall put in our best efforts
we shall act
we shall innovate.
We will communicate effectively:
we will involve and inspire the maximum number of people around us
we will use our resources in a fair and rational manner.

We will have a human touch:
we will do everything with humility and human touch.

ACF was established in 1991 with the objective of improving the social and economic status of the community around the plant site through human, managerial, technical, and natural resources on a sustainable basis. It was registered in 1993 as an independent, non-profit NGO under Section 25 of The Companies Act.

ACF aims to reach all segments of society for the management of human and natural resources for sustainable development. The mission is to make people productive and prosperous where they are, to improve the quality of life.

The primary need of the area in which ACF Kodinar is working is two-fold – increase groundwater recharge and reduce ingression of salinity in fresh water acquifers to sustain agricultural production. The solution lies in harvesting every drop of rainfall and minimising the use of groundwater through efficient irrigation practices, and cultivating low-water requiring and salinity resistant crops. Based on these felt needs, ACF is making concerted attempts to propagate groundwater recharging and horticultural activities in the area through its water resources development, agriculture development, and watershed development programme. The vision is to tap every drop of rainwater that falls and not allow it to be drained into the sea.

ACF provides professional, technical, financial support with the help of its own dedicated team and the support of volunteers from GACL. It acts as a catalyst for appropriate planning, implementation and post implementation care in its interventions by motivating and involving the communities concerned in all the stages of the work. ACF also coordinates the inputs of various supporting agencies.

ACF believes that direct involvement of the community through building capacities is the only answer to sustainable development. The emphasis is on making people knowledgeable and confident to participate in the planning, execution and management of their own developmental initiatives. The support of the elected representatives of the people is also solicited in this process of change.

To ensure effective planning, management, and maintenance of assets created in the village, villagers have been mobilised and organised into groups, committees, and associations. ACF facilitates the required technical and management inputs for the village institutions to carry out their tasks with confidence.

Watershed Development Committees and associations have been formed and registered with the help of ACF in the villages. These committees handle the day-to-day administrative and financial affairs concerning the project and constitute an important interface between ACF and the government. A series of basic and advanced accounts trainings are conducted for the committee members at the village office to empower them to independently handle the programme. ACF also collaborates with external agencies to build capacities of village level secretaries in handling of financial and administrative work.

The approach to empowerment of people underlying all these interventions is to facilitate the process for everybody to be in charge of their own lives and be able to address various situations they are faced with by themselves.

The major programmes of ACF are Water Resources Development, Soil and Water Conservation, Agriculture Development, Farm Forestry and Afforestation, Animal Husbandry, Health Programme, Non-conventional Energy Sources, Children and Women Development, and Drinking Water Programme.

As part of the Water Resources Development Programme several activities such as construction and renovation of check dams, renovation of percolation tanks, construction of farm ponds, well recharge, installation of drip and sprinkler irrigation sets have been initiated.

Under the Soil and Water Conservation Programme the interventions include construction of contour bunding and drainage channels on the private lands of farmers, and distribution of gypsum to farmers to reduce soil salinity.

The activities in the Agriculture Development Programme are field level extension, awareness raising, demonstrations, training programmes, and exposure visits for farmers.

Plantation along farm boundaries, road sides, in school compound and wasteland, and conducting motivational training to encourage farmers to grow trees on their farmlands are the activities undertaken in the Farm Forestry and Afforestation Programme.

A mobile community health programme for curative and preventive treatment of diseases, community health improvement, immunisation, vaccination for eradication of malaria and tuberculosis are taken up under the Health Programme.

Popularising solar cookers and raising awareness of conventional and non-conventional sources of energy are the focus of the Non-conventional Energy Sources Programme.

Emphasis on women's empowerment aims to ensure the involvement of women in mainstream development activities, promoting women's rights, opportunities, and capacities. *Mahila Vikas Mandals* (Women's Development Committees) are promoted for this purpose.

The activities undertaken in the Drinking Water Programme include construction of roof rainwater harvesting structures and conducting awareness trainings in water conservation/purification.

The Children's Development Programme undertakes school based training programmes for children, excursions and exposure visits to impart practical training.

ACF Kodinar work extends to 96 villages in its project area. The physical achievements of the various programmes over the decade 1991–2002 are presented in Table A 3–2.

Table 2. Achievement of activities at the ACF Kodinar unit.

Sr. No.	Activities	1991–01	2001–02	Cummulative Achievement
1	**Water Resource Development**			
	Check Dam Construction	16	2	18
	Check Dam Renovation	10	1	11
	Well Recharging	566	123	689
	Percolation Tank Renovation	27	7	34
	Waste Weir Construction	6	1	7
	Construction of Culvert	3	0	3
	Farm Pond Construction	601	115	716
	Drip Irrigation	50	18	68
	Link Channel	0	2.5 km	2.5 km
	Construction of Nalaplugs	0	22	22
2	**Soil and Water Conservation**			
	Area Treated (Ha.)	6697	663	7360
	Gypsum Distributed (Mt)	1197	0	1197
3	**Agricultural Development**			
	Demonstration Plots (No.)	2454	181	2635
	Horticulture Saplings Plantation (No.)	29644	22804	52448
	Installation of Bee Keeping Units	70	0	70
	Farmers Trained	2571	347	2918
	Farmers' Day Celebrated	10	1	10
4	**Farm Forestry and Afforestation**			
	Farm Boundary Plantation (trees)	682083	3870	685953
	School Compound Plantation (trees)	52039	0	52039
	Wasteland Plantation (trees)	206503	700	207203
	Road Side Plantation (trees)	596	0	596

[*Table 2. Contd.*

Contd. Table 2.]

5	**Health and Sanitation**			
	Mobile Dispensary (villages)	22	22	22
	Camp for Artificial Limbs / Callipers (no. of beneficiaries)	0	1225	1225
	Construction of Toilet Blocks	0	100	100
6	**Animal Husbandry**			
	Cattle Health Camps	42	3	45
	Cattle Treated	50026	4742	54768
	Farmers Benefitted	3000	425	3425
7	**Non Conventional Energy Sources**			
	Biogas Plants	420	10	420
	Smokeless Chullahs	320	154	474
	Solar Cookers	54	10	54
8	**Children and Women's Development**			
	Women Trained	1201	258	1459
	Children Trained	3202	1019	4221
	Self Help Groups Formed	0	51	51
9	**Drinking Water Programme**			
	RRWHS Constructed	128	57	185
	Renovation of Saline Wells	0	6	6
	Drinking Water Wells	2	3	5
	Drought Relief (drinking water supply)	31	24	55
10	**Workshops and Seminars**			
	Seminar for Farmers (participants)	103	72	175

The financial resources of ACF are generated from GACL as per annual plans submitted by the ACF team. The board of directors of ACF approves the annual plans and the budget. ACF has also developed programmes-based funding collaboration with the government and other national/international funding agencies.

In 2001–02 a sum of Rs. 263.98 lakhs was budgeted for ACF Kodinar by GACL. The total expenditure for the year was Rs. 229.17 lakhs (including earthquake relief work). Besides this, GACL also provides all the administrative support to ACF, infrastructure, production and duplication of materials, and volunteers to support the work. The total funds allocated in 2001–02 for all the units of ACF and support to other NGOs and to social-religious causes was Rs. 323.42 lakhs. GACL also responds to natural calamities like the cyclone in

Orissa and Kutch in Gujarat, the earthquake and drought in Gujarat.

ACF Kodinar is making a gradual and sustained attempt to use its internal financial resources to leverage developmental funds from different government departments and funding organisations. The diversification of sources of funds is essential to forge symbiotic partnerships, initiate innovative activities and replicate the successful models set up by ACF on a much larger scale. Macro-level influencing to advocate policy changes for greater improvement in the quality of life of the people is also pursued by ACF.

Case Study 3

Tata Chemicals Ltd.

Tata Chemicals Ltd. (TCL) was incorporated in 1939 and began producing soda ash in 1944. It is one of India's leading producer of inorganic chemicals such as soda ash, caustic, sodium bicarbonate, industrial and edible salts, and marine chemicals. It also produces cement, gypsum, and fertilisers. It is a pioneer in the iodised salt category and the market leader in branded salts. The inorganic chemicals complex in Mithapur, Gujarat is the largest and most integrated plant in India. The fertilisers unit at Babrala in Uttar Pradesh is the most energy efficient urea plant in the country. The very founding of the company was an act of defiance against international monopolies. This has instilled a sense of national pride and self-reliance in all the people at TCL.

A Tata Group company, it is among the top 20 companies in the Group which are referred to as core companies. The Tata Group is one of the oldest and highly respected industrial groups in India with a service track record of 124 years. The turnover of TCL was Rs. 1,512 crores in 2001–02. It employs about 2,900 people.

The Vision of the company is articulated in the following words: 'With our expertise in chemistry we shall create solutions and services that enrich the lives of people.'

The Mission Statement of the company is:

Our success will be achieved by attaining unassailable cost levels and becoming globally competitive in all our product and service offerings; by consistently enhancing shareholder value; by reinforcing our commitment to the environment and the community around us; by conducting ourselves with dignity.

Our people are our strength and we will create an environment which encourages innovation, teamwork and knowledge.

The Values the company cherishes are:

- Excellence
- Integrity
- Fairness
- Innovativeness

TCL has one of the largest solar salt works spread over an area of 36,000 acres. The company has achieved a high degree of integration and self reliance since solar salt and gypsum are raw materials, won from the sea, for its soda ash, caustic soda, and cement plants. The other raw material, limestone, is mined about 120 kms southwest of Mithapur and transported by rail and road. Lignite is transported by road from mines about 450 kms away and coal is usually imported (after liberalisation). Some of the coke is supplied by an ancilliary unit which imports coking coal and carries out the coking operations at a site 5 kms away. Continuous improvement in the water and energy conservation strategies adopted is pursued to increase productivity. TCL has received several national awards for energy conservation, pollution control, safety and productivity.

The Mithapur plant in the Okhamandal region of Gujarat is the major employer in the area since its inception. Okhamandal is linked to the mainland of Gujarat state by a narrow strip. It is quite isolated from the rest of the state and was even more so in the 1930s when the company was established. As such, employment opportunities are very scarce. When TCL was established a lot of people from the local area got work – directly as employees and indirectly as providers of a variety of services and facilities to the company. A very strong loyalty to the company has developed over the years, and being such a large company it continues to need people. There are many second and third generation employees at different levels in the company, even today, which reflects the strong bonding the people have with it.

The company's 500 acre Mithapur factory site and 4,000 acres township are the hub of activity in Mithapur. In keeping with the culture of the Tata Group, TCL also has been very conscious about its responsibility to the community where it is located and to society at large. TCL being located in a very barren and isolated part of the state, has taken on itself several responsibilities for providing infrastructure facilities for its employees such as water, electricity, phones, roads, market, hospital, school, varied recreation and entertainment facilities including a beach. Some of these facilities are also made available to the residents of Mithapur. The township is very green with trees, gardens, lawns. ISO 14001 has been awarded to the Mithapur township and this is the first time that an industrial township has been conferred with such a certification.

Over its entire history, TCL has largely been in a monopoly situation vis-a-vis its products and position in the industry. But with liberalisation of the Indian economy, it is gearing itself to face global and local competition to retain its leadership position. It has become a flatter organisation to face the post World Trade Organisation (WTO) reality and prepare itself for the post 2005 scenario. From thirteen levels in the hierarchy earlier, it now has six levels. A number of initiatives to consolidate and drive growth are being pursued such as restructuring the marketing function and becoming more customer focused, improving operational efficiencies by aggressively cutting costs, and improving supply chain management. An operational efficiency programme named Project Manthan is being implemented at Mithapur with the initial focus on four areas, viz., purchasing, marketing, manufacturing, and supply chain. It is expected that Project Manthan would result in significant cost savings and will help the company in achieving its mission of attaining unassailable cost levels towards becoming globally competitive.

As a part of the organisation building exercise, initiatives are being taken in the areas of leadership development and succession planning. This is being done through a combination of job enrichment, job rotation, and a selective infusion of external talent. The Balanced Score Card method is used to monitor organisational performance as part of the performance management system of the company. This has been linked to performance pay and has now been implemented for all management staff in the company. Many initiatives have been taken in the area of training and learning across the company. There is a strong system of internal controls based on an Enterprise Resource Planning (ERP) system which provides for checks and balances and improvements in controls. Regular reports are sent to the head office in Mumbai.

The company attaches great importance to implementing the Safety, Health, and Environment Policy (SHE Policy). The effort is to uphold its position as a leader in the chemical industry by conducting all its operations in a manner that is protective of the environment and health and safety of employees, customers, and the community. TCL seeks to increase shareholder value through SHE excellence.

The Tata Business Excellence Model (TBEM), based on the Malcom Balridge Model, is a key change driver for the companies in the Tata Group. TCL has started implementing an action plan for TBEM which will enable it to adopt world class business processes in all its functional areas. TCL has set itself a target of scoring the cut-off 500 points on the TBEM to be considered for the Tata Excellence Award. The activities of Tata Chemicals Society for Rural Development, described later, also contributes to the total score thus integrating the community development work of TCL completely with the business operations. The Company treats community development as a part of its business practice.

All Tata employees sign a Code of Conduct when they join a Tata Group company. This is a document with 25 key parameters which set a direction for employee conduct and behaviour in the Tata Group. As a core value, Corporate Citizenship is enshrined as an important clause, as can be seen from the following para of this document, thus expecting Tata employees to be individually responsible to the society at large. The Tata Council for Community Initiatives is a nodal agency responsible for creating an enabling condition for every Tata employee who chooses to volunteer in community development work.

> A Tata company shall be committed to be a good corporate citizen not only in compliance with all relevant laws and

regulations but also by actively assisting in the communities in which it operates with the objective of making them self-reliant. Such social responsibility would comprise of initiating and supporting community initiatives in the field of community health and family welfare, water management, vocational training, education and literacy by encouraging the application of modern, scientific and managerial techniques and expertise. This will be reviewed periodically in consonance with national and regional priorities. The company will not treat these activities as optional but will strive to incorporate them as an integral part of its business plan. The company will also encourage volunteering amongst its employees and help them to work in the communities. Tata companies are encouraged to develop social accounting systems and to carry out social audit of their operations.

Cross-section of Views on Empowerment

A cross-section of views on empowerment by the employees of TCL is presented as follows:

'Transforming from a person oriented system to a process oriented system is empowerment.'

'Community development must also have measurement and metrics. The loop must be completed – Community to business and Business to community. When this happens there are less legal problems, less unionisation, less disturbance, undermining, threat, et cetera and more support for work of the company. Hence business can do better which in turn can help the business give more to the community.

Energy, environment, sustainable development, community development are some of the main concerns of the company today.

A lean and thin organisation is preferred because it will perform better.

Among all the stakeholders – shareholders, employees, government, customers, suppliers, community – all others except community have the exchange relationship with the business defined. TCL is seriously applying itself to define the exchange relationship with the community also so that it can be monitored and improved in the same way as the exchange relationship with the other stakeholders. One measure of empowerment is defining the exchange relationship of the community with the business. We are trying to develop metrics for measuring empowerment.'

'Empowerment is freedom within reasonable limits, freedom where I can do my work in a reasonable way.'

'There is a family feeling here.

Empowerment is "whatever I have to do I am empowered to do".

Regular meetings are held and reports are sent every week to Mumbai.

There is good communication about decisions at the top so there is no room for speculation and gossip.'

'Empowerment is built into the design of the TBEM and its internalisation at every level.'

'This is a family like work place with good support and good working conditions. There is educational support to improve my academic qualifications and enrich my mental capacities – to the extent of B-school on the computer. I see empowerment as a loyalty-benefit matrix. I want to be in the high loyalty - high benefit segment of the matrix. This place is in such a segment.'

'Criticality of all inputs in a process plant – everybody has to work with full concentration and deal with any problem immediately if the plant has to run continuously. Empowerment means creating conditions for this to happen.'

'Empowerment is freedom to do my work well.

The TBEM and Performance Measurement System are the main forces which are activated now to bring the company in a new orbit. A re-orientation is happening in the company. Some are happy with the new system, some were happy with the old system. But everybody will eventually find the new system better.'

Since its inception TCL has been engaged in relief and welfare works for the community around it, and even for those who may be far away, during natural calamities like floods and cyclones. The employees and their family members get involved very easily in sharing responsibility during such crises to effectively manage large relief programmes. The company has always believed that the community it lives in is its home and must be cared for. Volunteering by employees for community initiatives is given a high premium by the company.

Many events and programmes are organised to channelise the energies of the township residents into constructive and educative activities. Various committees are formed for this purpose and a lot of initiative is taken by individuals (employees as well as family members) to manage these activities. This also helps in building a close knit family like atmosphere in the township.

The TCL Community Development Policy adopted in November 2000 reads:

Tata Chemicals Limited pledges itself to serve the community by:

- Designing, evolving and implementing sustainable community development programmes in its area of influence, that lead to measurable socio-economic development of the community.
- Involving the beneficiaries in all stages of the process, in the true spirit of participatory development.
- Having a focused and transparent beneficiary selection criteria, that provides for equal opportunity, favours the economically weaker sections, and promotes enthusiasm.
- Partnering and networking with the Central and State Governments, Development Agencies, Corporate Bodies and NGOs to implement appropriate community development programs.
- Involving the employees in volunteering for community development programs.

Tata Chemicals Society for Rural Development (TCSRD)

TCSRD was established as a consequence of TCL's involvement and concern for the rural population and its development. A comprehensive community service programme has been in operation for quite some time in Mithapur and Babrala. TCSRD was registered in 1991 as a trust. Its objectives are promotion and growth of the rural economy, development of facilities for public education, and upliftment of the people in the rural areas by becoming a catalyst in the socio-economic development of the region. The activities of the Mithapur unit are described here.

The Okhamandal region of Jamnagar district, where TCL is located, is highly susceptible to natural calamities like drought and cyclones. TCSRD has, over the years, also initiated many welfare and relief activities during such crises. These activities have included providing relief work, helping the villages to be self-sufficient in drinking water by supplying water through tankers, by deepening and desalting community wells, by constructing storage tanks in villages, and by constructing water tanks for cattle. Subsidised feed for the entire cattle population in Okhamandal has also been provided during times of drought.

As it became clear that rural development encompassed a great deal more than relief and welfare work, a project for the Integrated Regional Development of Okhamandal was launched in 1991. TCSRD has been working in all the 42 villages of Okhamandal region.

A comprehensive database of the socio-economic and the geo-physical aspects of the region was compiled and analysed to provide an understanding of the social, economic, and environmental features of the region. Based on this data and the suggestions and inputs of the local people in the region, experts, and local administration, development activities were launched. It is now more than ten years since this approach was adopted.

TCSRD is an integral part of TCL as indicated by its integration in the HR department of the company. The staff of TCSRD are regular employees of TCL but dedicated by the company for community development work. The budget sanctioned by TCL for TCSRD is used totally for programme activities because the overheads of salary, infrastructure, and other running costs of TCSRD are borne by TCL. The TCL/TCSRD contribution in 2001–02 for Mithapur and Babrala together was Rs. 31.80 lakhs. Other sources of funds from funding agencies, government programmes, and people's contribution are also leveraged. The total expenditure in 2001–02 from all sources was Rs. 69.40 lakhs.

The programmes of TCSRD in Mithapur area and the achievements till 2000–2001 include:

- Agriculture development – well recharging, horticulture promotion, wind break plantation. By the end of 2001–02, 37 villages of Dwarka taluka were included in this programme, specially targetting households having some source of water for irrigation.
- Watershed development – training, water harvesting, afforestation. Eight villages were covered in this programme.
- Health – health care projects are being implemented in 42 villages. Distribution of first aid kits and safe delivery kits as well as mid-wife training.
- Women's programme – formation of self help groups, economic activities, and handicrafts development. 38 self-help groups had been formed by 2001–02 with 480 women members in 32 groups and 108 men in 6 groups.
- Infrastructure projects – construction of schools, cattle sheds, repair of village and roads, provision of furniture and fittings to schools, and supply of PVC water pipes for water suppply. Special emphasis on house construction as part of the rehabilitation work after the January 2001 earthquake. Infrastructure projects have been taken up in 12 villages of Okhamandal taluka. Selection of villages is done in consultation with the district authorities.

The interventions are operationalised through groups of people in the villages. The TCSRD team facilitates the formation of groups and helps in building the capacities of the groups to manage the activities themselves. The guiding principle is that eventually the groups have to become self-reliant. As one member of the team puts it 'empowerment means more the community can do on its own without us the more empowered it is.'

Tata Council for Community Initiatives

All the Tata Group companies are encouraged to get involved in community initiatives. Being such a large group, the Tata Council for Community Initiatives has been formed as an umbrella support and integration mechanism for all the community initiatives of the

Group companies. The expenditure on social responsibility by the Tata Group as a whole was Rs. 150 crores in 2001–2002. TCL is a member of TCCI and is active in the regional group network. Concern for the community is an integral part of business for the Tatas, as succintly expressed by J. R. D. Tata:

> The wealth generated by Jamshedji Tata and his sons in half a century of industrial pioneering formed but a minute fraction of the amount by which they enriched the nation. The whole of that wealth is held in trust for the people and used exclusively for their benefit. The cycle is thus complete; what has come from the people has gone back to the people many times over.

The TCCI builds on this philosophy to define the guiding principles for social responsibility in the Tata Group as below:

> The guiding principles for social responsibility in the Tata Group evolve from its rich heritage and traditions of trusteeship as a way to redistribute the wealth created by the industrial society kept aside exclusively for the benefit of people at large. Building on this model, we also increasingly recognise that in modern industrial organisations, the connotation of wealth goes beyond the money donated to charitable causes. We therefore, recognise that wealth generated by a business enterprise also assumes the form of knowledge, expertise, talent, skills, networking and various inputs to organise and manage social work. As an extension to discharging social responsibilities, our efforts will encompass a collective Tata effort in finding various means to share the Tata Group's enormous managerial synergy to strengthen self-help initiatives through Tata volunteers to give back to the community a measurable contribution.

The Mission Statement of TCCI reads:

> We will evolve a common direction for community development programmes from diverse activities of all Tata business units through sharing and participatory networking.

We will strive together constantly to strengthen our professional and organisational abilities to fulfil our commitments towards society at large.

The Declaration of the TCCI on Social Responsibility reads:

- The community is central in the core values we adhere to in the Tata Group.
- Tata community programmes aim at building trust and improving the quality of life.
- Tata programmes facilitate sustainable change.
- We believe that community gives us valuable opportunities to learn
- Commitment to social responsibility is explicit in every Tata company.
- We network through our core competence to empower communities
- Tata volunteers are committed to the spirit of service.

Some quotes on social responsibility from the address of Shri Ratan N. Tata, Chairman of Tata Sons Ltd. and also Chairman of TCL, to the TCCI at its first meeting in May 1996 emphasise the significance of community involvement in the whole Group. These are:

'Let me start off by saying that I do believe that we in the Group have held a view and held a sense of purpose that our companies are not in existence just to run our business and to make profit – and that we are responsible and good corporate citizens over and above our normal operations... .'

'...We are not doing this for propaganda. We are not doing this for visibility. I think we should do it for the satisfaction of knowing that we have really achieved something worthwhile and given something to the community in which we are working... . There are companies (outside the group) who may do it for sake of publicity for what they do. That is not our intention. What I am trying to convey is that we are doing it because we really wish to do it (by choice).'

'...think that the message we should leave with our CEOs is that there is an integrated approach – that we want them to be profit oriented, we want them to be cost effective, we want them to be quality conscious, and we want them to be good corporate citizens.'

'... I would like to see our CEOs all share the same spirit: that they, as the CEOs of Tata companies, must be responsible and conscious of the communities which they serve.'

'... I think what we should try to do is to start off a movement that will consciously institutionalise what many of our companies have been doing for many years. And now what we are doing here, through the TCCI, is to institutionalise this strength into a common entity. And we should make sure that the CEOs of various companies feel that all this is part of the Tata ethos.'

'...What we must do is that, we must somehow find a way to make TCCI a part of the Tata brand and not create another 'brand'. All this should be seen as a part of the same thing because that is what we all stand for.'

TCL tries to operationalise all these nuances of meaning in its community development work. The written commitments and policies for social responsibility provide a strong anchor for everybody in the company to get involved in community initiatives.

Case Study 4

Gujarat Cooperative Milk Marketing Federation Ltd.

Gujarat Cooperative Milk Marketing Federation Ltd. (GCMMF) is the state level Federation of twelve District Milk Unions in Gujarat, which in 2001–02 had 10852 Dairy Cooperative Societies at the village level with 22.23 lakhs milk producers as members, spread over the twelve districts. The pioneering efforts at organising dairy cooperatives in the country on the Anand pattern, which began in Kaira district in Gujarat in 1946 with two village dairy cooperatives and fewer than two hundred milk producers as members, have grown to this scale in the state. GCMMF markets its products under the brand name 'Amul'. The White Revolution in the country was ushered in by the success of Amul. India is the largest milk producer in the world today with over 11 million farmers organised into dairy cooperatives. This movement has received a lot of national and international recognition as well as several awards for its pioneering work.

GCMMF was formed in 1973 by federating six District Milk Unions to strengthen the marketing base of the cooperative dairy industry in the state. It has grown to twelve members over the years. The turnover of GCMMF Ltd. in 2001–02 was Rs. 2336 crores. It is the largest food products marketing organisation in the country and also the largest exporter of dairy products. Nine of the twelve member District Milk Unions of GCMMF have ISO 9002 certification, one has ISO 9001 certification, three have ISO 14001 certification, and ten have HACCP

(Hazard Analysis and Critical Control Point) certification.

One District Union, The Kaira District Cooperative Milk Producers Union Ltd., better known as Amul Dairy, has been included in the study alongwith GCMMF.

The unique structure of the cooperative dairy industry in Gujarat and India has developed from the concern for building member owned, democratic, economic institutions which can strengthen the position of the cooperative members in society. Social, economic, and political change for the members has been made possible by the dairy cooperatives.

In the private sector tradition of intermediaries collecting milk from the village producers the guiding principles were – lowest possible price to the milk producers, highest possible price to the consumer, and lowest possible quality of milk and milk products for sale. The profits went to the intermediaries. Under the Amul system the reverse has been achieved – highest possible price to the milk producers, lowest possible price to the consumers, and highest possible quality of milk and milk products for sale. The profits are used for the milk producer's welfare.

The cooperative dairy industry in Gujarat has a three tier structure. At the village level a primary Dairy Cooperative Society is formed with individuals as members. They own milch cattle and bring the milk produced to the village society twice a day. The village cooperative is mainly concerned with purchase of milk from milk producers and acts as a channel for enhancing milk production.

The milk is sent to the District Milk Union which owns milk processing facilities in the form of a modern dairy and also other facilities for providing inputs for increasing the milk production of the milch cattle. The milk is purified and homogenised at the dairy and sold as liquid milk or processed and sold as milk products. The District Union is a secondary cooperative which has the primary village cooperatives as members. It looks after policy formulation, processing and marketing of milk, and provision of technical inputs to enhance milk production in animals like artificial insemination service, veterinary care, better feeds, etc.

The District Unions are federated into an apex Milk Marketing Federation at the state level which is a tertiary cooperative. The Federation coordinates the marketing function for all the milk and milk products produced by the member unions.

An integrated set of services is provided to the members in addition to the price of milk – such as veterinary care, artificial insemination, cattle feed, certified seeds for fodder, cattle insurance – so that the quality and quantity of milk produced can be increased which in turn will strengthen the whole chain of individual farmer, the village dairy cooperative, the district milk union, and the marketing federation. This whole integrated approach has become known as the Anand Pattern of dairy cooperatives.

This three tier structure functions on the principles of economic democracy. At the village level, the Dairy Cooperative Society consists of primary milk producers. To become a member, a milk producer pays an entrance fee and buys at least one share of Rs.10. The members elect a Managing Committee and the committee elects a Chairman. Each member has only one vote regardless of the number of shares he/she has. Committees work honorary and restrict their role to policy formulation and supervision. Salaried staff are employed for milk collection, fat-testing, clerical and accounting work, artificial insemination, etc.

The District Union is managed by a Board of Directors. Twelve directors are elected from among the Chairmen of village societies and one member from among the delegates of individual members. The Board elects a Chairman and a Vice-Chairman and appoints a professional Managing Director who in turn appoints supporting professionals. A nominee of the Registrar Cooperatives, a nominee member from the Federation, and a dairy management expert are also members of the Board. A nominee each of the District Central Cooperative Bank and the National Dairy Development Board (NDDB) are members of the Board (as long as the Union is indebted to them). The Board formulates policy while the professionals look after the day-to-day work. Village representatives on the Board are elected every three years but the Chairman is elected every year from amongst the village representatives.

The State Federation is also managed by a Board of Directors. The Chairman of each member Union becomes a member of the Board of Directors. In addition, the Registrar Cooperatives, one dairy management expert, and a nominee of the NDDB (as long as there are loans/interest outstanding to NDDB) are members of the Board of Directors. This body elects a Chairman for a period of three years and appoints a paid professional as the Managing Director. The MD is an ex-officio member of the Board and also the Member-Secretary. The Federation also employs professionals to look after the day-to-day affairs and they report to the MD.

The Anand Pattern of dairy cooperatives has demonstrated that farmers cooperatives can employ professionals, make use of modern technology, and harness market forces to serve their interest. To be a small producer is no more a disadvantage. In cooperative dairying there is a greater chance of rural development leading to the empowerment of the poor and the lowly.

Information technology and communications technology have been deployed effectively to network all the dairy cooperative societies. Electronic milk testers are used to simplify the process of milk testing for each individual member at the village level. Wireless sets are used for rapid communications and access to the veterinary services provided for the members. Computerised Automated Milk Colllection Systems are in place in 4000 villages with plans to cover 8000 villages by 2003. The country wide operations of the Federation are integrated through an 'Enterprise-wide Integrated Application System'. The GCMMF is among the top 100 IT users in the country. It was awarded the CIO Award for IT Excellence in Supply Chain Management and Customer Management by TMG for 2001.

The nineties brought in winds of change with the liberalisation of the Indian economy. There was a growing realisation in GCMMF of the need to manage the ever expanding milk business more effectively in tune with the changing times. There was concern about whether the dairy managers would be able to handle the business through existing systems and processes. Two factors called for attention (i) How to cater to ever changing aspirations of the customers, and (ii) How to improve the quality of products and services that GCMMF offered. The organisations had to brace themselves to effect the change fast and with as little pain as possible. Information technology had to be incorporated into the systems and the organisations had to be made learning organisations through continuous training and retraining.

In order to facilitate such a transformation, GCMMF decided to introduce the concept of Total Quality Management (TQM) in 1994, with its twin pillars of customer focus and continuous improvement. This approach entailed employee involvement, waste reduction, problem solving techniques, and improvement of the processes together with continuous training. Six years down the line the organisation has been transformed and continues to improve itself. GCMMF received the Rajiv Gandhi National Quality Award in 1999. It has set itself an ambitious target of growth by defining clear cut strategic thrust areas with a focused vision and mission.

This whole experience has had a cascading effect of extending the TQM approach upto the individual members of the village Dairy Cooperative Society on the production side and the whole distribution channel upto the salesmen on the marketing side. These efforts are continuing.

The effort at reorienting the distribution channel has initially focused on taking the wholesale dealers into the TQM fold to supplement the Federation's efforts to achieve customer delight. Internal Change Agents were trained who in turn trained the Federation marketing field force who then facilitated quality management initiatives with more than 2500 wholesale dealers. As a result, all the wholesale dealers have been organised into Quality Circles comprising 8–10 wholesale dealers of an area. Monthly Quality Circle meetings have become a reality all over the country, to address all issues of product distribution and sales. Almost every GCMMF wholesale dealer has visited Anand to participate in a unique programme called 'Amul Yatra'. During this programme, they are exposed to the philosophy of GCMMF, they see for themselves the Anand pattern of cooperatives and related activities as well as the operational systems and processes. GCMMF has also invited distributor's salesmen from all over the country to Anand for a training programme focused on the Federation's philosophy and developing their selling skills. This reorientation of the distribution channel is an initiative which perhaps few other businesses in the country can match.

For taking TQM to the farmer GCMMF has set a major goal is to transform each village Dairy Cooperative Society into a self reliant, growing business organisation and build professionalism in each of the operations. To achieve this goal, GCMMF has introduced the Change Management Process through which Union staff are encouraged and equipped to become consultants rather than supervisors, facilitators rather than decision-makers, trainers rather than doers. This field extension force would serve as internal professional consultants for village Dairy Cooperative Society management, encouraging them to plan and undertake quality assurance productivity enhancement, and member education programmes. Some 6100 village Dairy Cooperative Societies have been included in this effort so far. Fifty village Dairy Cooperative Societies have received ISO 9000 certification. And the effort continues.

A concerted effort is also being made to include women as members of the cooperative structure at all levels. The work of milk production is mainly done by the women in the villages. Systematic exposure and training is being provided to the women members to enable them to take on a more active role in running the Dairy Cooperative Societies. A target of 50 per cent membership of women in the dairy cooperatives by 2010 has been set. Conscious steps are being taken to achieve this, though it will not be easy.

GCMMF and Amul have established the Tribhuvandas Foundation to provide integrated health care services to the members of the village dairy cooperative societies.

CSR in the Context of Dairy Cooperatives

The meaning of Corporate Social Responsibility in the GCMMF context (vis-a-vis the community) becomes a little different from the meaning in the company context. The whole business intervention itself emerges as a response of members (the community) to help themselves – addressing the socio-economic concerns of the members leads to the development of the business venture.

In addition, each village Dairy Cooperative Society invests in the development of its village from its profits and reserves. Construction of infrastructure in the village such as school buildings, panchayat buildings, libraries, dispensaries and health centres, water works, drinking troughs for cattle, community centres, approach roads, electricity, telephone facilities are supported besides activities such as youth clubs, cattle relief and veterinary services like first aid and artificial insemination in its village. The infrastructure for the dairy cooperative itself such as office, collection centre, godown for cattlefeed, et cetera are also built by the dairy cooperative.

The District Union pools back the profits from the milk business to the members in the form of an integrated package of various services.

Over and above this, the District Union in collaboration with GCMMF, sets up a special body like the Tribhuvandas Foundation to address a district wide social need such as health care.

Cross-section of Views on Empowerment

A cross section of views on empowerment by the employees of GCMMF and Amul is as follows:

'Development is a manifestation of empowerment, empowerment is holistic development of a person.

Of the farmer, by the farmer, for the farmer.'

'Mataantar ho sakta hai, manaantar nahin hona chahiye. (We may have differences of opinion but not a divergence of hearts). In the Amul hierarchy work is done jointly – we sit together – don't treat people like employer-employee but like brother-brother. If there is any problem we help each other – spend time together after office hours to sit and chat and eat *nasta* (by dutch sharing). The interest of the farmer is to common purpose.

External force is needed to counterbalance the internal forces of the village cooperative and the working of the village community.

Balance of external and internal forces leads to sustainability of the village level institution.

There are two kinds of democracies:

micro democracy – grassroots democracy and

macro democracy – forces at the national level

How do the two influence each other?

The micro democracy is influenced by larger forces of vested interests at national level but it is also able to keep itself immune from the vested interest forces. The loss/gain is directly experienced by the same set of people in a grassroots democracy.

At the state and national level (macro democracy) the loss may be experienced by the public at large and the gain may be experienced by a few – so it becomes vulnerable. The external force in the form of the Cooperative Development team at the district level contributes to maintaining the vitality of the micro democracy. And that is the building block for realising the economic empowerment possible in this integrated structure of cooperatives. There is continuous need for farmer education and increasing awareness.'

'Empowerment and enforcement are two forces.

We believe in self determination where there are the legislative and executive functions, the political leadership and the managerial leadership.

The design is of mutual exclusivity and mutual dependence of these two functions and to work within a democratic framework.

Policy making to be informed by market forces.

Policy making to be educated by horizon broadening efforts like exposure, discussion, dialogue, classroom input.'

'Empowerment is the power to do whatever I wish to do and the options are open for that.'

'The right to speak, to ask questions, to raise issues is empowerment at village society level. Plus the right to represent a group of people at the Union level and at the Federation level.

Politically the elected leadership is powerful but in technical and managerial matters the professional management is very powerful.

At the Union and Federation level the bank account is operated by MD and accountant, not by Chairman – the fact that the budget is prepared and approved makes it possible.

Checks and balances are important.

One staff member of the Federation is on the Board of every Union as a nominee member. At the Federation level the MD is a full member of the Board and also the Member-Secretary.'

'Empowerment is enabling people to be in charge of the situation and see it through to achieve what they set out to do.

The organisational framework we have is not a vertical plane but a horizontal plane.

Consumers and producers interests are to be balanced.

Very tight margins and we have to deliver results in that situation.

Loyalty and involvement of distribution network is being developed – volumes make up for low margins.

Within the organisation there is scope for continuous improvement at every level up and down the line – your contribution to continuous improvement is recognised and rewarded through monetary incentives and through public recognition.

The *Hoshin Kanri* system of work implementation adopted by us is very helpful.'

'Your level of consciousness is true empowerment.

Consciousness at the physical, emotional and intellectual levels is obvious.

The spiritual level of consciousness is still not there in our employees and members – that is what sustains the inner fountainhead of responsible behaviour and a value system of cooperation and concern for all.'

Tribhuvandas Foundation (TF)

The late Shri Tribhovandas Patel, who pioneered this cooperation movement, was concerned about the health of the rural masses in Kaira district, particularly the women and children.

When he retired from the chairmanship of Amul, the milk producers of Kaira presented him with a parting gift of Rs. 6.5 lakhs. Tribhuvandas Patel expressed a desire to utilise this amount by starting a health programme linked with the milk cooperatives aimed at improving the health of women and children. A cooperative linked preventive human health care programme was framed as the objective of Tribhuvandas Foundation which was registered in 1975 as a trust. It became functional in 1980.

Over the last two decades Tribhuvandas Foundation has extended its activities to 644 out of 950 villages in Kaira/Anand districts through its centre in Anand and four subcentres in the district. TF visualises a cooperative based health care delivery system model at the district level by covering all the villages in the district.

In the approach of TF, the preventive and promotional aspects of health care and health education are given a high importance along with treating diseases and providing hospital services. The interventions of TF have been able to bring down significantly the infant and maternal mortality rates in the villages where they work. Infant Mortality Rate, for instance, has come down from 149.50 in 1983–84 to 56.37 in 1999–2000. The Neo-natal Mortality Rate has come down from 129.5 in 1983–84 to 44.17 in 1999–2000. The Maternal Mortality Rate has come down from 5.10 in 1987–88 to 2.88 in per thousand births 1999–2000.

The basic approach is to integrate economic and environmental aspects with health to focus on economic upliftment and a clean environment. The major programmes are:

- Maternal and Child Health/Primary Health Care
- Pre-school Non Formal Education – *Balwadi*
- Income Generating Activity for Women – Patchwork
- Environmental Sanitation

These programmes are operationalised through the following on-going activities:

– Primary health care through Village Health Workers
– Antenatal care
– Child care
– Immunisation
– Health education

- Special care for high risk pregnancies
- Family planning
- *Balwadi*
- Income generation activity for women - patchwork
- Construction of low cost latrines
- Distribution of portable *chullahs* (cooking stoves)
- Disposable delivery kit packing

Growth monitoring of children, anaemia control, tuberculosis control, and cancer programme are new activities which have been added. Table 3 gives the centre wise achievements of Tribhuvandas Foundation in the year 2001–02.

Individuals pay an annual membership fee to TF to avail of the health services. The Dairy Cooperative Society (DCS) pays annual contributions to TF to support the programme. The village appoints a Village Health Worker (VHW) who makes primary health care available in the village. The VHW is trained by TF. The DCS bears the cost of honararium to the VHW. The DCS also helps in collecting the annual membership fee from the members.

The extension network of TF is built through the participation of dairy cooperative societies at the village level.

A unique hospitalisation expenses subsidy programme was initiated in 2001 for the milk producers in collaboration with the Sardar Patel Arogya Mandal which has been formed for this purpose. Any dairy cooperative member who fulfils certain loyalty conditions in terms of selling milk to the cooperative can become a member of this scheme by paying a small annual membership. In return the scheme covers costs of hospitalisation for the member and his/her family members at designated hospitals in the district. An identity card is issued to the member which also mentions details of family members covered by the scheme. This card is sufficient to avail of the services by following the laid down procedure of intimating TF about the illness and hospitalisation required. The coordination with the hospitals and the payment of bills, etc etera is taken care of by TF.

Table 3. Centre wise achievement April 2001 to March 2002.

Achievement	**Anand**	**Kapadwanj**	**Balasinor**	**Kheda**	**Tarapur**	**Total**
Villages Covered	150	124	130	114	110	**628**
Patients Treated by VHW and Staff	227786	117004	124087	152994	212881	**834752**
Antenatal Registration	16316	5498	7483	8073	8100	**45470**
Safe Delivery Kit Use	9703	3503	4935	4743	5328	**28212**
Children Treated at NRC	330	138	258	18	130	**874**
Antenatal Women Treated at NRC	72	148	60	2	120	**402**
Postnatal Women Treated at NRC	5	16	14	1	51	**87**
Anaemic Women Treated at NRC	9	5	9	0	0	**23**
No. of Deliveries Conducted at NRC	0	0	0	0	0	**0**
Patients Treated at OPD	8062	8046	12285	7554	6610	**42557**
Patients Treated During Special OPD						
Medicine	0	0	0	0	0	**0**
Gynaecological	107	274	245	367	678	**1671**
Pediatric	0	208	248	162	95	**713**
TB	0	32	0	0	0	**32**
Cancer	0	0	0	0	0	**0**
Total	107	514	493	529	773	**2416**
Immunisation						
Hepatitis B (Children)	796	689	410	278	459	**2630**
Hepatitis B (Adult)	95	100	10	40	21	**266**
BCG	130	143	155	7	45	**480**
DPT (3 doses)	9	60	40	5	10	**124**
Polio (3 doses)	9	60	40	5	10	**124**

[*Table 3. Contd.*

Contd. Table 3.]

Measles	204	46	41	15	11	**317**
Tt Antenatal (2 doses)	11	97	394	32	148	**682**
Family Planning						
Camps Organised (LP + TL)	52	25	26	0	30	**133**
Laproscopic Operations	450	6	4	24	15	**499**
Tubectomy Operations	426	208	271	25	164	**1094**
Oral Pills	951	2645	1000	1118	1560	**7274**
Condom (Nirodh)	1596	3522	1127	3924	3011	**13180**
IUD	4	0	0	0	1	**5**
Infant Day Care Centre						
Villages Covered	23	14	1	7	3	**48**
Children Registered: Male	484	266	14	148	40	**952**
Female	470	249	25	136	49	**929**
Total	954	515	39	284	89	**1881**
Family Viability Patch Work						
Villages Covered (TF + Non-TF)	59	9	15	9	19	**111**
Beneficiaries	419	132	145	58	151	**906**
Beneficiaries Income in Rs.	170254	9640	29176	19212	41932	**270217**
Patch Work Sales in Rs. (Campus)	1644444	0	0	0	0	**1644444**
Environmental Sanitation						
Villages Covered	6	1	0	2	0	**9**
Portable Chullahs	344	31	25	0	0	**400**
Shala Swachata Sankulan (School Cleanliness)	13	0	0	0	0	**13**
Saur Fanas (Solar Lamps)	3	0	0	0	0	**3**
Sardar Awas Constructed	178	0	0	0	0	**178**
Improved Crematorium	2	0	0	0	0	**2**

Case Study 5

Indian Farmers Fertiliser Cooperative Ltd.

Indian Farmers Fertiliser Cooperative Ltd. (IFFCO) was established as the farmers own initiative in the cooperative sector in 1967 with proposed plants at Kalol and Kandla in Gujarat. Till the mid-sixties the agricultural cooperatives in India had no production facility inspite of marketing nearly 70 per cent of fertilisers.

To overcome the demand supply gap in the country a new cooperative society was conceived to specifically cater to the requirements of farmers. It was a unique venture in which farmers of the country, through their own cooperative societies, joined hands with the Government of India and created this new institution to safeguard their interests. It was started in 1967 with 57 cooperative societies which has grown to 36,114 societies in 2001–02. All cooperative societies associated with agricultural activities are eligible to be members of IFFCO. It is the largest producer of fertilisers in the country with a turnover of Rs. 5,072 crores in 2001–02.

The mission of IFFCO is to enable farmers to prosper through supply of timely, high quality, agricultural inputs and services in an environment sustainable manner and to undertake other activities to improve their welfare.

IFFCO is a multi unit cooperative society registered under the Multi State Cooperative Societies Act. The Representative General Body

(RGB), which is the General Body, forms the supreme body that guides the various activities of IFFCO. The RGB consists of:

i. Members of the Board of Directors.

ii. One delegate from each of the Member Societies holding shares of the value of Rs. 1,00,000 and above; such delegates shall be as per the provisions of the Multi State Cooperative Societies Act/Rules as amended from time to time.

iii. Delegates to be elected from amongst the representatives of Member Societies (other than Members holding shares of the value of Rs. 1,00,000 and above) in each State/Union Territory at the rate of one delegate for every 200 societies or part thereof. However the maximum number of such delegates from any State/Union Territory shall not exceed 25. Such elected delegates shall be as per the provisions of the Multi State Cooperative Societies Act/Rules.

The Board of Directors of IFFCO carry out all functions as specified under the Multi State Cooperative Societies Act/Rules. The Board of Directors frame policies, direct the various activities of the Society and undertake any other activities conducive to overall growth and development of the Societies. The Board is headed by the Chairman.

The Managing Director is the Chief Executive of the organisation with responsibilities for general conduct, supervision and management of day-to-day business and affairs of IFFCO. The Finance Director oversees the financial aspects and the Marketing Director looks after the marketing function of IFFCO. These three functional directors are assisted by Senior Executives who are experts in various fields.

Every member shall subscribe to at least one share. However, the rights of the members will only be available if they achieve the basic minimum level of utilisation of the services/products or the business of IFFCO as may be determined by the Board from time to time. No member shall hold more than such proportion of shares as may be prescribed in terms of Section (33) of the Multi State Cooperative Act.

IFFCO has plants at Kalol and Kandla in Gujarat, and at Phulpur and Aonla in Uttar Pradesh. The Kalol plant has been included in the study. The Kalol unit manufactures ammonia, urea, and dry ice and employs 800 people.

The fertilisers are produced in these plants and marketed through 36,114 cooperative societies and 167 farmers service centres. The state level apex cooperative marketing federations act as wholesalers.

The Kalol unit was the first plant of IFFCO, commissioned in 1975, and was the first in the fertiliser industry to receive ISO 9002 international certification for Quality Assurance in Production, Installation and Services in 1996. It has been recertified by BVQI (Bureau Veritas Quality International) in 1999 for its Quality Systems. It has received the National Energy Conservation Award – 2000. Over the years, IFFCO Kalol unit has also received several national and industry awards for safety and productivity. Despite being one of the oldest plants in the country, the unit is still maintaining a very good performance level due to retrofits and revamps carried out from time to time.

IFFCO has been a frontrunner in adoption of latest technologies in the plants to minimise emission of pollutants and maintain the emission levels at much below the permissible levels stipulated by the statutory authorities. IFFCO Kalol unit has been awarded ISO 14001 certification in 2000 for its Environmental Systems. The employees at Kalol unit like to refer to their unit as 'a plant in a garden' because of the clean and green plant site.

In addition to the effective pollution control measures in the plants, IFFCO is also concerned about the environmental systems in the areas surrounding the plants and in its townships. Plantation of trees and green belt development, water and energy conservation, and domestic sewerage treatment are some of the aspects for which facilities have been provided by IFFCO. The township of IFFCO Kalol unit is the first township in the country selected by United States Agency for International Development (USAID) for ISO 14001 certification as a single identity.

IFFCO has been continuously improving its cost efficiencies particularly with the liberalisation of the Indian economy in the nineties. There has been consistent pressure to reduce the subsidy on fertilisers and IFFCO has been gearing itself up to face this challenge. A plan called 'Vision 2000' had been initiated in 1992 and the efficiency targets set have been met. Encouraged by the success of growth plan

'Vision 2000' which helped IFFCO become a leader in the field of fertiliser production and marketing, it has embarked upon another five year plan called 'Mission 2005' for its further growth and development. 'Mission 2005' aims at exploitation of global resources by forming joint ventures abroad for sourcing raw material from overseas at economic rates either for production of complex fertilisers in India or for production of urea in the same country and importing it to India.

IFFCO today is a leading player in India's fertiliser industry and is making substantial contributions to the efforts of the Indian Government to increase foodgrain production in the country. Continuously improving the services to the farmers and member cooperatives, commitment to quality, and harnessing mother nature's bounty to drive hunger away from India in an ecologically sustainable manner is the prime concern at IFFCO.

Right from the beginning the culture of commitment to work has been created at the Kalol unit. Discipline, teamwork, and prompt response to problems have been highly valued. Efforts are made to create a happy atmosphere at the workplace to increase motivation to work. A participatory decision making culture has helped to share work related information and create transparency in dealings. A value system has been developed where management and workers both work together on the same side of the table rather than as antagonists – both have a common stake in the plant running well, in increasing productivity, in achieving targets, and in helping each other. This has proved very helpful in harmonious interaction and high levels of cooperation are visible. Open communication between individuals, departments, levels in the hierarchy is practiced.

Almost all the people who joined when the IFFCO Kalol unit was formed have continued to work there until retirement. 80 per cent of workmen are local residents from the surrounding villages.

The Code of Honour for senior excecutives of IFFCO is reflective of the commitment they have to IFFCO:

> The security, prestige and welfare of my organisation comes first always and everytime. The development, welfare and comfort of our employees comes next. My own ease, comfort and career interests comes last always and everytime.

IFFCO believes in taking good care of its employees at the workplace and outside. The township of Kalol unit is well equipped with good infrastructure facilities like a shopping centre, hospital, swimming pool, multipurpose hall and recreation club, all amidst beautiful lawns and parks. Good transport facilities are provided by IFFCO for employees to come to work from the township and from Ahmedabad city. School admissions assistance, transport facilities for children from the colony to go to school in Ahmedabad, and other required administrative support is provided to the employees.

The Marketing Division manages the centralised marketing function for all the plants of IFFCO. As the use of fertilisers is dependent on farmers knowledge, soil conditions and the prevalent agricultural practices, IFFCO has integrated agricultural extension and fertiliser use promotion programmes for farmers in its marketing function. The Gujarat state level marketing office has five area offices in the state with 5–6 extension officers attached to each area office. The two major emphases of the marketing function are (i) sales and logistics related, and (ii) education of farmers and promotion of the product related.

The emphasis on education of farmers is a reflection of IFFCO's community involvement. In addition, it has set up a separate trust called Cooperative Rural Development Trust for further strengthening the farmers. A separate effort called the Integrated Rural Development Programme is also initiated. The Kisan Sewa Fund and the Insurance Facility through IFFCO-TOKIO are recent developments to provide a multi-faceted support to the farmers. In the case of IFFCO too, the meaning of CSR is a little different than that in companies. The business of producing fertilisers itself is a member owned enterprise. The farmers' interests are looked after through the marketing function of IFFCO and also through the separate bodies created for specific purposes.

IFFCO has always been an active advocate of balanced fertilisation and focused its agricultural extension activities to educate the farmers in the concept of balanced fertiliser use for sustainable agriculture through its dedicated team at the grassroots level. Educational and promotional programmes like field demonstrations, field days, farmers meetings, seed multiplication, village adoption, crop seminars, training and visit programmes, special campaigns like bio-fertiliser campaigns, soil testing campaigns, women training programmes, supply point personnel training have consistently proved to be effective in transfer of technology. The Farmers Service Centres also play an important role in this process. They provide technical guidance and make available all vital agro-inputs under one roof especially for small and marginal farmers.

The services to farmers include:

- Promotion of balanced fertilisation programmes
- Adoption of villages for all round socio-economic development and primary cooperative society adoption
- Farmers visits to various agricultural institutes and research farms
- Mobile soil testing laboratories with audio-visual aids

The extension officers at the area office are responsible for this work. During the year 2001–02 the extension work for Gujarat included holding:

- 600 farmers meetings
- 66 field days
- 124 supply point personnel training
- 10 crop seminars
- 3 training and visit programmes
- 4 women training programmes
- 124 soil testing campaigns
- 31 bio-fertiliser campaigns
- 20 special sales campaigns
- 80 plot demonstrations
- 5 veterinary check-up camps
- 5 group visits to Agricultural University Research Station
- 550 CIP kits distributed
- 11 villages provided with agricultural equipment.

A district cooperative meeting of member and non-member

cooperative societies is called a month and a half before every cropping season to promote sales.

There is a State Advisory Committee of about 20 officials which meets for planning and review of performance of the marketing function. This group has directors of IFFCO, Director Agriculture, Registrar Cooperatives, State Cooperative Bank officials, State Apex Cooperative Marketing Federation (GUJCOMASOL) as members.

Special projects on different aspects of hi-tech agriculture such as drip irrigation, bio- pesticides, use of plastics in agriculture, agriculture implements, watershed management, wasteland development, micro-irrigation, et cetera have also been launched.

Strengthening the nation's cooperative fabric has been IFFCO's principal concern. To make grassroots cooperative societies healthy and strong, IFFCO has been regularly paying patronage rebates. In order to further improve the economic viability of cooperative societies, IFFCO has been developing some of the adopted societies as 'IFFCO Franchisee' by giving them the business of rake handling, transportation and warehousing of IFFCO fertilisers besides providing them guidance to undertake educational and promotional activities. 257 societies have taken up the activity of warehousing and 356 societies have undertaken transportation of fertilisers from warehouses to their godowns.

IFFCO is taking initiative to bring the benefits of Information Technology (IT) to the doorsteps of Indian farmers with specific focus on meeting the requirements of agriculture and cooperative sector. Measures are being taken to develop web based services to provide exhaustive information on Agriculture, Fertiliser Industry, Agro-chemicals, and on the Cooperative Sector.

An ambitious GIS (Geographical Information System) based decision support system has been initiated by IFFCO in association with Indian Space Research Organisation utilising their Satellite Imagery. The Information system includes data on IFFCO's logistics and infrastructure for efficient decision making in the areas of marketing and distribution. In addition, the information will also include data on district wise land use, land cover information, monthly crop changes, irrigation/rain fed area, soil types, data on weather such as analysis of rainfall based on historical data, and satellite images.

IFFCO would set up computers in 'Cooperative Kiosks' where this information would be available to farmers through internet apart from other internet based products and services devoted to rural India.

It has instituted *'Sahakarita Ratan'* and *'Sahakarita Bandhu'* Awards.

Cross-section of Views on Empowerment

A cross section of views on empowerment from the employees of IFFCO Kalol unit is as follows:

'Empowerment is delegation and team work.'

'This is a good place to work in. I get all the support I need. My potential gets a chance to be utilised.'

'By force of personality one can be empowered. By creating an image of oneself such that others seek your input and help.'

'To organise people and improve the economic situation of people is empowerment.'

'Empowerment is to authorise.'

'Empowerment is trust. If I feel reassured that things are happening as they should be, if the data in reports are correct, if what a person says is the truth then I can have a high degree of trust in the people around me. This trust makes it possible to delegate, to hand over, which leads to empowerment.'

'Empowerment is to authorise. The position I hold enables me to act in a particular way to get work done.'

'Empowerment is to activate the inner self in each person to do your best – more numbers of people activated, more empowerment.'

'Empowerment is trust and reliability.'

'What you can contribute to empowerment – what you think and what you do are both aspects to be borne in mind. Empowerment cannot be defined, it is experienced. They say that power is not given, it is enjoyed. You have to do your work, your activities in such a way that people around you look up to you and of their own do what you wish them to do – that power is empowerment.

Power is not through holding office only – even without office you can be powerful. You cannot limit the process of empowerment by trying to define it because defining it means putting a limit on it. It is always expanding and increasing and improving.'

'Pooling of everyone's strength, unity of purpose, openness, fearlessness, trust, these are some of the processes which lead to empowerment. When the workers and management are both concerned about the well being of the plant, then everyone's interest is met better.

To utilise each one's special talents and recognise it. Transparency in operations – the last worker also knows the discussions being undertaken by their leaders – information is shared. Dialogue all the time – channelise the energy of people to improve their work rather than trying to be destructive.

Internal union is better than external political affiliated union to achieve this kind of work atmosphere.

Knowledge is power, information is power, trust is power.'

'Power is financial power and position and authority. At another level, power is whatever you do – others eyes are on you. I do not have any financial power – I don't sign any cheques – but whatever work I do is so central – the whole system is centred around me – that is also power'. Whatever I want my subordinates and team members to do – I must have that much in the relationship with them – even if they do not stand up when I go there – but they must do what I tell them to do.

What is the use of their standing up when I go there to show that I am in power but when they don't do what I tell them to do'.

'Empowerment of people is to be able to reach out and include the last person in the activities we undertake. We can empower others and be empowered ourselves in a mutual way.'

'Empowerment is experienced. It cannot be described.'

Cooperative Rural Development Trust (CORDET)

IFFCO has promoted the Cooperative Rural Development Trust

(CORDET) as a separate trust in 1979 to provide education and training to farmers on various aspects of crop production, horticulture, animal husbandry, farm machinery, et cetera to provide assistance to rural people; and to conduct research on agriculture and related aspects. The broader aim is to undertake integrated rural development programmes for the benefit of the farmers. There are three CORDET centres presently – one each at Kalol and Kandla in Gujarat and the third at Phulpur in Uttar Pradesh.

The activities of Kalol CORDET include:

- Soil testing
- Production and supply of improved seeds
- One day/three day/weekly training camps to educate farmers and farm women in modern agriculture technology, dairying, animal husbandry, and home science
- Afforestation
- Rural development programme in the surrounding villages

The achievements of CORDET, Kalol in 2001–02 included:

- conducted 56 trainings with 3,210 participants
- 309 quintals of seeds were produced and distributed
- 27,570 soil samples were tested and farmers advised about the right mix of fertilisers for their soil
- 17,000 fruit and vegetable saplings were distributed.

A forest and fruit nursery has been started to raise saplings for distribution to farmers in the surrounding areas and more than 10,000 have been distributed in around 20 villages.

CORDET Kalol brings out several training materials in Gujarati for the farmers relating to various crops and improved agricultural practices, importance of soil and water testing, guidelines for collecting soil and water samples.

The Integrated Rural Development Programme (IRDP) of IFFCO Kalol is implemented jointly with CORDET staff. A fund of Rs. 20 lakhs is allocated every year by IFFCO Kalol for assisting in the infrastructure development of the villages within a radius of 30 kms of the plant. Applications are received by a committee constituted for this purpose. The village raises a part of the requirement for any particular facility it needs from its own resources and seeks the balance as support from IFFCO. The focus is now shifting to concentrated efforts in select villages to facilitate multi-dimensional agricultural development. Under IRDP, various activities like construction of classrooms, providing drinking water facilities, arranging medical aid and veterinary camps, building approach roads, et cetera are carried out.

The expenditures on all services to farmers by IFFCO in the whole country were Rs. 762.53 lakhs in 2000–01 out of which Rs. 110 lakhs were for the CORDET centres. A fixed amount is dedicated to CORDET for every tonne of fertiliser sold by IFFCO every year.

Kisan Sewa Fund

IFFCO has established the Kisan Sewa Fund (KSF) after the major earthquake in Gujarat in January 2001. It was felt necessary to be prepared for such eventualities as natural calamities are a regular feature in India. Farmers being one of the most vulnerable groups affected by natural calamities, led to the creation of the Kisan Sewa Fund with the objective of relief and welfare of the victims of natural calamities including Gujarat earthquake victims. KSF has been created out of contributions as shown below:

IFFCO	Rs. 10 crores
KRIBHCO	Rs. 5 crores
Employees of IFFCO	Rs. 1 crore
Cooperative societies and Others	Rs. 4 crores
Total	Rs. 20 crores

IFFCO will make a continuous contribution to the KSF every year and so will the employees. The emplyees contribute Rs. 20 every month and IFFCO contributes Rs. 40 per employee every month to the KSF to continually increase the size of the fund.

This fund will be utilised for relief, rehabilitation and reconstruction of IFFCO adopted villages which have been identified in consultation with the state government.

Group Insurance under IFFCO-TOKIO

IFFCO has entered into a joint venture with the Tokio Marine and Fire Insurance Co. Ltd. of Japan in the year 2000, called IFFCO-TOKIO General Insurance Ltd., to diversify into General Insurance.

The scope of IFFCO-TOKIO is to provide rural insurance business, crop insurance business, fire insurance business, marine insurance business, miscellaneous business.

One of the products offered is a rural based Group Personal Accident Insurance cover called 'Sankat Haran Bima Yojana' which was launched in September 2001. Under this product, any farmer buying a minimum of one bag of IFFCO fertiliser during the year is covered by the group insurance. The terms are as follows:

i. Compensation in the event of injury causing permanent fatal disability or death for a sum of Rs. 4000 per bag of 50 kg of fertiliser purchased through cooperatives and farmers service centres.

ii. Maximum capital sum assured for a farmer will be Rs. 1 lakh irrespective of the number of bags he/she has purchased.

iii. The policy will be effective for a period of 12 months from the date of purchase.

iv. The cash receipt or the debit memo will serve as the Insurance Cover.

v. The cash receipt or the debit memo must contain the following:

   a. Name of farmer alongwith father's name

   b. Address of village

   c. Date of issue of receipt or cash memo

   d. Number of bags of each brand of IFFCO / KRIBHCO / IPL products.

   e. Name of nominee

vi. Compensation is provided as per the details below for each bag of the product purchased by the farmer:

Accident death	Rs. 4000
Loss of any two limbs	Rs. 2000
Loss of sight of both eyes	Rs. 2000

Loss of any one limb	Rs. 1000
Loss of sight of any one eye	Rs. 1000
Permanent total disability	Rs. 2000

The bill for the purchase of fertiliser is treated as the insurance policy and the purchase itself is treated as the payment of premium thus reducing the need for elaborate paperwork. The marketing network of the cooperatives also become the agents for selling this insurance product and forwarding the claims thus reducing the need for a network of agents. In case of accident the person is eligible to get claims of specified amounts for varying degrees of incapacity. A gross premium of Rs. 5 crores has been generated so far and insurance cover has been provided to more than 1 crore farmers in the country under this service.

Select Bibliography

Applegarth, Mike and Posner, Keith, *The Empowerment Handbook,* New Delhi: Research Press, 1998.

Aga Khan Rural Support Programme (India), *Annual Report 2003*, Ahmedabad.

Basu, Kishanjit and Jindal, Krishan (eds) *Microfinance – Emerging Challenges,* New Delhi: Tata McGraw-Hill, 2000.

Bava, Noorjahan, (ed), *Non-Governmental Organisations in Development – Theory and Practice*, New Delhi: Kanishka Publishers, 1997.

Bede, Griffith, *The Marriage of the East and the West*, London: Collins Fount, 1983.

Bedi, K., Jeet Singh, P. and Shrivastava, S., *Government @ Net – New Governance Opportunities for India*, New Delhi: Sage, 2001.

Bishoprick, D. W. and Rice, G. H. *Conceptual Models of Organisation*, New York: Appleton-Century-Crofts, 1971.

Bhatnagar, Subhash and Schware, Robert (eds) *Information and Communication Technology in Development – Cases from India,* New Delhi: Sage, 2000.

Bharwada, Charul and Mahajan, Vinay, 'Government-NGO-CBO Participation for Low Income Settlement Improvement Programmes (Dharavi Redevelopment Programme) –Alternative Institutional Framework', Research Report 15, Human Settlement Management Institute, HUDCO, New Delhi.

Blumberg, Paul, *The Predatory Society*, New York: Oxford University Press, 1989.

Brewer, J. et al., *Irrigation Management Transfer in India – Policies, Processes and Performance*, New Delhi: Oxford University Press and IBH Publishing, 1999.

Carr, M., Chen, M. and Jhabvala, R. (eds), *Speaking Out – Women's Economic Empowermen in South Asia,* New Delhi: Vistaar, 1997.

Carroll, Archie B. and Buchholtz, Ann K., *Business and Society – Ethics and Stakeholder Management*, Ohio: Thompson, South-Western, 2003.

Chakraborty, S. K. and Bhattacharya, Pradip (eds), *Leadership and Power*, New Delhi: Oxford University Press, 2001.

Chakraborty, S. K., *Against the Tide – The Philosophical Foundations of Modern Management*, New Delhi: Oxford University Press, 2003.

Confederation of Indian Industry, *CII – Exim Award for Business Excellence – Guidelines for Companies, Self Assessment 1998,* New Delhi.

Confederation of Indian Industry, *Business as a Social Partner – A Compendium of Case Studies*, Volumes I, II, and III, New Delhi, 2001.

Confederation of Indian Industry and Partners in Change, *Proceedings of Conference on Corporate Social Responsibility in South Asia – Mapping the Ground*, New Delhi, 2001.

Conger, J. A., *The Charismatic Leader,* San Francisco: Jossey-Bass, 1989.

Cross, Rob and Parker, A., *The Hidden Power of Social Networks*, Boston, MA: HBS Press, 2004.

Dantwala, M L., Sethi, Harsh and Visaria, Pravin, *Social Change Through Voluntary Action*, New Delhi: Sage, 1998.

Department for International Development (DFID, UK), *Strategies for Achieving the Millenium Development Targets – Making Government Work for Poor People* Consultation Document, 2000.

Department for International Development (DFID, UK), *Institutional Development* Technical Note-14, n.d.

Edwards, Michael and Hulme, David, *Making a Difference – NGOs and development in a changing world,* London: Earthscan Publications, 1992.

Elkington, John, *Cannibals with Forks,* Capstone, 1997.

Fisher, Julie, *Non-Governments – NGOs and the Political Development of the Third World*, Jaipur: Rawat Publications, 2003.

Farrington, John et al., *Non-Governmental Organisations and the State in Asia – Rethinking Roles in Sustainable Agricultural Development*, London and New York: Routledge, 1993.

Galbraith, J. K., *The Anatomy of Power,* Boston: Houghton Mifflin Co., 1983.

Galliara, Meena, *Sahaveeryam – Manual for Managing and Sustaining Partnerships for Sustainable Development*, New Delhi: Business and Community Foundation, 2000.

Ghoshal, Sumantra and Bartlett, Christopher A., *The Individualised Corporation,* London: Heinemann, 1998.

Gibson, J. L., Ivancevich, J. M., and Donnelly, J. H. (Jr.), *Organisations: Structure, Processes, Behaviour,* Dallas: Business Publications Inc., 1973.

Government of India, *National Policy for the Empowerment of Women, 2001,* New Delhi: Department of Women and Child Development, Ministry of Human Resource Development, 2001.

Government of India, *National Human Development Report 2001, New Delhi:* Planning Commission, *The Economic Survey 2001–02, 2002–03,* and *2003–04,* New Delhi.

______, *Annual Report 2001–02, Ministry of Health and Family Welfare,* New Delhi.

Government of India, Government of Sweden, Government of Rajasthan, *Participatory Approach to Human and Land Resources Development (PAHAL) Project, Dungarpur – Phase II,* Reference Document, February 1998.

Greiner, Larry E. and Schein, Virginia. E., *Power and Organisation Development,* Reading, MA.: Addison-Wesley Publishing Company, 1988.

Gulhati, Ravi and Gulhati, Kaval, *Strengthening Voluntary Action in India*, New Delhi: Konark Publishers, 1995.

Hammer, Michael, *Beyond Reengineering – How the Process-Centred Organisation is Changing Our Work and Our Lives,* London: Harper Collins Business, 1996.

Harman, W.W. and Porter, Maya (eds), *The New Business of Business*, S.F.: Berrett-Koehler, 1997.

Harper, Malcolm, *Public Services Through Private Enterprise – Micro-privatisation for Improved Delivery*, New Delhi: Sage, 2000.

Hazarika, Anjali (ed), *Corporate Social Responsibility and the Oil Industry – Global Experiences,* New Delhi: Tata McGraw-Hill, 1998.

Hindustan Times, Delhi edition, 16 September 2004.

Howes, Mick, 'NGOs and the Institutional Development of Membership Organisations', *IDS Research Report 36*, Sussex, July 1999.

Human Development Report 2002, New York: UNDP, 2002.

Hunt, Daniel V., *Process Mapping – How to Reengineer Your Business Processes,* New York: John Wiley and Sons, Inc., 1996.

Huntington, S.P., *The Clash of Civilisations*, New Delhi: Penguin Books, 1997.

International Conference on Population and Development, 1994, *Programme of Action.*

Jumani, Jyoti (ed), *Partnership for Poverty Alleviation,* New Delhi: Tata McGraw-Hill , 2003.

Jumani, Usha, 'Process Lag and Individual Stress in Organisations: A Diagnostic Basis for OD' Doctoral Thesis, Indian Institute of Management, Ahmedabad, March 1979.

Kamat, Sangeeta, *Development Hegemony – NGOs and the State in India*, New Delhi: Oxford University Press, 2002.

Kelly, Marjorie, *Beyond the Bottom Line*, S.F.: Berrett-Koehler, 1999.

Khandwala, Pradip, *Revitalising the State – A Menu of Options,* New Delhi: Sage, 1999.

Kinlaw, D.C., *The Practice of Empowerment,* Aldershot-Hampshire: Gower, 1995.

Kooiman, Jan, *Governing as Governance*, New Delhi: Sage, 2003.

Korten, D.C., *Getting to the 21st Century: Voluntary Action and the Global Agenda,* West Hartford: Kumarian Press, 1990.

Kumar, R., Murphy, David F., and Balsari, Viraal, *Altered Images – the 2001 state of corporate responsibility in India poll*, New Delhi: TERI, 2001.

Lashley, Conrad, *Empowerment – HR strategies for service excellence,* Oxford: Butterworth-Heinemann, 2001.

Laverack, Glenn, *Health Promotion Practice, Power and Empowerment*, London: Sage, 2004.

Logan, David and Tuffrey, Michael, *Companies in Communities: Valuing the Contribution,* London: Charities Aid Foundation, 1999.

Maharishi, Anuradha and Dhillon, Rasna (eds.), *A Common Cause – NGOs & Civil Society*, New Delhi: National Foundation of India, 2002.

May, Nicky, 'Conference Report on Performance and Accountability in the New World Order', *Development in Practice,* Volume 5, Number 1, 1995.

Mayoux, Linda (ed), *Sustainable Learning for Women's Empowerment – Ways Forward in Micro-Finance*, New Delhi: Samskriti, 2003.

Morgan, Sandra and Bookman, Ann (eds) *Women and the Politics of Empowerment,* Philadelphia: Temple University Press, 1988.

Morganthau, Hans, *Politics Among Nations,* 3rd ed., New York: Knopf, 1967.

Narayan, Deepa (ed), *Empowerment and Poverty Reduction – A Source book,*

Washington D.C.: The International Bank for Reconstruction and Development, 2002.

Nelson, Jane, *Business as Partners in Development,* The Prince of Wales Business Leaders Forum in collaboration with The World Bank and The UNDP, London: 1996.

Nelson, Jane, *Building Competitiveness and Communities,* The Prince of Wales Business Leaders Forum in collaboration with The World Bank and The UNDP, London: 1998.

Oakley, Peter et al., *Projects with People,* Geneva: International Labour Organisation, 1991.

Osborne, David and Gaebler, Ted, *Reinventing Government: How the Entrepreneurial Spirit is Transforming the Public Sector from School House to State House, City Hall to Pentagon,* Reading, MA: Addison-Wesley, 1992.

Pachauri, R. (ed), *Business Unusual – championing corporate social responsibility,* New Delhi: TERI, 2004.

Padaki, Vijay and Vaz, Manjulika, *Institutional Development in Social Interventions – Towards Inter-Organisational Effectiveness*, New Delhi: Sage, 2003.

Partners in Change, *Strategy Paper 2001–2005 – Putting Equitable Social Development at the Centre of Corporate Social Responsibility,* New Delhi, n.d.

Pawar, S.N., Ambekar, J.B. and Shrikant, D. (eds), *NGOs and Development – The Indian Scenario,* Jaipur: Rawat Publications, 2004.

Planning Commission, Government of India and UNDP, *Successful Governance Initiatives and Best Practices – Experiences from the States*, New Delhi: Academic Foundation, 2003.

Planning Commission, Government of India, 'Action Plan to Bring About a Collaborative Relationship Between Voluntary Organisations and Government', New Delhi, 1994.

Plender, John, *A Stake in the Future: The Stakeholding Society*, Nicholas Brealey, 1997.

Purushothaman, Sangeetha, *The Empowerment of Women in India – Grassroots Women's Networks and the State*, New Delhi: Sage, 1998.

Rowlands, Joanna, *Questioning Empowerment: Working with Women in Honduras*, Oxford University Press: Oxfam Publications, 1997.

Rubenstein, Doris, *The Good Corporate Citizen – A Practical Guide,* New Jersey: Wiley, John Wiley and Sons, Hoboken, 2004.

Sahavikasa – Newsletter published by Cooperative Development Foundation from Hyderabad, India, May 2003.

Sen, Amartya, 'Goals, Commitment and Identity', *Journal of Law and Economic Organisation,* Vol. 1, no. 2, 1985.

Sen, Amartya, *Development As Freedom,* New Delhi: Oxford University Press, 1995.

Sen, G., Germain, A. and Chen, L. (eds), *Population Policies Reconsidered: Health, Empowerment and Rights,* Boston, MA: Harvard School of Public Health, 1994.

Shah, T., *Catalysing Co-operation: Design of Self-governing Organisations*, New Delhi: Sage, 1996.

Sharma, Kumud, 'Grassroots Organisations and Women's Empowerment: Some Issues in the Contemporary Debate' in *Samya Shakti,* Centre for Women's Development Studies, New Delhi, Volume VI, 1991–92.

Sharma, Mukul, *Improving People's Lives – Lessons in Empowerment from Asia*, New Delhi: Sage in association with The Commonwealth Foundation, 2003.

Sharma, Subhash, *Management in New Age – Western Windows and Eastern Doors*, New Delhi: New Age International, 1996.

Shrivastava, Harsh and Venkateswara, Shankar, *The Business of Social Responsibility,* Bangalore: Books for Change, 2000.

SinghaRoy, Debal (ed), *Social Development and the Empowerment of Marginalised Groups: Perspectives and Strategies,* New Delhi, Sage Publications, 2001.

Sriram, M.S., Fisher, Thomas and Harper, Malcolm, *Beyond Microcredit – Putting Development Back into MicroFinance*, New Delhi: Visataar, 2002.

SustainAbility and UNEP, *Engaging Stakeholders,* 1997.

SustainAbility Ltd., UNEP, ACCA, The Prince of Wales Business Leaders Forum, *The CEO Agenda: Can Business Leaders Satisfy the Triple Bottom Line,* London, 1997.

Tandon, R. and Mohanty, R., *Does Civil Society Matter?,* New Delhi: Sage, 2003.

Tata Quality Management Services, *Tata Business Excellence Model, Criteria for 2001,* Mumbai.

The Associated Chambers of Commerce and Industry of India, *Accelerating Socio-Economic Rural Development* (Study Report), New Delhi, 1991.

Thompson, Grahame, *Between Heirarchies and Markets – The Logic and Limits of Network Organisations*, Oxford: OUP, 2003.

Townsend, Janet Gabriel, et al., *Women and Power: Fighting Patriarchies and Poverty*, London: Zed Books, 1999.

Underwood, Barry, 'Village Institutions and Federations', Unpublished Paper, Aga Khan Rural Support Programme (India), Ahmedabad, 1997.

Vikram Sarabhai Center for Development Interaction (VIKSAT), *Annual Report 2003–04*, Ahmedabad.

______, *Joint Forest Management – A Status Report*, VIKSAT, Ahmedabad, 2002.

Williams, Suzanne et al., *The Oxfam Gender Training Manual - Handout 33*, Oxfam (UK and Ireland), 1994.

World Development Report, 1997, The State in a Changing World, Washington DC: The World Bank, 1997.

World Development Report, 2003, Sustainable Development in a Dynamic World – Transforming Institutions, Growth, and the Quality of Life, Washington D.C.: The World Bank. 2003.

World Summit for Social Development, 1995 *Declaration of the World Summit for Social Development,* Geneva, United Nations.

Index